Morning by Morning

Morning by Morning

A Fresh NIV Edition of the Classic Daily Devotional

Charles Haddon Spurgeon

Edited by Randy Petersen

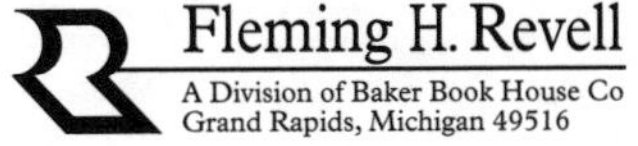
Fleming H. Revell
A Division of Baker Book House Co
Grand Rapids, Michigan 49516

Published by Fleming H. Revell
a division of Baker Book House Company
P.O. Box 6287, Grand Rapids, MI 49516-6287

Printed in the United States of America

Library of Congress Cataloging-in-Publication Data

Spurgeon, C. H. (Charles Haddon), 1834–1892.
Morning by morning / Charles Haddon Spurgeon ; edited by Randy Petersen.
p. cm.
ISBN 0-8007-5481-6
1. Devotional calendars—Baptists. I. Petersen, Randy.
[BV4811.S667 1993]
242′.2—dc20 93-13463

Verses marked KJV are from the King James Version of the Bible.

Preface

Charles Haddon Spurgeon broke the rules. An upstart from the beginning, this teenage country preacher was brought into a big-city London church to bolster its flagging attendance. He succeeded so well that they had to move services down to the music hall to accommodate the crowds.

Spurgeon's simple style attracted a broad cross-section of people. He did not put on airs—that was one of the rules he broke. Class-conscious London society wasn't too crazy about the rabble his sermons dragged in. The papers had a field day with him. He was a popularizer, they said, a vulgarizer, dragging religion down from its noble position.

But this country preacher wouldn't stand for ceremony. As his fame spread in the last half of the 1800s, he learned to hobnob with the upper crust. But he was always a bit ill at ease with them. His job was to preach God's Word; as he saw it, God's Word was open to everybody.

Many of Spurgeon's contemporaries in the Victorian era paid more attention to style than substance. Descriptions would go on for pages, always hinting at the truth of the matter, never coming right out and saying it. Circumlocution, you might call it. Spurgeon might say, "Beating around the bush."

But Spurgeon's style is decidedly different from his contemporaries'. He chooses strong words to say what he means. He grabs a metaphor and throws it at you. The edges are sometimes rough. The images aren't always perfect. He mixes metaphors on occasion. But you always come away with a solid understanding of what he means. In some ways, he was ahead of his time. It is a modern convention to ditch style for substance.

As an editor, my work has largely been translation. The goal was to present Spurgeon's writing in a way that would sound fresh to modern ears. I tried to combine my appreciation for his lush language with a sense of modern syntax. I have probably erred often on one side or the other, but the whole, I think, should be satisfying. There is a new generation of believers out there who do not know our favorite Christian phrases. "The sweet bye and bye" sounds to them like a commercial for a new diet plan. I tried, wherever possible, to avoid the trite expressions in favor of direct explanation.

At the same time, I tried to stay away from obvious anachronisms. When Spurgeon talked about a "cartload" of God's blessings, should I change that to "truckload"? No, I decided. Trucks would probably be unknown to Spurgeon. It's better to stay within his context. Yet one clear anachronism is the use of the New International Version. I felt the use of a modern translation was essential. Wherever possible, I have adapted Spurgeon's comments to the NIV. On some occasions, as you'll see, his whole lesson depends on the unique wording of the King James Version. Since those are legitimate translations of the original text, I have allowed those few verses to stand.

I'd like to think that Charles Haddon Spurgeon is smiling from heaven on this enterprise, but he is probably too busy glorifying his beloved Savior.

Randy Petersen

January 1

That year they ate of the produce of Canaan.
(Joshua 5:12)

Israel had completed its weary wanderings. The people had attained their promised rest: no more moving tents, fiery serpents, fierce Amalekites, and howling wildernesses. They came to a land that flowed with milk and honey, and they ate the corn of this new land.

Perhaps this year, you may rest in Christ. Our "promised rest" is to be with Jesus. If we are living by faith, that prospect should fill us with joy. Those marked by unbelief shudder with fear at the thought of crossing that "Jordan River" that lies between our present life and the life to come. But we can rest assured that we have already experienced more ills than death at its worst can cause us. We should banish those fearful thoughts and rejoice greatly in the possibility that maybe this year we will begin to be "forever with the Lord."

But what if we remain here on earth this year? What if we tarry here to do service for the Lord? This New Year's text still applies. As Paul says in Hebrews, "Now we who have believed enter that rest" (Hebrews 4:3). The Holy Spirit is the down payment on our inheritance. To those who believe, he gives a foretaste of heavenly glory.

Heaven is a place of security; but we on earth are kept safe in Jesus. Heaven is a place of triumph; but we have victories, too. Those in heaven enjoy communion with the Lord; but this is not denied to us. They rest in his love, but we also have perfect peace in him. They sing his praises; and it is our privilege to bless him, too. In all these ways in this coming year, we will gather celestial fruits on earthly ground. Faith and hope have turned this desert into the garden of God. The Israelites ate angels' food (Psalm 78:25) in the wilderness—why shouldn't we?

I pray that we might feed on Jesus this year and so eat of the produce of our Promised Land.

January 2

Devote yourselves to prayer.
(Colossians 4:2)

It is interesting to note how much of Scripture is concerned with the subject of prayer, in furnishing examples, enforcing precepts, or pronouncing promises. We hardly open the Bible before we read, "At that time men began to call on the name of the Lord" (Genesis 4:26). And just as we are about to close the volume, the "Amen" of an earnest supplication meets our ears (Revelation 22:20).

Instances are plentiful. Here we find a wrestling Jacob; there a Daniel who prayed three times a day; and a David who called upon his God with all his heart. We see Elijah on the mountain, Paul and Silas in the dungeon. We have multitudes of commands and myriads of promises. What does this teach us, but the sacred importance and necessity of prayer?

We can be sure that whatever God has made prominent in his Word he wants to be conspicuous in our lives. If he has said a great deal about prayer, it is because he knows we need it a great deal. In fact, we need it so deeply that we should never stop praying until we get to heaven.

You say you don't need anything? Then I'm afraid you don't know your own poverty. So you don't feel you need to pray for the Lord's mercy? Maybe he will mercifully show you your own misery. A prayerless soul is a Christless soul. Prayer is the lisping of the believing infant, the shout of the fighting believer, the requiem of the dying saint falling asleep in Jesus. It is the breath, the watchword, the comfort, the strength, the honor of a Christian. If you are God's child, you will seek your Father's face and live in your Father's love.

Pray that this year you may be an example and a blessing to others, that you may live more to the glory of your Master. The motto for this year must be "Devote yourselves to prayer."

January 3

I . . . will make you to be a covenant for the people.
(Isaiah 49:8)

Jesus Christ himself is the sum and substance of the covenant. As a gift of the covenant, he is the property of every believer. Can you imagine what that means? Can you fully estimate all that you have gotten in Christ? "For in Christ all the fullness of the Deity lives in bodily form" (Colossians 2:9).

Consider the word *God*, in all its infinity. Then meditate on *perfect man*, in all its beauty. All that Christ, as God and man, ever had or will have is yours—from God's free favor, handed over to you, to be your inheritance forever.

Our blessed Jesus, as God, is omniscient, omnipresent, omnipotent. Will it not console you to know that all these great and glorious attributes are now yours?

Jesus has power, doesn't he? That power is yours to support and strengthen you, to overcome your enemies, and to preserve you to the end.

He has love, doesn't he? Well, there is not a drop of love in his heart that is not yours; you may dive into the immense ocean of his love, and you may say of it all, "It is mine!"

He has justice, too. This may seem like a stern attribute, but even this is yours, for by his justice he will see to it that everything promised to you in the covenant of grace will actually come to you.

In addition, all that Jesus has as *perfect man* is yours. As a perfect man, Jesus enjoyed the Father's perfect delight. He stood accepted by the Most High God. Believer, God's acceptance of Christ is your acceptance. Don't you know that the love the Father bestowed on Christ he is bestowing on you now? For all that Christ did is yours. That perfect righteousness that Jesus worked out through his stainless life, as he kept the law and made it honorable, is yours; it is credited to your account. Christ is in the covenant.

January 4

But grow in the grace and knowledge of our Lord and Savior Jesus Christ. (2 Peter 3:18)

Grow in grace"—we should be growing in every aspect of our Lord's grace.

That means growing in *faith*, the root of grace. Believe the promises more firmly than ever. Let your faith grow fuller, steadier, and simpler.

Grow also in *love*. Ask God to make your love more extensive, more intense, more practical, influencing every thought, word, and deed.

Grow in *humility* as well. Try to lie very low, learning more about your own nothingness. As you grow downward in humility seek also to grow upward, growing closer to God in prayer.

May God's Holy Spirit also enable you to "grow in the . . . knowledge of our Lord and Savior." The one who refuses to grow in the knowledge of Jesus is turning down a great blessing. To know him is eternal life. Obviously the one who has no desire to know Jesus better does not know him at all. Whoever has sipped this heavenly wine will thirst for more. This is not to say that Christ doesn't satisfy, but it is so great a satisfaction that it doesn't extinguish our appetite; it whets it.

If you know the love of Jesus, you will pant like a thirsty deer (Psalm 42:1) after deeper and deeper drinks of it. Absence from Christ is hell, but the presence of Jesus is heaven. So we must not be content with merely a passing acquaintance with Jesus. We should seek to know more of him, more of his divine nature, his human relationships, his finished work of salvation, his death and resurrection, his present intercession for us, and his future return as king.

Stay close to the cross. Study the mystery of his wounds. As we grow in his grace we will love him more and understand more fully his tremendous love for us.

January 5

God saw that the light was good, and he separated the light from the darkness. (Genesis 1:4)

Light sprang from God's first fiat, "Let there be light" (Genesis 1:3). We who enjoy light should be very grateful and see more of God in it and by it.

Solomon said that *physical* light was sweet (Ecclesiastes 11:7), but the light of the *gospel* is infinitely more precious, for it reveals eternal things and ministers to our immortal natures. When the Holy Spirit gives us *spiritual* light, opening our eyes to behold the glory of God in the face of Jesus Christ, we see sin in its true colors and ourselves in our real position. We see the Most Holy God as he reveals himself, the plan of mercy as he displays it, and the world to come as the Word describes it.

Spiritual light has many beams and prismatic colors—knowledge, joy, holiness, and life. All are divinely good. If the light *we* see is this good, imagine what the very *essence* of God's light must be like. O Lord, since light is so good, give us more of it and more of yourself, the true Light.

As soon as a good thing comes into the world, a division is necessary. Light and darkness have no communion with each other. God divided them; we must not confuse them. Children of light must not have fellowship with the deeds, doctrines, or deceits of darkness. The children of the day must be sober, honest, and bold in their Lord's work, leaving the works of darkness to those who live in darkness.

In judgment, in action, in hearing, in teaching, in association, we must discern between the precious and the vile, maintaining that great distinction the Lord made on the world's first day.

O Lord Jesus, be our light throughout this whole day.

SENT THIS VERSE TO LZ ON THE SAME DAY - NOT KNOWING OF THIS DEVOTION - JUST RECEIVED IN THE MAIL 1/6! 1/6/09

…s for you.

It … *for me*. Chris-
t… ng so worried
all … Your heavenly
Fat… s you stagger.
You…
… sed over you.
He … you need. Do not let despair drag you down; hope, always hope. Take up the arms of faith against a sea of troubles, and your trusting opposition will end your worries.

There is One who cares for you. His eye is fixed on you, his heart beats with pity over your sorrow, and his powerful hand will yet bring you the help you need. The darkest cloud will scatter itself in showers of mercy. The blackest gloom will give way to morning. If you belong to the Lord, he will bind your wounds and heal your broken heart.

Do not doubt God's grace when you face trouble. Believe that he loves you just as much in tough times as in happy times. What a serene and quiet life you could lead if you would just let the God of providence worry about providing for you. With a little oil in the jar and a handful of meal in the bin, Elijah outlived a famine (1 Kings 17); you can, too. If God cares for you, why do you need to worry? If you trust him with your soul, why not trust him with your body as well? He has never refused to bear your burdens; he has never staggered under their weight. So put away your anxiety! Leave your concerns in the hands of a gracious God.

January 7

For to me, to live is Christ.
(Philippians 1:21)

A person begins to live for Christ when the Holy Spirit convinces him of his sin and when by grace he sees the Savior's sacrifice cleansing his guilt. For believers, Jesus is the "pearl of great price" (Matthew 13:45–46), for whom we are willing to part with all we have. He has completely won our love; our hearts beat only for him. For his glory we live; for his gospel we would die. He is the pattern of our life; we sculpt our character with him as our model.

Paul's words mean more than most people think. Reading this verse, most assume that the aim or purpose of Paul's life was Christ. No, his *life itself* was Jesus. Jesus was his very breath, the soul of his soul, the heart of his heart. Paul ate, drank, and slept eternal life.

Do you live up to this ideal? Can you honestly say, "To me, to live is Christ"? Your daily work—are you doing it for Christ? Or are you doing it for self-aggrandizement or even for your family?

"What's wrong with that?" you might ask. But for the Christian, who professes to live for Christ, to have any other primary purpose in life amounts to spiritual adultery. Many of us live for Christ, *somewhat*. But who can truly say that he lives totally for Jesus? Yet Jesus *is* our life—its source and sustenance. The way we live, our purpose, all rolled into one name: Christ Jesus.

Lord, accept me. I put myself at your disposal, wanting only to live in you and for you.

January 8

He will bear the guilt involved in the sacred gifts.
(Exodus 28:38)

These words reveal a great deal. We should pause a while to reflect on this sad sight. The "guilt" involved in our public worship—the hypocrisy, formality, lukewarmness, irreverence, wandering of heart, and forgetfulness of God. Or consider our work for the Lord—its selfishness, carelessness, laziness, and unbelief. Or our private devotions—their laxity, coldness, neglect, sleepiness, and vanity. Yes, our "sacred gifts" contain far more guilt than we would think.

One minister has written, "My parish, as well as my heart, very much resembles the garden of the sluggard. And what is worse, I find that many of my desires to improve both proceed from pride or vanity or indolence. I look at the weeds taking over my garden, and I wish they were gone. Why? It may be that I want to walk out and say to myself, 'My garden is kept in fine order!' This is *pride*. Or I may want my neighbors to look over the wall and say, 'Your garden looks great!' This is *vanity*. Or I may just want the weeds to go away because I am tired of pulling them up. This is *indolence*."

Even our desires for holiness may be polluted by wrong motives. Worms hide under the greenest sods; we don't need to look very long to find them. It is encouraging to note that the high priest, bearing the guilt of the sacred gifts, wore a turban that bore these words, "Holy to the Lord." In the same way, Jesus bears our sin, presenting to the Father not our unholiness, but his own holiness.

January 9

I will be their God.
(Jeremiah 31:33)

Christian, here is all you need. You want something that *satisfies*; isn't this enough? If you could pour this promise into a cup, wouldn't you say with David, "My cup overflows" (Psalm 23:5)? If God is your God, don't you have everything?

Desire is as insatiable as death. But the One who "fills everything in every way" (Ephesians 1:23) can fill it. Who can measure the full capacity of our wishes? But the immeasurable wealth of God exceeds it.

I ask you, are you not complete when God is yours? Do you want anything else? If all else should fail, isn't his all-sufficiency enough to satisfy you?

Ah, but you want more than quiet satisfaction; you want *rapturous delight*. With God you have music fit for heaven, for he is the Maker of heaven. All the music of the sweetest instruments cannot compare to the melody of this sweet promise: "I will be their God." Here is a deep sea of bliss, a shoreless ocean of delight. Bathe in it; swim in it; dive into it. "I will be their God."

If this does not make your eyes sparkle and your heart beat faster, then your soul must not be in a healthy state.

You say you want more? More than present delights? You crave *hope* for the future. Where can you find greater hope than in this promise: "I will be their God"? This is the masterpiece of all promises.

Dwell in the light of the Lord and let your soul be ravished with his love. Live up to your privileges and rejoice with unspeakable joy.

January 10

Now there is in store for me a crown of righteousness.
(2 Timothy 4:8)

Have you ever doubted that you would make it to heaven? Don't worry. All the people of God will enter there.

I love the saying of the dying man who exclaimed, "I have no fear of going home. I have sent everything before me. God's finger is on the latch of my door, and I am ready for him to enter."

"But," someone asked, "aren't you afraid that you might miss out on your inheritance?"

"No," he answered, "no. There is one crown in heaven that the angel Gabriel could not wear. It will fit no head but mine. There is one throne in heaven that Paul the apostle could not fill. It was made for me, and I shall have it."

O Christian, what a joyous thought! Your inheritance is secure. "But can't I lose it?" you may ask. No, if you are a child of God, you cannot lose it. It is yours as surely as if you were already there.

Come with me, believer, and let us sit on top of Mount Nebo and view that good land, Canaan (Deuteronomy 32:48–49). Do you see that little river of death glistening in the sunlight? Across that river, do you see the pinnacles of the eternal city? If you could fly across that city, you would see a sign on each mansion: THIS IS RESERVED FOR SO-AND-SO. HE WILL LIVE HERE FOREVER WITH GOD. One of those mansions is your inheritance.

If you believe in the Lord Jesus, if you have repented of sin and have a renewed heart, you are one of the Lord's people. There is a place reserved for you, a crown set aside, a harp ready for you to play.

January 11

They have no root.
(Luke 8:13)

My soul examines itself this morning in the light of this text. I have received the Word with joy. My feelings have been stirred. Scripture has made a lively impression on me. But remember, it is one thing to hear the Word with one's ears; it is quite another to let Jesus into one's soul.

Superficial feeling is often linked with an inward hardness of heart. A lively impression is not always a lasting one.

In one of the scenes in this parable, the seed fell on ground that had a rocky base, covered with a thin layer of soil. When the seed began to take root, its downward growth was stopped by the hard rock. Therefore, it spent all its strength pushing its green shoot as high as it could. But since it had no moisture coming from the roots, it withered away.

Is this my case? Have I been putting on a good show on the outside, without any true life on the inside? Good growth takes place upward and downward at the same time. Am I rooted in sincere faith and love for Jesus?

If my heart remains unsoftened, unfertilized by grace, the good seed may bloom for a season, but it eventually withers. It cannot flourish when the heart is rocky, unbroken, unsanctified.

I don't want a godliness that sprouts up like Jonah's gourd (Jonah 4), but doesn't last. Let me count the cost of following Jesus. Let me feel the energy of his Holy Spirit. Then I will have a thriving *and lasting* seed in my soul.

If my mind stays as hard and obstinate as it naturally is, the hot sun of each trial and temptation will scorch my faith. My hard heart will only reflect the heat back onto the seed. My faith will soon die, and I will lose hope.

Therefore, O heavenly Sower, plow me first. Then cast the truth into me. And let me yield a bountiful harvest for you.

January 12

And you are of Christ.
(1 Corinthians 3:23)

You belong to Christ, because you have been donated to him by the Father. You have been bought by his blood. You have been dedicated to his service. You have been adopted by him, named by his name, made a brother and joint heir.

Show the world that you are the servant, the friend, the bride of Jesus. When you are tempted to sin, say, "I can't do this sinful thing, because I belong to Christ." It just does not make sense for a friend of Christ to sin.

When temptation dangles money before you, money you can win through sin, don't touch it. Remember that you are Christ's.

When you encounter difficulties and dangers, be strong. You are Christ's.

Do you work with people who are lazy, who cheat the employer by sitting down on the job? Rise and do your work with all your might. When you tire, when you're tempted to sit around like the others, say, "No, I cannot stop. I am Christ's. He has bought me with his blood. I owe him my full service."

When the siren song of pleasure tries to tempt you from the path of right, reply, "Your music cannot charm me; I am Christ's."

When the cause of God invites you, give yourself to it. When the poor need you, give your goods and even yourself away, for you are Christ's.

If you have professed faith in Christ, that is your profession. Act like a Christian. Let the way you talk make people think of Christ. Let your conduct conjure up pictures of heaven. Let everyone know, by the way you live, that you belong to the Savior. Let them recognize his love and holiness in you, because you are of Christ.

January 13

Now Jehoshaphat built a fleet of trading ships to go to Ophir for gold, but they never set sail—they were wrecked at Ezion Geber. (1 Kings 22:48)

Solomon's ships had returned safely with foreign treasures, but Jehoshaphat's fleet never reached the land of gold. In his providence, God allows one to prosper and frustrates another—doing the same business, in the same spot. Yet the Great Ruler is still as good and wise as ever.

May we have the grace to praise God not only for the shiploads of blessings he gives us, but also for the ships broken at Ezion Geber. We should not envy the more successful. Nor should we complain about our losses, as if we were the only ones who suffered misfortunes. Like Jehoshaphat, we may be precious in the Lord's sight, even though our schemes end in disappointment.

Why did Jehoshaphat lose his ships? A prophet announced the cause of his disaster: "Because you have made an alliance with Ahaziah, the Lord will destroy what you have made" (2 Chronicles 20:37).

This is worth noting. Ahaziah was the wicked king in the northern kingdom of Israel. He came from a very sinful family. Good king Jehoshaphat had no business allying himself with this evil ruler.

Apparently Jehoshaphat learned his lesson. After this, he refused to let his men sail with Ahaziah's (1 Kings 22:49).

This king's experience should serve as a warning to the rest of God's people. We should avoid being "unequally yoked together" with unbelievers (2 Corinthians 6:14). A life of misery generally awaits believers who are united in marriage or in some other bond with people of the world. We must love Jesus so much that we remain holy, undefiled, separate from sinners. Otherwise, we may expect to hear this same report: "The Lord will destroy what you have made."

January 14

Mighty to save.
(Isaiah 63:1)

Here we read an immense amount in a few, small words. "To save" speaks of God's entire work of mercy. Christ is not only "mighty to save" those who repent, but he is able to make people repent. Yes, he will carry to heaven those who believe. But he shows his might also in giving people new hearts and establishing faith inside them.

Christ is mighty enough to make the man who hates holiness love it. He can make the woman who despises his name bend her knee before him. And even this does not fully capture the meaning of these few words.

The life of the believer is a series of miracles performed by this "mighty" God. The bush burns, but it is not consumed. He is mighty enough not only to make his people holy, but to keep them holy. He preserves them in his fear and love, until he welcomes them into the full delights of heaven. Christ does not bring a person to repentance and then let him shift for himself. He who begins the work carries it on (Philippians 1:6). He who puts the first germ of life in the dead soul strengthens it, until it breaks the bonds of sin and the soul leaps from the earth, perfected in glory.

Believer, this is real encouragement. Are you praying for a loved one? Don't give up—Christ is "mighty to save." You may be unable to reclaim this rebel, but the Lord is almighty. Grab onto that mighty arm and implore him to use its strength.

Or maybe you are in need yourself. His strength is sufficient for you, too. With others or with you, Jesus is "mighty to save." The best proof lies in the fact that he has already saved *you*.

January 15

Do as you promised.
(2 Samuel 7:25)

God's promises were never meant to be thrown aside like wastepaper. He wants them to be used. God's gold is not miser's money, hoarded away, but it is minted to be traded with. Nothing pleases our Lord more than to see his promises put in circulation. He loves to see his children bring them up to him, and say, "Lord, do as you promised."

We glorify God when we plead his promises. Do you think that God becomes any poorer when he gives you the riches he has promised? Will he be any less holy after he gives you holiness? Will he be any less pure because he washes your sins away? He has said, "Come now, let us reason together. . . . Though your sins are like scarlet, they shall be as white as snow; though they are red as crimson, they shall be like wool" (Isaiah 1:18).

Faith grabs the promise of pardon. It does not hesitate, saying, "I wonder if it's really true?" It goes straight to the throne and pleads, "Lord, here is your promise. Do as you have promised."

When a Christian grasps a promise, if he does not take it to God, he dishonors him. But when he rushes to the throne of grace and cries, "This is all I have to stand on—your promise," then his desire is granted.

Our Heavenly Banker loves to cash his own checks. Never let a promise rust. Draw the sword of God's Word out of its scabbard, and use it with holy power. Don't think that God will be bothered when you keep reminding him of his promises. Does the sun get tired of shining? Does the fountain get tired of flowing? No. God loves to hear the requests of needy souls. It is his nature to keep his promises. He delights in giving out favors. He is more ready to hear than you are to ask.

January 16

"I myself will help you," declares the Lord.
(Isaiah 41:14)

This morning Jesus is speaking to each one of us. "I myself will help you. Of course I will help you! Look at what I have done for you already. I bought you with my blood. I have died for you. Help you? Of course I will help you!

"Helping you is the least of the things I do for you. I have done far more—and I will continue to do more. Before the world began, I chose you. I made a covenant for you. I laid aside my glory and became a man for you. I gave my life for you. And if I did all this, I will surely help you now.

"In helping you, I am giving you what I have already bought for you. If you needed a thousand times more help, I would give that, too. Your need is small compared to what I am ready to give. Help you? Have no fear, I will help you.

"If there were an ant at the door of your silo full of grain, and if that ant were asking for food, it would not ruin you to give him a handful of wheat. It would be nothing to you. In the same way, you are like a tiny insect at the door of my all-sufficiency. *I will help you.*"

Do you need any more assurances, my friend? Do you need more than the omnipotence of the Trinity? Do you want more wisdom than the Father has, more love than the Son, more power than the Spirit? Bring your empty pitcher. This well will fill it. Gather up all your wants and bring them here—your emptiness, your sorrows, your needs. The river of God is flowing; it is ready to supply your needs. What else can you want?

You can go forth with this assurance: The Eternal God is your helper. "So do not fear, for I am with you; do not be dismayed, for I am your God. I will strengthen you and help you; I will uphold you with my righteous right hand" (Isaiah 41:10).

January 17

Then I looked, and there before me was the Lamb, standing on Mount Zion. (Revelation 14:1)

The apostle John had the privilege of looking inside the gates of heaven. Describing what he saw, he starts by saying, "There . . . was the Lamb."

This teaches us something very important. The major object of contemplation in the heavenly city is "the Lamb of God, who takes away the sin of the world" (John 1:29). That's what captured John's attention. Nothing else was as important as that Divine Being, who redeemed us by his blood. He is the theme of the songs of all glorified spirits and holy angels.

Fellow Christian, here is your joy. You have looked, and you have seen the Lamb. Through your tears you have seen the Lamb of God taking away your sins. So rejoice! In a little while, when the tears have been wiped away from your eyes, you will see the same Lamb *exalted on his throne*.

It is a joyous experience to have daily fellowship with Jesus. We will have the same joy in heaven, but to a higher degree. We will enjoy the constant vision of his presence. We will live with him forever.

"I looked, and there . . . was the Lamb." Why, that Lamb is heaven itself. As one scholar has said, "Heaven and Christ are the same thing." To be with Christ is to be in heaven and to be in heaven is to be with Christ. This scholar went on to write, "O my Lord Christ, if I could be in heaven without you, it would be a hell. And if I could be in hell, and still have you, it would be a heaven to me, for you are all the heaven I want."

All that you need to be content, to be truly blessed, is to be with Christ.

January 18

There remains, then, a Sabbath-rest for the people of God. (Hebrews 4:9)

Our situation in heaven will be much different from what it is here. Here we are born to work hard and grow weary. But in the land of the immortal, no one knows fatigue. Anxious to serve our Master, here on earth we find that our strength never matches our zeal. We are always crying, "Lord, help me to serve you."

If we are very active, we soon reach our limit. Not a limit of what we *want* to do for God, but what we are *able* to do. We cry, "Lord, I am not tired *of* your work, but I am tired *in* it."

But our days of weariness will not last forever. The sun is nearing the horizon. It will rise again in a brighter day than you have ever seen. It will rise upon a land where they serve God day and night—and they still have rest.

Here, our rest is partial. There, it is perfect. Here, we remain unsettled; we feel there is always so much more to do. There, all are at rest; they have reached the top of the mountain; they rest in the bosom of God himself. They can go no higher.

Think of that, if you are weary from your labors. Think of that eternal rest. Can you even imagine it? It is a rest that "remains." Here on earth, my best joys are mortal. My fairest flowers fade. My sweetest birds fall to death's arrows. My most pleasant days are shadowed into nights.

But there, everything is immortal. The harp does not rust. The laurel crown does not wither. The eye does not dim. The voice does not falter. The immortal being is totally absorbed in infinite delight. That will be a truly happy day, when mortality is swallowed up by life and the Eternal Sabbath will begin.

January 19

I looked for him but did not find him.
(Song of Songs 3:1)

Tell me where you lost track of Christ, and I will tell you where you will probably find him. Did you lose him in the prayer closet by neglecting regular prayer? Then that is where you should look for him.

Did you lose Christ when you turned to sin? Then find him by giving up the sin and restraining your desires. Did you lose Christ by neglecting the Scriptures? Then find him in the Scriptures.

As the saying goes, "Look for a thing where you dropped it." Look for Christ where you lost him. He has not gone away.

But it is hard work to go back for Christ. As John Bunyan indicated in *Pilgrim's Progress*, the hardest road for the pilgrim to travel was the road back to the Arbor of Ease, where he lost his supplies. It is easier to go twenty miles forward than to go one mile back to retrieve something you have lost.

So when you do find your Master again, be sure to cling to him. How could you have parted with such a precious friend, whose presence is so sweet, whose words are so comforting, whose company is so dear to you? You would think that you would watch him every moment, never let him out of your sight.

But since you have let him go, it is good that you are seeking him again. It may be painful to seek him here and there, but keep seeking! It is dangerous to be without your Lord. Without Christ you are like a sheep without a shepherd, like a tree without water at its roots, like a dry leaf in a windstorm, not bound to the tree of life.

Seek him with your whole heart, and you will find him. Give yourself thoroughly to this search, and once again he will be your joy and gladness.

January 20

Now Abel kept flocks.
(Genesis 4:2)

Abel, the shepherd, offered a sacrifice of blood, dedicating it to God. And "the Lord looked with favor on Abel and his offering" (Genesis 4:4). Clearly, Abel serves as an early symbol of Jesus. Like the first streak of light that tinges the eastern sky at sunrise, it does not reveal everything, but it clearly indicates that the sun is coming. So Abel is a shepherd and a priest, since he offers a sweet-smelling sacrifice to God. In him, we see our Lord Jesus, who brings before his Father a pleasing sacrifice.

Abel was hated by his brother, hated without cause. So was our Savior. The natural and carnal man hated the accepted man, who bore the Spirit of God's grace and did not rest until his blood was shed. Abel fell and sprinkled his altar and sacrifice with his own blood. In the same way, Jesus was slain by human enemies while serving as a priest before the Lord.

"The good shepherd," he said, "lays down his life for the sheep" (John 10:11). Let us weep over him as we see him slain by the hatred of humanity, staining the horns of his own altar with his blood.

Abel's blood speaks! The Lord told Cain that his brother's blood cried out from the ground (Genesis 4:10). So the blood of Jesus has a mighty tongue. But it cries out for mercy, not vengeance. It is a very precious thing to stand at the altar of our Good Shepherd, to see him bleeding there as a slaughtered priest, and then to hear his blood speaking peace to his whole flock. He speaks peace to our consciences, peace between Jew and Gentile, peace between God and humanity, peace throughout eternity for blood-washed souls.

Abel is the first shepherd in human history, but our hearts give Jesus first place in order of excellence.

January 21

And so all Israel will be saved.
(Romans 11:26)

When Moses sang at the Red Sea, it was his joy to know that *all* Israel was safe. Not a drop of spray fell from that wall of water until the last Israelite had safely planted his feet on the other side. When that was done, the floods rushed back to their proper place—but not until then.

Part of Moses' song was "In your unfailing love you will lead the people you have redeemed" (Exodus 15:13). And at the end of time, when all God's chosen ones will sing the song of Moses and of the Lamb, this will be the boast of Jesus—"None has been lost" (John 17:12). There will be no vacant thrones in heaven.

All the ones God has chosen, all those redeemed by Christ, all those the Spirit has called, all who believe in Jesus, will safely cross the dividing sea. We have not all crossed over yet, but we are on the way. The vanguard of our army has already reached the shore. We are marching through the depths. Right now we are following our Leader into the heart of the sea.

But let us rejoice. We in the rear guard will soon be where the vanguard is. Soon the last of the chosen ones will have crossed the sea. Then when all are safe, will the song of triumph be heard.

If one were absent, if one of God's chosen family were left behind, it would create an eternal discord in the song of the redeemed. It would cut the strings of the harps of paradise, so that they would never make music again.

January 22

Son of man, how is the wood of a vine better than that of a branch on any of the trees in the forest? (Ezekiel 15:2)

These words are for the humbling of God's people. They are called God's vine, but does that mean they are naturally better than any other nation? By God's goodness, they have been fruitful, planted in good soil. The Lord strung these vines on the walls of his sanctuary, and they bear fruit for his glory. But what are they without God? What are they without the continual influence of the Spirit, making them fruitful?

Get rid of pride, believer. You have no reason for it. Whatever you are, you have nothing to be proud of. The more you have, the more you are in debt to God. And no one should be proud of that which makes him a debtor.

Consider where you came from. Look back at what you were. Where would you be without God's grace? Look at yourself as you are now. Doesn't your conscience bother you? Don't your thousands of sins stand before you, telling you that you are unworthy to be called God's child?

If you amount to anything right now, it is because of God's grace. That's what makes you different from anyone else. You may be a great believer now, but you would be a great sinner if God had not changed you. You may be valiant in the cause of God's truth, but if grace had not grabbed you, you would be just as valiant in unholy causes.

So do not be proud. What a strange fixation this is—that you, who have borrowed everything, would think of exalting yourself. You are just a poor pensioner, dependent on the Savior's goodness.

January 23

I have exalted a young man from among the people.
(Psalm 89:19)

Why was Christ chosen from among the people? That is, why was our Lord "among the people" at all? Was it not so that he might be *our brother*? What a relationship this is!

The believer can say, "I have a Brother in heaven. I may be poor, but I have a Brother who is rich. He is a king, and will he let me suffer want while he is on the throne? No! He loves me. He is my Brother."

Believer, wear this blessed thought like a necklace of diamonds around the neck of your memory. Put it like a golden ring on the finger of your thoughts. Use it as the king's own signet ring, stamping the petitions of your faith with confidence in his approval. He is a brother born for adversity. Treat him as such.

Christ was also "among the people" so that he might know our needs and sympathize with us. He "has been tempted in every way, just as we are—yet was without sin" (Hebrews 4:15). In all our sorrows we have his sympathy. Temptation, pain, disappointment, weakness, weariness, poverty—he knows them all, for he has felt them all.

Remember this, Christian, and let it comfort you. However difficult and painful your road may be, it is marked by the footsteps of the Savior. Even when you reach the dark valley of the shadow of death and the deep waters of the surging Jordan, you will find his footprints there. Wherever you go, he has gone. Each burden we have to carry has at one time been laid on the shoulders of Immanuel.

January 24

Surely he will save you from the fowler's snare.
(Psalm 91:3)

God saves his people from the fowler's snare in two ways: *from* and *out of*. First he saves them from the snare by keeping them away from it. But if they should get caught in the snare, he gets them out of it. For some, the first promise is most precious. For others, the second.

How does God save us *from* the snare? He often uses *trouble*. God knows that our backsliding leads to our destruction. In mercy, he sends the rod of affliction. We say, "Why, Lord?" not knowing that our trouble has been God's way of protecting us from a far greater evil. Many have been saved from ruin by their sorrows and trials—they are like birds frightened away from the net.

At other times, God saves us from the snare by giving us spiritual strength. Then when we are tempted to do evil, we say, "How can I do this great evil and sin against God?"

But what happens when a believer does fall into the net? God still delivers him *out of* it. If you are a backslider, you should feel uncomfortable, but do not lose hope. Hear what your Redeemer says: "Return, O backsliding children; I will have mercy upon you."

But you say you cannot return; you are a captive. Then listen again to this promise—"Surely he will save you from the fowler's snare." He can bring you out. He will receive you. He will give you joy and gladness. Even the bones that he has broken will rejoice. No bird of paradise will die in the fowler's net.

January 25

I will tell of the kindnesses of the Lord, the deeds for which he is to be praised, according to all the Lord has done for us.
(Isaiah 63:7)

What kindnesses have you experienced? You may be gloomy now, but are you forgetting that blessed hour when Jesus met you and said, "Come to me"? Can't you remember that rapturous moment when he snapped your fetters, dashed your chains to the ground, and said, "I came to break your bonds and set you free"?

Or if you have forgotten these moments of first love, surely there is some precious milestone along the road of life that you can remember—some sign not quite grown over with moss, some memorial to his mercy?

Did you ever have a sickness that he healed? Were you ever in need, and he supplied it? Were you ever in dire straits, and he delivered you?

Get up and go to the river of your experience. Pull up a few bullrushes. Weave these into a tiny ark, a basket in which your infant faith may float safely on the stream. Do not forget what God has done for you. Open up the book of your memories and consider the days of old.

Have you never been helped in a time of need? I know you have. Go back, then, to the choice mercies of yesterday. It may be dark now, but if you light up the lamps of the past, they will glitter through the darkness. They will help you trust in the Lord until the day breaks and the shadows flee.

January 26

Your heavenly Father.
(Matthew 6:26)

God's people are doubly his children. They are his offspring by creation, and they are his sons by adoption in Christ. And so they are privileged to call him, "Our Father in heaven" (Matthew 6:9).

Father! Oh, what a precious word that is! Here is *authority*. Because he is our Father, we owe him obedience. Here is *affection* mingled with authority. God's authority does not provoke rebellion. The obedience he demands is most cheerfully given. It would not be held back, even if it could be.

The obedience that God's children show him must be *loving* obedience. Don't go about God's service as slaves might go about their taskmaster's toil. Enjoy it, because it is your Father's desire. Yield your bodies as instruments of righteousness, because righteousness is what your Father wants, and his will should also be the will of his child.

Father! Here we find honor and love. How great is a father's love for his children! It goes beyond friendship. It goes beyond mere benevolence. These will not even attempt what a father's heart and hand must do for his children. They are his offspring—he must bless them. They are his children—he must defend them with all his strength.

If an earthly father watches over his children with constant love and care, how much more does our heavenly Father? Abba, Father! He who says this produces sweeter music than any cherub can chirp. There is heaven in the depth of this one word—*Father*!

January 27

From the fullness of his grace we have all received one blessing after another. (John 1:16)

There is fullness in Christ. In him is the fullness of the deity. "For God was pleased to have all his fullness dwell in him" (Colossians 1:19).

Christ also has the fullness of perfect manhood. In his body, the Godhead was revealed. There is fullness in the atoning power of his blood, for "the blood of Jesus, his Son, purifies us from all sin" (1 John 1:7).

There is also fullness in the justification he offers. "Therefore, there is now no condemnation for those who are in Christ Jesus" (Romans 8:1). There is fullness in his deliverance, for "he is able to save completely those who come to God through him, because he always lives to intercede for them" (Hebrews 7:25).

There is fullness of victory in his death, for through death he destroyed the power of death. There is fullness of power in his resurrection, for "in his great mercy he has given us new birth into a living hope through the resurrection of Jesus Christ from the dead" (1 Peter 1:3).

There is a fullness of blessings of every sort and shape—a fullness of grace to forgive us, to make us new, to make us holy, to keep us safe, to make us more like Christ.

There is fullness for all situations—a fullness of comfort in affliction, of guidance in prosperity. There is a fullness of every divine attribute, of wisdom, power, love. It would be impossible to survey this fullness, much less explore it.

Come, believer, get all your need supplied. Ask for much, and you will get much. This fullness is inexhaustible, and it is stored up where all the needy may reach it—in Jesus.

January 28

Perfect in Christ.
(Colossians 1:28)

You are not perfect. You know that in your soul. Every day teaches you that. Every tear in your eye weeps, "Imperfection!" Every sigh that bursts from your heart cries, "Imperfection!" Every harsh word that comes out of your mouth mutters, "Imperfection!" You know your heart too well to even dream for a moment of any perfection *in yourself*.

But in the middle of this sad situation, there is comfort for you—you are "perfect *in Christ*." In God's sight, you are "complete in him." Right now, you stand accepted by God.

Yet we have a second perfection, too, that is yet to be realized. We can look forward to the time when every stain of sin will be removed from us. We will be presented faultless before God's throne, without spot or wrinkle. The church of Christ will be so pure that not even the eye of the omniscient God will see a spot or blemish in us. Dressed in Jesus' spotless garments, we will be holy.

Then we will know and taste and feel the happiness of this vast but short phrase: "Perfect in Christ." Not until then will we fully comprehend the heights and depths of our salvation. Doesn't your heart leap for joy at the very thought of it? As filthy as you are now, you will be clean. Christ takes a worm and transforms it into an angel. Christ takes a deformed thing and gives it beauty.

January 29

We fix our eyes not on what is seen, but on what is unseen.
(2 Corinthians 4:18)

In our Christian pilgrimage, it is good to look forward. Our crown is in front of us, our goal lies ahead. Looking ahead with the eyes of faith, we see the hope, joy, comfort, and inspiration of the future. We see sin cast out, the body of sin and death destroyed, the soul made perfect. We see ourselves as partakers of the inheritance of the saints.

Looking even further, the believer's enlightened eyes see the crossing of death's river and the climbing of the hills of light, on which stands the celestial city. The believer can see himself entering the pearly gates, hailed as a conqueror, crowned by Christ, embraced in the arms of Jesus, glorified with him, offered a seat on his throne.

These thoughts of the future may relieve the dark memories of the past and the gloom of the present. The joys of heaven will certainly compensate for the sorrows of earth.

That vision banishes my fears. This world is only a narrow span; it will soon be past. My doubts are gone. Death is just a small stream; it will soon be crossed. Time is short, but eternity is long. I will soon be there.

January 30

As soon as you hear the sound of marching in the tops of the balsam trees, move quickly. (2 Samuel 5:24)

The members of Christ's church should always be prayerful. We should always seek the anointing of God's Spirit in our hearts. We should pray for the coming of Christ's kingdom, that his "will be done on earth as it is in heaven" (see Luke 11:2).

But there are some times when the Lord seems to pour out his special favor on his people. In these times he is doing special things.

We ought to pay attention to these events as "the sound of marching in the tops of the balsam trees." We should be doubly prayerful, doubly diligent, wrestling more at God's throne than usual. Our action should be prompt and vigorous. The tide is flowing; we need to row strongly toward the shore.

There are times when the "sound of marching" is heard in your personal life. You become especially powerful in prayer. The Spirit gives you joy and gladness. The Scripture is open to you, and you apply its promises. You are walking in the light of God's presence. Your dedication to Christ is full and free, and you stay in close communication with him.

Now is the time to "move quickly." Get rid of some evil habit. Spread your sails and take advantage of the Spirit's breezes. Ask God to help you make new strides in your devotion to him at this time when your faith is strong. Develop new habits of prayer in this time when you feel close to Christ. Learn new ways to be holy now that you are tapping into Christ's power.

January 31

The Lord Our Righteousness.
(Jeremiah 23:6)

It should give the Christian a sense of calm, a sense of quiet peace, to think about the perfect righteousness of Christ. Yet so many are downcast and sad! I don't think they ought to be, and I don't think they would feel that way if they could see their perfection in Christ.

Some people always talk about corruption, the depravity of the heart, the innate evil of the soul. All of this is quite true, but why not go a step further and remember that we are "perfect in Christ Jesus"? No wonder they look so downcast! But if we call to mind Christ's righteousness, we should be of good cheer.

Though distress may afflict me, though Satan assaults me, I can rest in the fact that Christ has made me righteous. On the cross he said, "It is finished!" If it is finished, then I am complete in him, and I can rejoice—"not having a righteousness of my own that comes from the law, but that which is through faith in Christ" (Philippians 3:9).

There is no one holier than those who have received Christ's righteousness. When the believer says, "I live by Christ alone. I rely on only him for my salvation. I believe that, as unworthy as I am, I am still saved in Jesus," then a sense of gratitude springs up. The believer goes on to say, "Well, then, shouldn't I live for him? Shouldn't I love him and serve him?"

We have had righteousness *imputed* to our account. That helps us value the righteousness *imparted* to our lives.

February 1

May they sing of the ways of the Lord.
(Psalm 138:5)

When do Christians begin to sing? When they leave their burden at the foot of the cross. Not even the songs of angels seem as sweet as the first songs that gush from the forgiven soul. In *Pilgrim's Progress*, John Bunyan described how Pilgrim dropped his burden at the cross, took three great leaps, and went on his way singing.

Do you recall the day when your fetters fell off? Do you remember the place when Jesus met you and said, "I have loved you with an everlasting love" (Jeremiah 31:3), "I have swept away your offenses like a cloud, your sins like the morning mist" (Isaiah 44:22)?

Oh, what a great time that is, when Jesus takes away the pain of sin. When the Lord first forgave my sin, I was so happy I could hardly keep from dancing. On the way home that day, I felt that I had to tell my story to the stones in the street! I wanted to tell every snowflake of the wondrous love of Jesus, who had swept away the sins of one of his chief rebels.

But it is not only at the beginning of their Christian lives that people have a reason to sing. As long as they live, Christians keep discovering reasons to sing of the ways of the Lord. Their daily experience makes them say, "I will extol the Lord at all times; his praise will always be on my lips" (Psalm 34:1). Magnify the Lord today!

February 2

Without the shedding of blood there is no forgiveness. (Hebrews 9:22)

This is an eternal truth. Sin cannot be pardoned without atonement. That means that there is no hope for me outside of Christ, for there is no other blood that can truly take away my sin.

Are you, then, believing in him? Is the blood of his atonement applied to your soul? All of us are equal in our need of him. We may be moral, generous, friendly, or patriotic—but there is no exception to the rule. Sin will yield to nothing less powerful than the blood of the Savior. We should be glad that we have a way to be forgiven! Why go looking for another?

Those who follow a merely formal religion don't understand us. How can we rejoice that all our sins are forgiven in Christ? Their works and prayers and ceremonies keep them busy, but they don't give them rest. And with good reason: they are neglecting the single source of true salvation. They are trying to get forgiveness without blood.

Sit down and look at it. God is just. He must punish sin. The Lord Jesus took that punishment upon himself, shedding his blood. We should be falling at his feet in gratitude.

We don't need to "feel" saved. If your conscience troubles you, don't look for "proofs" of your salvation. Look to the cross. See Jesus suffering for you. Trust in his blood for your forgiveness.

February 3

Therefore, brethren, we are debtors.
(Romans 8:12 KJV)

As God's creatures, we are all debtors to him—to obey him with all our bodies, souls, and strength. Since we have all broken his commandments, we are debtors to his justice. We owe him a vast amount that we are not able to pay.

But we can say that the *Christian* owes nothing to God's justice, since Christ has paid our debt. The Christian owes more to God's love. I am a debtor to God's grace and forgiving mercy, but I am no debtor to his justice, for he will never accuse me of a debt already paid.

Christ said, "It is finished!" Whatever his people owed was wiped from the books. Christ has satisfied the divine justice. The account is settled. The bill has been nailed to the cross. The receipt has been given.

But then, because we are not debtors anymore in *that* sense, we become ten times more God's debtors in another sense. Pause and ponder for a moment. Think about how much you owe to God's sovereignty, to his unmerited love, to his forgiving grace. After ten thousand insults, he still loves you as infinitely as ever.

Think about what you owe to his power, how he has raised you from death, how he has energized your spiritual life, and how he has kept you from falling.

Think about what you owe to his unchanging nature. Though you have changed a thousand times, he has not changed once.

You owe God a great deal. You owe yourself and all that you have. So give yourself as a living sacrifice. It is only your reasonable service (Romans 12:1).

February 4

As the Lord loves the Israelites.
(Hosea 3:1)

Look back through your experience. See how the Lord has led you through the wilderness, how he has fed and clothed you every day, how he has put up with your bad manners and complaining.

When you longed to go back to "Egypt," he opened up the rock to supply your needs, and he fed you with manna from heaven.

Think of how his grace has been sufficient for you in all your troubles, how his blood has pardoned all your sins, and how his rod and staff have comforted you.

After you have looked back on the way the Lord has loved you in the past, let your faith anticipate his future love. The one who has loved and pardoned you will never stop loving and pardoning. He is Alpha, but also Omega. He is first, but he will also be last. So when you pass through the valley of the shadow of death, you do not need to fear any evil, for he will be with you. When you stand in the cold River Jordan, don't be afraid. Even death cannot separate you from his love.

When you enter the mysteries of eternity, there will be no need to tremble. "For I am convinced that neither death nor life, neither angels nor demons, neither the present nor the future, nor any powers, neither height nor depth, nor anything else in all creation, will be able to separate us from the love of God that is in Christ Jesus our Lord" (Romans 8:38–39).

Doesn't this refresh your own love? Doesn't this make you love Jesus? The more we meditate on the way "the Lord loves the Israelites"—and how he loves us—the more our hearts burn within us. We long to love him more.

February 5

The Father has sent his Son to be the Savior of the world.
(1 John 4:14)

Jesus Christ did not come to us without his Father's permission. He had the Father's full authority, consent, and assistance. We tend to forget that, although there are three distinct *persons* in the Trinity, there are no distinctions of *honor*. That is, we often credit Jesus Christ for our salvation more than we credit the Father. This is a very great mistake.

Yes, Jesus came to us. But didn't his Father send him? Jesus spoke wondrously, but didn't the Father pour grace into his lips so that he might proclaim the new covenant? The one who truly knows the Father, Son, and Holy Spirit never sets one above another. He loves them equally. He sees them at Bethlehem, at Gethsemane, and on Calvary, equally involved in the work of salvation.

Have you put your confidence in Christ Jesus? Have you placed your faith solely in him? Are you united with him? Then you are also united with the God of heaven. If you have close, brotherly fellowship with Jesus, that links you with the Eternal God. The "Ancient of Days" is therefore your Father and your friend.

Have you ever considered the depth of Yahweh's love, when he equipped his Son for this great mission of mercy? Meditate on this today. The *Father* sent him! Jesus does what the Father plans. In the wounds of the dying Savior, see the love of the great I AM. Every time you think of Jesus, think of the eternal loving Father who sent him.

February 6

And pray in the Spirit on all occasions.
(Ephesians 6:18)

Think of all the prayers you have prayed, ever since you first learned how. Our first prayer is a prayer for ourselves—we ask God to have mercy and blot out our sin. He heard that prayer of yours and blotted out your sin, but then there were more prayers.

We have prayed for grace to help us live holy lives, for a fresh assurance of our salvation, for the application of God's promises, for deliverance from temptation, for strength to do God's work, for comfort in times of testing. We are like beggars, regularly approaching God to ask for whatever our souls need.

Where else will we find what our souls need?

All the bread your soul has eaten has come from heaven, all the water your soul has drunk has flowed from the living rock—Christ Jesus. Your soul has not grown rich on its own. It is dependent, relying on God for its daily allowance of blessing. That is why we pray for the whole range of spiritual mercies we need.

Our wants have been countless, but God's supplies have been infinite. Our prayers have been as varied as the mercies are plentiful.

As you think about your lifetime of prayers, don't you want to say, "I love the Lord, for he heard my voice; he heard my cry for mercy" (Psalm 116:1)? He has heard you in your day of trouble. He has strengthened you and helped you, even when your prayers were full of trembling and doubting.

Remember this, and let it fill your heart with gratitude. "Praise the Lord, O my soul, and forget not all his benefits" (Psalm 103:2).

February 7

Get up, go away! For this is not your resting place.
(Micah 2:10)

All of us will hear this message sooner or later. "Get up! It's time to leave your home, your business, your family, and your friends. It is time to take your final journey."

What do we know about that journey? What do we know about the land where we are going? We have read a little, and the Spirit has revealed some to us, but we still know very little of our future home.

We know that there is a dark and stormy river called death. God tells us to cross it, promising to be with us. And what comes then? What world of wonder will open up to us? No traveler has ever returned to tell us.

Yet we know enough about the heavenly land to rejoice when we are finally summoned there. The journey of death may be dark, but we can travel without fear. God is with us as we walk through the gloomy valley. We need to "fear no evil" (Psalm 23:4). We will be leaving all we have known and loved here, but we are headed for our Father's house, to that royal "city with foundations, whose architect and builder is God" (Hebrews 11:10). We will be with Jesus.

This will be our last move. We will live forever with the Lord we love and with all his people. Christian, meditate on heaven as much as you can; it will help you to press on, to forget how difficult the journey can be. This valley of tears is only the pathway to a better country. This world of woe is the stepping-stone to a world of bliss.

February 8

You are to give him the name Jesus.
(Matthew 1:21)

When a person is precious to you, everything connected with him becomes precious. Jesus is so precious to believers that everything about him is precious. "All your robes are fragrant with myrrh and aloes and cassia," said David (Psalm 45:8), as if the very vestments of the Savior were so sweetened by his being that David couldn't help but love them.

Certainly, every spot where his holy feet have walked, every word his blessed lips have spoken, every thought that comes to us in his written Word—these are all precious to us, beyond price.

This is also true of the names of Christ. They are all sweet in the believer's ear. Whether he is called the Husband of the Church, her Bridegroom, her Friend; whether he is styled as the Lamb slain from the foundation of the world—the King, the Prophet, or the Priest—every title of our Master—Emmanuel, Wonderful, the Mighty Counselor—every name is like the honeycomb dripping with honey.

But if there is one name sweeter than any other, it is the name *Jesus*. Jesus! It is a name that moves the harps of heaven to make beautiful melody. Jesus! It is woven into the very fabric of our worship. Many of our hymns begin with it, and hardly any, if they're worth anything, end without mentioning it. It is the sum total of all delights. It is the music ringing from the bells of heaven, an ocean of things to think about in just a droplet of speech, a matchless oratorio in two syllables. It gathers up all the hallelujahs of eternity in just five letters.

Jesus!

February 9

So David inquired of the Lord.
(2 Samuel 5:23)

When David made this inquiry, he had just fought the Philistines. He had won a great victory. The Philistines came at him in great numbers, but with God's help, David routed them.

Then they came at him a second time. David did not go right out to fight them. He inquired of the Lord *again*. After one victory, most of us would have said, "I will win again. I did it once; I can do it again. Why bother to ask the Lord about it?"

Not so David. He had won the first battle by God's strength. He would not attempt another until he knew he had God's strength behind him. He asked, "Shall I go and attack the Philistines?" and he waited for God's answer.

Learn this from David. Take no step without God. If you want to stay on the right path, let God be your compass. If you want to steer your ship safely through the storm, let God's hand rest on the tiller. We will avoid many rocks, many shoals and quicksands, if we let our Father take the helm.

A Puritan writer once said, "As sure as ever a Christian carves for himself, he'll cut his own fingers." This is true. Another preacher has said, "He that goes before the cloud of God's providence goes on a fool's errand." So he does. We must let God's providence lead the way. If we run ahead, we'll have to run back again.

God promised his people, "I will instruct you and teach you in the way you should go" (Psalm 32:8). So let's take all our pressing questions to him. Ask him, "What should I do?" Don't leave your room this morning without inquiring of the Lord.

February 10

I know how to abound.
(Philippians 4:12 KJV)

Many of us know "how to be abased." We trust God in hard times. But few of us have learned "how to abound." Put us on top, and we get dizzy; we fall.

The Christian is more apt to disgrace his faith in prosperity than in adversity. It is a dangerous thing to be prosperous. The material bounty that God gives us often leads us to neglect spiritual things. Our souls grow lean as our bodies grow fat.

But this does not have to be. Paul tells us he knew how to abound. When he had much, he knew what to do with it. Abundant grace enabled him to bear abundant prosperity.

It takes more than human skill to carry the brimming cup of mortal joy with a steady hand, but Paul had learned that skill. He says, "I have learned the secret of being content in any and every situation, whether well fed or hungry" (Philippians 4:12). Only God can teach us this, and it is a difficult lesson to learn. Whenever the Israelites were "well fed," it seems, they did something to earn God's wrath.

Many have asked for God's blessings in order to satisfy their own desires. They are full of God's providential mercies, but they lack God's grace, and they have little gratitude for what they have received. When we are full, we tend to forget God. We grow satisfied with earth; we can do without heaven.

Rest assured, it is harder to know how to be full than it is to know how to be hungry. Because of our pride and forgetfulness, prosperity is difficult for us. So be sure to ask God to teach you how to abound.

February 11

They took note that these men had been with Jesus.
(Acts 4:13)

A Christian should be a striking likeness of Jesus Christ. You may have read accounts of the life of Christ, beautifully pulled together from the Gospels, but the best "life of Christ" is his living biography, written out in the words and actions of his people.

If we were what we profess to be, we would be pictures of Christ. In fact, we would be such a striking likeness that people would not have to hold us up to the light and say, "Well, this Christian seems *sort of* like Christ." No, the immediate reaction would be "He has been with Jesus. He has been taught by him. He is like him. He has caught the whole idea of the holy man of Nazareth, and he works it out in his life and everyday actions."

A Christian should be like Christ in his *boldness*. Never blush to claim your faith. Your Christianity will never disgrace you; be careful not to disgrace it.

Imitate Jesus in your *loving spirit*. Think kindly, speak kindly, and act kindly—so that people will say about you, "He has been with Jesus."

Imitate Jesus in his *holiness*. He was zealous; you should be, too, always going about doing good. He was self-denying; you should be, too. He was devout; you, too, should be fervent in your prayers. He submitted to his Father's will; and so should you. He was patient; and you, too, must learn to endure.

Above all, try to forgive your enemies, as Jesus did. Forgive as you hope to be forgiven. Heap coals of fire on the head of your foe by being kind to him (Romans 12:20). Remember that repaying good for evil is God-like. So be God-like in all you do and say, so that everyone who sees you may say, "He has been with Jesus."

February 12

For just as the sufferings of Christ flow over into our lives, so also through Christ our comfort overflows. (2 Corinthians 1:5)

The Ruler of All holds a set of scales. In one side he puts his people's trials. In the other he puts their comforts. When the trial side is nearly empty, so is the comfort side. When the trials are great, so are the comforts.

When the black clouds gather, the light comes through more brightly. When the night approaches and the storm threatens, the heavenly Captain is especially close to his crew. This is a wonderful thing. The more we are distressed, the more we are lifted up by the Spirit.

Why? For one thing, *trials make more room for comfort*. Trouble is like a shovel that digs a deep reservoir for comfort. The deeper it digs, the more comfort the reservoir will hold. Great hearts can only be made by great trials.

Or picture this: God comes into our heart—he finds it full. He begins to break our comforts and make it empty. Then there is more room for grace. The needy person always gets more comfort, because he is more able to receive it.

Another reason is this. When we have troubles, *we have our closest dealings with God*. When the barn is full, we think we can live without God. When our purses are bursting, we can try to get along without prayer. But clean the idols out of the house, and then we must honor the true God.

The psalmist wrote: "Out of the depths I cry to you, O Lord" (Psalm 130:1). There is no prayer half so hearty as that which comes up from the depths of the soul, through deep trials and afflictions. These bring us to God, and we are happier.

So do not fret over your heavy troubles. They are the heralds of great mercies.

February 13

How great is the love the Father has lavished on us, that we should be called children of God! And that is what we are! The reason the world does not know us is that it did not know him. Dear friends, now we are children of God. (1 John 3:1–2)

When we consider the kind of people we were and how corrupt we still feel sometimes, this adoption is truly amazing. We are the children of God! What an honored relationship this is, and what privileges it brings! What care and tenderness the child expects from his father, and what love a father feels toward his child! All of that—and more—we now have through Christ.

There is, however, a temporary drawback. The world does not recognize our heritage. But we accept this as an honor—it did not recognize Jesus either. We are content to be unknown with him, because we know we will be exalted with him.

Do you feel like a child of God this morning? How is it with your heart? Are you in the lowest depths of sorrow? Does a desire to sin rise up within you? Does grace seem like a fading spark, trampled underfoot? Does your faith almost fail you? Don't worry. You are not to live by your feelings or even your gracious acts. You must live simply by faith in Christ.

Wherever we are, even in the depths of sorrow, the message comes to us: "Now we are children of God."

"But wait," you say. "Look how I'm dressed. I'm not wearing any fancy graces. My righteousness does not shine with dazzling glory."

But read the rest of verse 2: "What we will be has not yet been made known. But we know that when he appears, we shall be like him."

The Holy Spirit will purify our minds. Divine power will reshape our bodies. And we will see our Lord as he is.

February 14

Day by day the king gave Jehoiachin a regular allowance as long as he lived. (2 Kings 25:30)

The conquered King Jehoiachin was released from prison and treated with honor. But he was not given provisions to last for months. He was given a daily allowance. In this, he models the ideal position of all God's people. A daily allowance is *all anyone really needs*.

We don't need tomorrow's supplies. That day has not yet dawned; its wants are still unborn. The thirst we suffer in the month of June cannot be quenched in February. If we have enough for each day, as the days arrive, we will not be in need. The fact is, that's all we can really enjoy.

We cannot eat or drink or wear more than one day's supply of food and clothing. Any surplus just gives us the trouble of storing it and the worry of guarding against thieves. If a traveler has one staff, that helps. But if he has a bundle of staffs, that's a burden. "Enough for the day" is not only *as good as* a feast—it is all that even the hungriest glutton can enjoy.

This is all we should expect. When our Father does not give us more, we should be content with his daily allowance. Jehoiachin's situation is ours. We have a regular allowance from the King himself; it is enough for the day, and it will last forever. This is surely something to be thankful for.

My friend, in matters of grace, *you need a daily supply*. You cannot store up spiritual strength. Day by day you must seek God's help. You can be sure that a daily allowance will be offered—in God's Word, through ministry, in meditation, in prayer, in waiting on the Lord. Everything you need is there for you. So enjoy your allowance. Never go hungry while the daily bread of grace is on the table of mercy.

February 15

To him be glory both now and forever.
(2 Peter 3:18)

Heaven will be full of unending songs to Jesus. He will receive glory through all eternity. Is he not a "priest forever in the order of Melchizedek" (Hebrews 7:17)? To him be glory. Is he not an eternal king, "King of kings and Lord of lords" (1 Timothy 6:15), "the Everlasting Father" (Isaiah 9:6)? To him be glory forever. His praises will never cease.

The purchase he made with his blood will last through all eternity. The glory of the cross will never be eclipsed. The luster of the empty grave and the glorious resurrection will never be dimmed. O Jesus, you will receive our praise forever! As long as immortal spirits live, as long as the Father's throne endures, forever and forever, unto you be all the glory.

Believer, you are eagerly anticipating the time when you will join the saints in giving eternal glory to Jesus. But are you glorifying him now? Peter says, "To him be glory both *now* and forever."

Why not make this your prayer today? "Lord, help me to glorify you. I am poor, but help me to glorify you by being content. I am sick, but help me to honor you with my patience. I have talents; help me to use them for you. I have time, Lord; help me to redeem it so that I can serve you. I have a heart that feels things deeply, Lord; let my heart glow with a flame of passion for you. I have a head that thinks, Lord; fill it with thoughts of you and thoughts that please you. You have put me in the world for something, Lord. Show me what that is.

"I cannot do much for you, Lord. But, as the widow put in her two coins [Luke 21:1–4], so I throw my time and eternity into your treasury. I am yours. Take me, and show me how to glorify you *now*."

February 16

I have learned to be content whatever the circumstances.
(Philippians 4:11)

Contentment is not a natural propensity of man. Covetousness, discontent, and complaining are as natural to us as weeds are to soil. We don't need to plant weeds; they come up by themselves. In the same way, we don't have to teach people to complain; they do so well enough without any education.

But the precious things of the earth must be cultivated. If we want wheat, we have to plow and plant. If we want flowers, we must garden. Now contentment is one of the flowers of heaven. If we want it, we must cultivate it. It will not grow naturally. Only the new nature can produce it, and even then we must take special care of the grace God has planted inside us.

Paul says, "I have *learned* to be content." Apparently there was a time when he did not know how. It cost him some pains to grasp that great mystery. No doubt there were times when he thought he had it down pat and then broke down. When he finally was able to say this, he was an old, gray-haired man nearing his grave, a poor prisoner shut up in Nero's dungeon in Rome.

Do not indulge the notion that you can be content without learning. And you can't learn without discipline. Contentment is not a power we have naturally. It's a science that we acquire gradually. We know this from experience.

So my brother or sister, hold back your next complaint, however natural it may be, and continue as a diligent pupil in the College of Contentment.

February 17

Isaac . . . lived near Beer Lahai Roi.
(Genesis 25:11)

Hagar had met the angel of God at the well called Beer Lahai Roi (Genesis 16:7–14). It may have been here that God graciously provided water for Hagar and her son, Ishmael (Genesis 20:19). The name means "the well of the Living One who sees me." The seeing God met their needs.

But these seem to have been momentary occurrences. This sort of thing happens to many people, even unbelievers. They pay a casual visit to the Lord when it suits them, in a time of need. They cry to him in trouble, but ignore him when things are going well.

Isaac *lived* there. He made the well of the living and all-seeing God the source of his livelihood. This is the true test of a person—where does his soul *live*?

Perhaps Isaac had heard of Hagar's experience. Perhaps its name made it special to him. His frequent meditations in that area would have made him familiar with it. Certainly the memory of his first glimpse of Rebekah there would make his spirit feel at home. But best of all, here he enjoyed fellowship with the living God.

We should learn to live in the presence of the living God. He should be a well for us—delightful, comforting, unfailing, springing up to eternal life (John 4:14). When we rely on other people, their water supplies ultimately dry up. But the well of the Creator never fails to nourish us.

The Lord has shown himself to be a true helper. His name is Shaddai, the all-sufficient God. Our hearts have enjoyed his company. "In him we live and move and have our being" (Acts 17:28). So let us live in close fellowship with him, drawing daily from his well.

February 18

Tell me what charges you have against me.
(Job 10:2)

Are you being tested like Job? Perhaps the Lord is trying to develop some aspects of your character—faith, love, and hope. Some of these might never be discovered if it weren't for trials.

Faith never looks as big in summer as in winter. Love is often like a glowworm, showing little light except when surrounded by darkness. Hope is like a star, not seen in the sunshine of prosperity, but only in the night of adversity.

Hard times are often the dark background against which God sets the jewels of his children's faith, hope, and love—they shine all the brighter.

Weren't you praying just recently, "Lord, I'm afraid I have no faith; let me know that I have faith"? You may not have known it, but in a way you were praying for trials. How can you know you have faith until you have to put it to work?

Count on this: God often sends us trials to help us discover new attributes of our Christianity and not only to discover them, but to *grow in them*. God often takes away our comforts and privileges in order to make us better Christians. He trains his soldiers not in tents of ease and luxury, but by putting us through a boot camp of forced marches and hard service. He makes us ford streams and swim across rivers and climb mountains and walk miles with heavy knapsacks of sorrows on our backs.

Well, Christian, does this help explain your troubles? Isn't God helping you to grow?

February 19

This is what the Sovereign Lord says: Once again I will yield to the plea of the house of Israel and do this for them.
(Ezekiel 36:37)

Prayer is the forerunner of mercy. Search through sacred history, and you will find that hardly ever did a great mercy come to this world without prayer paving its way. You have found this true in your own life, I'm sure. God has given many blessings without being asked, but still, great prayer has always preceded great mercy.

When you first found peace with God through the blood of the cross, you had been praying a great deal, earnestly asking God to remove your doubts. Prayer led to new assurance. As you think about the great joys of your life, you have to see them as answers to prayer. When you have been delivered out of dire troubles, you have been able to say, "I sought the Lord, and he answered me; he delivered me from all my fears" (Psalm 34:4).

Prayer is always the preface to blessing. It is like a blessing's shadow. As the sunlight of God's mercy rises on our needs, it casts the shadow of prayer. To use another illustration, when God piles up a hill of mercies, he himself shines behind them, and the shadow of prayer falls on our spirits.

So we see the value of prayer. If we had the blessings without asking for them, we would take them for granted. But prayer makes our mercies more precious than diamonds. The things we ask for are precious, but we do not realize how precious until we have earnestly asked God for them.

February 20

But God, who comforts the downcast.
(2 Corinthians 7:6)

Who can comfort us like God? Go to some poor, melancholy, distressed child of God. Tell him sweet promises, whisper words of comfort in his ear. What happens? He is like a deaf snake that refuses to be charmed, no matter how skillful the snake charmer is. Comfort him as you may, you will only get a note or two of mournful resignation from him. You will bring forth no psalms of praise, no hallelujahs, no joyful sonnets.

But let *God* come to his child, and the mourner's eyes glisten with hope. *You* may not be able to cheer up the sufferer, but God does it easily. He is the "God of all comfort" (2 Corinthians 1:3). There is no balm in Gilead (Jeremiah 8:22), but God himself is a healing balm for his people. One sweet word from God will make whole songs for Christians. One word from God is like a piece of gold, and the Christian is like the goldsmith, who hammers out that promise for weeks on end.

So then, poor Christian, you don't need to sit down in despair. Go to the Comforter. Ask him to give you consolation. You are a poor, dry well. But as you may know, when a pump is dry, you must first pour water down into it, and then you will get water. So Christian, when you are dry, go to God. Ask him to dowse your soul with joy. Then your joy will be full. Don't go to earthly friends. They will probably turn out like the comforters of Job. But go first and foremost to the God who comforts the downcast, and you will soon find yourself saying, "When anxiety was great within me, your consolation brought joy to my soul" (Psalm 94:19).

February 21

God has said.
(Hebrews 13:5)

If we grasp these words by faith, we have an all-conquering weapon in our hand. This two-edged sword will slay all doubt. This arrow from the bow of God's covenant will pierce every fear with a deadly wound. When we hide ourselves within the fortress of this statement—"God has said"—all the distresses of life, all its traps and trials, seem light and easy to bear.

This simple truth gives us delight in times of quiet meditation, and it gives us strength for our daily battles. It shows us the great value of searching the Scriptures. There may be a promise in God's Word that would fit your situation exactly, but you may not know of it, so you miss out on its comfort. You are like a prisoner in a dungeon, with a ring of keys. One of the keys would unlock the door and free you. But if you don't look for it, you will remain a prisoner, though your liberty is so close at hand.

There may be a powerful medicine in Scripture's pharmacy. But you will remain sick until you search for what "God has said."

Besides just reading the Bible, shouldn't you fill your memory with God's promises? Maybe you can quote the sayings of great men; you memorize the verses of famous poets. Shouldn't you be just as diligent in your knowledge of God's words, so that you can recall them when you need them?

"He has said" is the source of all wisdom. Let it dwell in you richly.

February 22

But his bow remained steady, his strong arms stayed limber, because of the hand of the Mighty One of Jacob. (Genesis 49:24)

God gave Joseph *real* strength, not just boasted courage, the fictitious kind that people claim and usually end up just blowing smoke. God gives to all his Josephs *divine* strength.

Why did Joseph resist temptation? God helped him. We can do nothing without God's power. All true strength comes from "the Mighty One of Jacob."

Notice *how* God gave Joseph his strength. The mention of God's hand paints a picture of him placing his hands on Joseph's hands. As a father teaches his children, so God empowers Joseph's arms with his own arms. What a wonderfully familiar scene! God puts his arms on us, his children. God Almighty, Eternal, All-Powerful stoops from his throne and lays his arms upon our arms to strengthen us.

The strength God gives is also *covenant* strength, since it is ascribed to the God "of Jacob." Now, whenever you read of the God of Jacob, you should remember the covenant with Jacob. We Christians love to think of God's covenant. All the power, grace, blessings, and mercies of God—all that we have—flow through God's covenant. If there were no covenant, we would have no hope, for all God's grace proceeds from it, as light and heat from the sun. No angels ascend or descend except on that ladder that Jacob saw—and at the top of that ladder was God, making a covenant with him.

Dear Christian, you may have been wounded by enemy archers, but your bow is still strong. Be sure to give all the glory to "the Mighty One of Jacob."

February 23

Never will I leave you.
(Hebrews 13:5)

Whatever God has said to one saint, he says to all. When he opens a well, all may drink from it. When he opens the door of the storehouse to give out grain, he may be doing so for one starving man, but all hungry saints may come and be fed.

It does not really matter whether he said something to Abraham or Moses—he has said it to you, as a member of the family, a partaker in the covenant. There is no blessing too great for you, no mercy too far reaching. Lift your eyes to the north and south, to the east and west—it is all yours. Climb to the top of Mount Pisgah with old Moses, and view the territory God has promised—it belongs to you. There is no brook of living water that you may not drink from. If the land flows with milk and honey, eat the honey and drink the milk—both are yours.

Be bold to believe, because he has said, "Never will I leave *you*, never will I forsake *you*." In this promise, God gives his people everything. Suddenly all the attributes of God are there for our use. Is he mighty? He shows his strength on behalf of those who trust him. Is he love? Then he lovingly shows us his mercy. Anything you could want, anything you could ask for, anything you would need in time or eternity—this text contains it all. Everything living or dying, in this world or the next, now and on the resurrection morning—it is all here for you. God tells you, "Never will I leave you."

February 24

I will send down showers in season; there will be showers of blessing. (Ezekiel 34:26)

Who can say this but God? One voice alone can speak to the clouds and tell them to rain. Only God can send showers upon the vegetation of earth. Grace is like that, too. It is a gift of God; we cannot create it ourselves.

Grace is also like rain in another way. It is *needed*. What would the ground do without showers? You may plow your soil, you may sow your seeds, but what can you do without rain? Divine blessing is just as needed. All our works are useless until God sends the saving shower of his grace.

God's grace is also *plentiful*. God did not say, "I will send drops." He sends showers, and so it is with grace. If God gives a blessing, he usually gives it in such proportions that we don't have room to receive it all. Think about that for a moment: God's plentiful grace. We want that in our lives, don't we? Grace to keep us humble, to make us prayerful, to make us holy. Grace to make us zealous, to get us through this life and on to heaven. We cannot do without the saturating showers of God's grace.

God's grace, like rain, is also *seasonable*. It comes at the right time. What is your season this morning? Are you in a drought? Then that is the season for God's showers. Is it a season of weariness and dark clouds? Then that is the time for God's blessing. Look up today, O parched plant, and open your leaves and flowers for a heavenly watering.

February 25

The coming wrath.
(Matthew 3:7)

Have you ever walked in the country after a rainstorm? It is great to smell the freshness of the grass and to see the drops glistening like diamonds in the sun. That is the situation for the Christian. He walks through a land where a storm has just been—it has fallen upon our Savior. If there are still a few drops falling, they fall from clouds of mercy. Jesus assures us that no storm will destroy us.

How terrible it is to see the approach of a thunderstorm. We see the signs of its coming. The birds in the air droop their wings. The cattle drop their heads in terror. The sky grows black. The sun does not shine through. The heavens seem angry and frowning. It is even worse as a hurricane approaches. We wait in terrible apprehension for the wind to wreak its havoc, furiously tearing up trees from their roots, forcing rocks from cliffs and hurtling them down on human residences.

Yet sinner, this is your present situation. No hot drops have yet fallen, but a shower of fire is coming. No terrible winds howl around you, but God's hurricane is gathering up its awesome artillery. The floodgates are still dammed up by God's mercy, but soon they shall open. God's thunderbolts are still in his storehouse, but he will soon be marching out in his fury. Then where will you flee?

God's hand of mercy is now outstretched, offering to lead you to Christ. He will shelter you from the storm. You know you need him. Believe in him, throw yourself upon his mercy, and let the approaching storm of God's wrath blow over you.

February 26

Salvation comes from the Lord.
(Jonah 2:9)

Salvation is the work of God. Only he can bring life to the soul that is "dead in . . . transgressions and sins" (Ephesians 2:1). Only he can maintain the soul in its spiritual life. He is both Alpha and Omega (Revelation 21:6). Salvation comes from the Lord.

If I am prayerful, it's because God makes me so. If I have faith or hope or love, they are God's gifts to me. If my life is steady and consistent, that's because God upholds me with his hand. I can do nothing to preserve myself, except what God does first inside of me. Whatever I have, all my goodness comes from God. When I sin, that's my doing. But when I act rightly, that is totally from God.

If I have fought against some spiritual enemy and beaten him down, it's because the Lord's strength steadied my arm. Do I live a holy life in this world? If so, it is not I, but Christ living in me. Am I forgiven for my sins? I did not cleanse myself; God did it. Am I growing toward God and away from this world's temptations? That is entirely because God is disciplining me properly. Am I growing in knowledge? The great Instructor is teaching me.

All my jewels have been crafted by heavenly design. I find in God all that I want, though I find in myself only sin and misery. "He alone is my rock and my salvation" (Psalm 62:2).

Do I feed on the Word? That Word would not nourish me at all unless the Lord made it nourishing and fed it to me. Am I continually receiving fresh strength? Where does that strength come from? My help comes from heaven's hills (Psalm 121:1–2). Without Jesus I can do nothing. As a branch cannot bear fruit unless it remains in the vine (John 15:4), neither can I, unless I remain in Jesus.

February 27

If you make the Most High your dwelling—
even the Lord, who is my refuge. (Psalm 91:9)

In the desert the Israelites were continually exposed to change. Whenever the fiery cloud stopped, they pitched their tents. But the next day, before the sun had risen, the trumpet sounded, the ark was up and moving, and the cloud led them through the canyons, up the hillsides, or along the arid wastelands. They hardly had time to rest before they heard, "Get up! This is not your resting place! You must keep traveling toward Canaan!" They were never very long in one place. Even wells and palm trees could not detain them.

Yet they had an enduring home in their God. His fiery cloud was their roof, its flame their household fire. They had to go on from place to place, always on the move, never settling down, never saying, "Now we are secure, this is our dwelling place."

"Yet," says Moses, "though we are always changing, Lord, you have been our dwelling place through all generations."

The Christian knows no change when it comes to God. He may be rich today and poor tomorrow. He may be sick today and well tomorrow. He may be happy today and distressed tomorrow. But there is no change in where he stands with God. If God loved me yesterday, he loves me today. My blessed Lord is my unmoving mansion of rest.

Let all my prospects fall through; let my hopes be blasted; let my joy wither—I will never lose what I have in God. He is my safe dwelling place. I am a pilgrim in this world, but at home with God. On the earth I wander, but in God I live in peace.

February 28

My hope comes from him.
(Psalm 62:5)

If we are looking for any satisfaction from this world, our hopes will be dashed. But if we look to God to supply our wants, both temporal and spiritual, we will be satisfied. We may always draw from the bank of faith and have our needs supplied out of the riches of God's loving-kindness. This I know: I'd rather have God as my banker than all the Rothschilds. My Lord never fails to honor his promises. When we bring them to his throne, he never sends them back unanswered. Therefore, I will wait, hat in hand, only at his door. He always opens it with a hand of bountiful grace.

But we also have hopes beyond this life. We will die soon, and then our hope is truly in him. We expect that God will send angels to our sickbed to carry us home. We believe that when the pulse is faint and the heart heaves heavily, some angelic messenger will stand and look with loving eyes upon us. "Come away, Sister Spirit," he will say, "Come away!"

And as we approach the heavenly gate, we hope to hear the welcome invitation, "Come, you who are blessed by my Father; take your inheritance, the kingdom prepared for you since the creation of the world" (Matthew 25:34). We expect harps of gold and crowns of glory. We hope soon to be among the multitudes of shining ones before the throne. We look forward to and long for the time when we will be like our glorious Lord, when "we shall see him as he is" (1 John 3:2).

If these are your hopes, my friend, then live for God. Live with the desire to glorify him. Only through his grace do you have hope of future glory.

February 29

I have drawn you with loving-kindness.
(Jeremiah 31:3)

God uses the thunders of the law and the terrors of judgment to bring us to Christ. But he wins his final victory with loving-kindness.

The Prodigal Son set out for his father's house with a great sense of need. But his father saw him a long way off and ran to meet him. That boy took the last few steps toward his father's house with a kiss still warm on his cheek and the welcome music ringing in his ears (Luke 15).

As an old poem puts it:

Law and terrors do but harden
All the while they work alone;
But a sense of blood-bought pardon
Will dissolve a heart of stone.

The Master came one night to the door and knocked with the iron hand of the law. The door shook and trembled on its hinges. But the man inside piled every piece of furniture he could find against the door. "I will not let him in," he said.

The Master turned away, but eventually he came back and knocked again. This time he used his own soft hand, especially that part that the nail had penetrated. The knock was soft and tender. This time the door did not shake, but strange to say, it opened. There, on his knees, the once-unwilling host was gladly receiving his guest. "Come in," he said. "Come in. Your knock has touched me. I could not think of your pierced hand leaving its blood mark on my door, and turning you away homeless. I yield. Your love has won my heart."

In every case, loving-kindness wins the day. What Moses could never do with his tablets of stone, Christ does with his wounded hand. May he continue to draw me with his love, until I finally sit down at the wedding feast of the Lamb.

March 1

Awake, north wind, and come, south wind! Blow on my garden, that its fragrance may spread abroad. (Song of Songs 4:16)

Anything is better than the dead calm of indifference. It would be better to call forth the north wind of trouble, if that could somehow be sanctified to carry the fragrance of our spiritual growth. As long as it cannot be said that "the Lord was not in the wind" (1 Kings 19:11), we will not shy away from even the most wintry blast.

Didn't the "beloved" in the Song of Songs submit herself to her Lover's will? She only asked him to send his grace in some form—any form, north or south, it didn't matter. Yet she seems so weary of deadness and unholy calm that she longed for any visit at all that would spur her to action.

But note that she wants the warm south wind of comfort, too, the smiles of divine love, the joy of the Redeemer's presence. These, too, can effectively arouse one's sluggish life. She calls for one or the other or both. She only wants to delight her Lover with the spices of her garden. She can't stand being useless, and neither can we.

We can honestly welcome any trial or even death itself, if that will help to please our Immanuel. We would let our heart be crushed to atoms, if only that would bring glory to our sweet Lord Jesus.

But those Christian virtues that we do not exercise are like the fragrant nectar that stays slumbering in the cups of the flowers. Yet when our wise Gardener allows the winds of both affliction and comfort to blow on us, these winds catch our aromas of faith, love, patience, hope, resignation, joy, and so on, spreading them far and wide.

March 2

So all Israel went down to the Philistines to have their plowshares, mattocks, axes and sickles sharpened. (1 Samuel 13:20)

We are engaged in a great war with the Philistines of evil, and we must use every weapon within our reach. Preaching, teaching, praying, giving, all must be brought into action. Talents that were once thought useless must now be employed. Mattock and ax and sickle may all be useful in slaying Philistines. Rough tools may deal hard blows, and killing need not be elegantly done, as long as it does the job. Each moment is precious, in season or out of season. Each fragment of ability, trained or not, each opportunity, favorable or unfavorable, must be used. Our foes are many and our forces are small.

Most of our tools need sharpening. We need quickness of perception, tact, energy, promptness—we must adapt everything for the Lord's work. Practical common sense is scarce among Christians. We could learn a thing or two from our enemies. In doing so, we make the "Philistines" sharpen our weapons.

This morning, let's just consider a few of the lessons we can learn from others. Various false religions use great energy in spreading their views, crossing land and sea to proselytize. Should they have a monopoly on missionary zeal? In many lands, idol worshipers go through great tortures to serve their false gods. Should they be the only ones practicing patience and self-sacrifice? See the work of the prince of darkness, persevering in his efforts, bold in his attempts, daring in his plans, shrewd in his schemes, and energetic in everything! The devils are united in their rebellion, while we believers are divided as we try to serve Jesus. We hardly ever work together. We should learn from our enemies how to bless, not curse, and how to truly serve our true Lord.

March 3

I have chosen thee in the furnace of affliction.
(Isaiah 48:10 KJV)

Comfort yourself with this thought. Don't the words come like a soft shower, dowsing the furious flames? Isn't it like asbestos armor, shielding you from the heat? Let affliction come—God has chosen me. Poverty may stride in through my door, but God is already in the house—and he has chosen me. Whatever may happen to me in this valley of tears, I know that he has chosen me.

If you need even greater comfort, remember this: You have the Son of Man with you in the furnace. In your quiet room, there is someone sitting beside you whom you have never seen, but whom you love. Often in your times of affliction, when you don't even realize it, he makes your bed and smoothes your pillow. You may be in poverty, but the Lord of life and glory is a frequent visitor in your lonely house. He loves to visit his chosen ones in desolate places. This friend sticks closer than a brother (Proverbs 18:24).

You can't see him, but you can feel the pressure of his hands. And don't you hear his voice? Even in the valley of the shadow of death he says, "So do not fear, for I am with you; do not be dismayed, for I am your God" (Isaiah 41:10).

Don't be afraid, Christian. Jesus is with you. In all your fiery trials, his presence is both your comfort and safety. He will never leave one whom he has chosen as his own. So take hold of him and follow where he leads.

March 4

My grace is sufficient for you.
(2 Corinthians 12:9)

If none of God's saints were poor and troubled, we would never know the comfort of God's grace. When we find a wanderer with nowhere to lay his head, who still says, "I will keep trusting in the Lord"; when we see a pauper starving on bread and water, who still glories in Jesus; when we see a bereaved widow overwhelmed with grief, who still has faith in Christ, what honor it reflects on the gospel! God's grace is illustrated and magnified in the poverty and trials of believers. God's chosen ones bear up under every discouragement. They know that all things work together for good, that out of this apparent evil will ultimately arise something good. They expect their God to work—either to quickly get them out of their troubles or to support them as long as the troubles last. This patience of the saints proves the power of divine grace.

There is a lighthouse out in the middle of the sea. It is a calm night. I can't tell whether the lighthouse is firmly built. But when a storm rages around it, then I know how sturdy it is. So it is with the Spirit's workmanship in building us. If we never had to face storms, we would never know how strong the Spirit has made us. The masterworks of God are those people who stand firm in the midst of difficulties.

He who wants to glorify God can count on facing many trials. No one can truly shine for Christ without enduring many conflicts. So if you have a difficult path, rejoice in it. You are demonstrating the all-sufficient grace of God. Will he ever fail you? Don't even dream of it—hate that thought. The God who has been sufficient until now should be trusted to the end.

March 5

Let us not be like others, who are asleep.
(1 Thessalonians 5:6)

There are many ways to promote Christian wakefulness. Let me suggest one: We should talk with each other about the Lord. In *Pilgrim's Progress*, Christian and Hopeful were journeying toward the Celestial City. They said to themselves, "To prevent drowsiness in this place, let us fall into good discourse."

And soon they began to sing this song:

> When saints do sleepy grow, let them come hither,
> And hear how these two pilgrims talk together;
> Yea, let them learn of them, in any wise,
> Thus to keep open their drowsy slumb'ring eyes.
> Saints' fellowship, if it be managed well,
> Keeps them awake, and that in spite of hell.

Christians who isolate themselves and walk alone are liable to grow drowsy. Join with other Christians, though, and you will stay awake, refreshed, encouraged, and will make quicker progress on the road to heaven. But as you converse with other believers, make sure that your theme is Jesus. Let the eye of faith always be looking to him. Let your heart be full of him. Let your lips speak of his worth.

My friend, live close to the cross, and you will not sleep. Try to impress yourself with a deep sense of the value of the place where you are going. You are headed toward heaven! That thought alone should keep you alert. And if you keep in mind that hell is behind you, and the devil pursuing you, you will not loiter.

Christian, do you really want to be sleeping when the pearly gates are opening for you, when the angels are singing a song of welcome, when a crown of gold awaits you? Of course not. So continue to "watch and pray" (Matthew 26:41), in fellowship with other Christians, so that you don't enter into temptation.

March 6

You must be born again.
(John 3:7)

Regeneration is the very basis of salvation. We should make sure that we are really "born again," for there are many who fancy that they are, but really aren't. To call oneself a Christian is not the same as being a Christian. Being born in a Christian land and even professing a Christian religion does not count for much—unless you are "born again" by the power of the Holy Spirit.

Being born again is a matter so mysterious that human words cannot describe it. "The wind blows wherever it pleases. You hear its sound, but you cannot tell where it comes from or where it is going. So it is with everyone born of the Spirit" (John 3:8).

Yet as mysterious as it is, it is a change that can be *known* and *felt*. There is an experience of grace that we feel, and we recognize the change in our lives, a greater tendency toward holy actions.

This great work of rebirth is also *supernatural*. A person cannot do this by himself. God infuses a whole new principle in a person's heart, renewing the soul, affecting one's entire life. It is not a change of my name, but a renewal of my nature. I am not the man I used to be, but a new man in Christ Jesus. You can wash and dress a corpse, but you can't bring it back to life. Only God has that power.

So if you have been born again, your prayer is this: "Lord Jesus, everlasting Father, you are my spiritual parent. If your Spirit had not breathed into me the breath of a new, holy, and spiritual life, I would still be 'dead in transgressions and sins.' My spiritual life is totally derived from you, and I owe it all to you. My life is hidden with Christ in God. It is no longer I who live, but Christ living in me."

May the Lord give us full assurance on this matter, because without rebirth we are unsaved, unpardoned, without God, and without hope.

March 7

Have faith in God.
(Mark 11:22)

Faith gives feet to the soul. With faith, the soul can march along the road of God's commandments. Love can make the feet move more swiftly, but faith *is* both feet.

Faith is the oil that enables the wheels of holy devotion and earnest piety to move well. Without faith, the wheels grind to a halt.

With faith, I can do everything. Without faith, I have neither the inclination nor the power to do anything to serve God. If you are looking for the people who serve God the best, look for those with the most faith. A little faith is enough to save you, but not enough to do great things for God. The person of little faith will go to heaven but cannot defeat those monsters that threaten our spiritual advancement here on earth. The person of little faith is afraid to journey closer to God. The road may be rough, thorny, and dangerous. But the person of great faith boldly steps forward. She is willing to venture through any difficulty, to get closer to her Lord. The person of little faith bemoans his own misfortune, becoming more and more depressed with each pitfall. But the person of great faith fords the raging streams, knowing that God is there, too. That brings joy in even the most trying circumstances.

So do you want to be comfortable and happy? Do you want to enjoy religion? Do you want to be cheerful rather than gloomy? Then "have faith in God." If you love darkness and are satisfied with gloom and misery, then a little faith is enough for you. But if you love sunshine and want to sing songs of rejoicing, go after this great gift of great faith.

March 8

We must go through many hardships to enter the kingdom of God. (Acts 14:22)

God's people have their trials. God never intended for his chosen people to be exempt from difficulties. They were chosen in a furnace of affliction. He never promised that they would only experience worldly peace and earthly joy. He never said they would have utter freedom from sickness and the pains of mortality. When the Lord drew up their "bill of rights," he included chastisements, discipline, and trials as part of their inheritance.

Trials are part of our lot. They were predestinated for us in God's decrees and bequeathed to us in Christ's last legacy. As surely as the stars have been fashioned by his hands and their orbits fixed by him, so are trials allotted to us. He has planned their time and their place, their intensity, and the effect they will have on us.

Good people must never expect to escape troubles. If they do, they will be disappointed. None of their predecessors have gone without troubles. Note the patience of Job. Remember Abraham—his faith in the midst of trials made him "father of the faithful." Read the biographies of all the patriarchs, prophets, apostles, and martyrs, and you will find that all those great vessels of mercy had to pass through fires of affliction.

But although tribulation is the path of God's children, they have the comfort of knowing that their Master has walked this path first. They have his presence and sympathy to cheer them, his grace to support them, and his example to guide them. And when they reach his kingdom, it will be worth it all.

March 9

He is altogether lovely.
(Song of Songs 5:16)

The superlative beauty of Jesus is all-attracting. It is not so much to be admired as to be loved. He is more than pleasant, more than fair—he is lovely. This golden word is especially appropriate, because Jesus is the object of our warmest love, a love founded on his intrinsic excellence, the complete perfection of his charms.

Disciples of Jesus, look to your Master's lips and say (with Solomon's beloved), "His mouth is sweetness itself" (5:16). Don't his very words make your heart burn within you as he talks with you on your journey (Luke 24:32)? You who worship Immanuel, look to his lovely head, crowned with gold (Song of Songs 5:11), and tell me—aren't his thoughts precious to you? Isn't your adoration sweetened with affection as you humbly bow before him? He is as excellent as the cedars of Lebanon (Song of Songs 5:15). There is charm in his every feature. His whole being is fragrant with choice scents.

Is there any part of him that is not attractive? Is there some portion of his being that fails to draw us closer to him? We love not only his loving heart, but also his powerful arm. We anoint his whole person with the expensive perfume of our fervent love.

We want to imitate his whole life. We want to duplicate his whole character. In everyone else there is some flaw, but he has only perfection. Even the best of his saints have had a few stains on their garments or wrinkles on their brows—but our Lord is nothing but loveliness. All earthly suns have their spots. Even our beautiful earth has its deserts. As much as we may love any earthly thing, we cannot love every part of it. But Christ Jesus is the purest gold, light without darkness, bright glory unclouded. He is *altogether* lovely.

March 10

When I felt secure, I said, "I will never be shaken."
(Psalm 30:6)

Give a person wealth. Let his ships bring home rich cargoes. Let the winds and waves bear his vessels quickly over the sea. Let his lands yield abundant crops. Let the weather be seasonable. Let uninterrupted success accompany him. Let him stand as a successful merchant in society. Let him enjoy continuing health. Let him march through the world with braced nerve and a brilliant eye, living happily. Give him a buoyant spirit. Let him have a song always on his lips. Let his eyes sparkle with joy.

What will happen? Immobility. As David said, "I will never be shaken." You may be the best Christian that ever lived, still, with all the security, you will not budge.

Brother or sister, beware of the smooth places along the way. When the way is rough, thank God for it. If God always rocked us in the cradle of prosperity, if we were always dandled on the knees of fortune, if there were never clouds in the sky, if there were never any bitter drops in the wine of this life, we would become intoxicated with pleasure. We would be like a man standing on some precarious pinnacle. "I am standing!" the man might well say—but he is actually in quite a dangerous situation. We are like a sailor asleep on the mast. He may dream of safety, but he is in danger every moment.

Let us bless God, then, for our afflictions. Let us thank him for our changes. If he did not chasten us like this, we would feel too secure. Continued worldly prosperity is a fiery trial.

March 11

So that . . . sin might become utterly sinful.
(Romans 7:13)

Beware of light thoughts of sin. When we are first converted, our consciences are tender. We are afraid of even the slightest sin. Young Christians have a holy timidity, a godly fear that they may be offending God. But all too soon the fine bloom of these ripe fruits is removed by the rough handling of the surrounding world. The sensitive plant of young piety turns into a willow in later life, too pliant, too easily yielding. It is sadly true that even a Christian may grow callous by degrees, so that the same sin that once startled him does not alarm him in the least.

By degrees people grow familiar with sin. The ear in which the cannon has been booming will not notice slight sounds. At first a little sin bothers us, but soon we say, "Well, it's just a little one." Then comes another, larger, and then another, until we begin to regard sin as unimportant. Then we rationalize further: "I have not fallen into open sin. True, I tripped a little, but generally I stood upright. I may have uttered one unholy word, but most of my conversation has been consistently Christian."

So we throw a cloak over our sin. We call it by dainty names. Christian, beware of this. By thinking lightly of sin, you may be falling little by little.

How can sin be a *little* thing? Isn't it a poison? It may seem little, but it is capable of great destruction. Don't the "little" foxes spoil the grapes (Song of Songs 2:15)? Doesn't the tiny coral organism build reefs that can wreck navies? Don't "little strokes fell lofty oaks"?

This "little" thing of sin circled our Savior's head with thorns; it made him suffer anguish. If you could weigh even the smallest sin on the scales of eternity, you would run from it as from a serpent. You would abhor even the least appearance of evil. Look on all sin as that which crucified the Savior, and you, too, will see that it is "utterly sinful."

March 12

Love your neighbor.
(Matthew 5:43)

What if your neighbor is rolling in riches? And what if you are poor? You live in a tiny cottage next to his lordly mansion. Every day you see his vast estates, his fine clothing, his splendid banquets. God has given him these gifts. Do not covet his wealth, and do not think badly of him. Be content with what you have. Try to improve your fortunes, if you can, but do not try to drag your neighbor down. Love him, and then you won't envy him.

But maybe you are the rich one. Near you there are poor people. Do not look down on them. Be proud to call them neighbors. Own up to your responsibility to love them. The world calls them your inferiors. But why? They are certainly more equals than inferiors, since God has made us all. Your coat may be better than your neighbor's coat. Does that make you a better person? Your neighbor is a human being. Can you claim any more than that? Be sure to love your neighbor, even if he is in rags, in abject poverty.

Perhaps you are saying, "I'd like to love my neighbors, but whenever I do anything, they return ingratitude and contempt." Well, that gives you more opportunity for the heroism of love. Love is no feather bed; it's a battle. The one who dares the most will win the most. If the path of love is rough, tread it boldly. Love your neighbors through thick and thin. Heap "coals of fire" on their heads (Romans 12:20), and if they're hard to please, then just try to please your Master. Even if they spurn your love, your Master does not spurn it. Love your neighbor, for in that way you are following the footsteps of Christ.

March 13

Why stay here until we die?
(2 Kings 7:3)

This book is mainly intended to strengthen believers, but if you are still unsaved, my heart yearns for you. I want to say something that speaks to your situation, too.

Open your Bible and read the story of the lepers (2 Kings 7:3–11). Note their position; it was much the same as yours. If you remain where you are, you will die. You have nothing to lose by coming to Jesus. "Nothing ventured, nothing gained," says the old proverb. In your case, the venture is not great.

Look at it this way. Of those who refuse to look to Jesus for salvation, no one escapes final damnation. Now, you may not be absolutely certain that Jesus will save you, but at least you can see that he has saved others. So why not you? As the Ninevites said, "Who knows?" (Jonah 3:9). Act upon this same hope. Try the Lord's mercy.

The fact is, without his mercy, you have no hope at all. Perishing is such an awful thing that you should be grabbing at any straw. Your very instinct of self-preservation should make you reach out.

So far, I have been talking to you on your own unbelieving ground. But I assure you, there is no uncertainty: If you seek the Lord, you will find him. Jesus turns away no one who comes to him. You will not perish if you trust him. On the contrary, you will find treasures even greater than those that the poor lepers gathered up in the Syrian camp.

I pray that the Holy Spirit will embolden you to get up and go to Jesus. It will not be in vain. When you yourself are saved, broadcast the good news to others. Don't hold back. Tell the King's household first and join with them in Christian fellowship. Then proclaim the good news everywhere. May the Lord save you before the sun goes down today.

March 14

So, if you think you are standing firm, be careful that you don't fall! (1 Corinthians 10:12)

It is a curious fact that there is such a thing as being proud of grace. Someone may say, "I have great faith. I will never fall. Someone who has less faith may fall, but not I."

Or someone else may say, "I have fervent love. This will keep me standing. There is no danger of my going astray."

But he who boasts of grace has little grace to boast of. He may think that his faith and love will preserve him, but he doesn't realize that the stream must always flow from the source—or else it runs dry. It makes no sense to glory in your own faith and love. Let your confidence be in Christ and his strength. Only he can keep you from falling.

Spend more time in prayer. Take time to adore him. Read the Scriptures more often—and more earnestly. Watch your life carefully; live closer to God. Let your life-style reflect heavenly patterns. Let your heart be perfumed with a concern for people's souls. Live in a way that makes people sit up and take notice of the fact that you have been with Jesus.

Then when that happy day has finally come, when your beloved Lord says, "Come up higher," then you may be blessed enough to hear him say, "You have fought a good fight; you have finished the race; and now there is an eternal crown of righteousness awaiting you." Until then, we press on with care and caution, with holy fear and trembling. With faith and confidence in Jesus alone, we pray, "Uphold me according to your Word."

Only he is "able to keep you from falling and to present you before his glorious presence without fault and with great joy" (Jude 24).

March 15

Be strong in the grace that is in Christ Jesus.
(2 Timothy 2:1)

Within himself, Christ has grace beyond measure. But he does not keep it to himself. As a reservoir empties itself into pipes, so Christ has emptied out his grace for his people. "From the fullness of his grace we have all received one blessing after another" (John 1:16). He stands there like a fountain, always flowing, in order to supply the empty pitchers and thirsty lips of his people. Like a tree, he bears sweet fruit, not to hang on the branches, but to be picked by those who need it.

Grace, whether its work is to pardon, to cleanse, to preserve, to strengthen, to enlighten, to bring to life, or to restore—grace is always available from him freely and without price. He has not withheld any kind of grace from his people.

Just as the blood of our bodies flows from the heart, but belongs equally to every part of our bodies, so the effects of God's grace belong to every saint who belongs to him. Here is the sweet communion between Christ and his church: They both receive the same grace. Christ is the head on which the oil is poured, but the oil runs down to the hem of the garments—so that even the least of Christians has the same precious anointing as the head. The sap of grace flows from the stem to the branch, nourishing both. This is true communion. Day by day we receive grace from Jesus. As we learn to recognize that this grace comes from him, we will sense our communion with him and enjoy this fellowship all the more.

Let us use these daily riches of grace. Let us keep coming back to him to supply all we need. He is there to provide grace for us—we can come to him as boldly as people take money from their own wallets.

March 16

I dwell with you as an alien, a stranger.
(Psalm 39:12)

I may be a stranger, but I am still dwelling *with* you, Lord. I am naturally alienated from you, but your grace has brought me close to you. Now, in fellowship with you, I walk through this sinful world as a pilgrim in a foreign country. *You* are a stranger in your own world, Lord. People forget you, dishonor you, set up new laws and strange customs, and do not recognize you.

Your dear Son "came to that which was his own, but his own did not receive him" (John 1:11). "He was in the world, and though the world was made through him, the world did not recognize him" (John 1:10). Never was a foreigner such an oddity among the citizens of any land as your beloved Son was among his mother's people. It should be no surprise, then, if I—living the life of Jesus—should be unknown, a stranger here below.

Lord, I don't want to be a citizen in a world where Jesus was a stranger. His pierced hands have loosened the cords that used to bind my soul to this earth. Now I, too, am a stranger here. My speech seems outlandish, a foreign tongue, to these "Babylonians" who live around me. My manners seem odd to them, my actions seem strange.

But here is the good part: I am a stranger *dwelling with you*. You are my fellow sufferer, my fellow pilgrim. And you are great company. My heart burns within me as we walk and talk together. Though I am a sojourner, I am far more blessed than those who sit on thrones. I am far more at home than those who live in palaces.

March 17

Remember the poor.
(Galatians 2:10)

Why does God allow so many of his children to be poor? He could make them all rich, if he wanted to. He could lay bags of gold at their doors. He could provide a guaranteed income or fill their homes with provisions as he once rained manna on the Israelites and piled up the quail around their camp.

There is no need for his people to be poor, except that he must want it that way. The "cattle on a thousand hills" belong to him (Psalm 50:10)—he could give them to his poorer children. He could make the richest, greatest, and mightiest people in this world bring all their wealth and power to the feet of needy believers. But he does not choose to do so. He allows them to suffer want. He allows them to pine away in poverty.

Why is this? There are many reasons. For one, he wants to give those of us who have enough an opportunity to show our love for Jesus. Now we show our love for Jesus by singing and praying to him, but also by giving to those in need. If we had no poorer brothers and sisters, we would lose the sweet privilege of showing our love in this way. He wants us to show our love not only in our words, but also by our actions. If we truly love Christ, we will care for those whom he loves.

Those who are dear to him will be dear to us. We should not look on this as a duty but as a great privilege. Remember Jesus' words: "Whatever you did for one of the least of these brothers of mine, you did for me" (Matthew 25:40). Surely this is a strong enough motive to make us want to help others with a willing hand and a loving heart. Everything we do for God's needy people is accepted by Christ as a gift for himself.

March 18

You are all sons of God through faith in Christ Jesus.
(Galatians 3:26)

The fatherhood of God is common to all his children. You may have said, "If I only had the courage of those who have great faith, I could do great things for God. But I shrink from every obstacle." Listen, you are just as much a child of God as the person with great faith. Peter and Paul, those highly favored apostles, were members of God's family—and so are you. A weak Christian belongs to this family just as much as a strong one. As an old hymn puts it: "The strong, the feeble, and the weak are one in Jesus now."

All the names are in the same family register. One may have more faith or love than another, but God, our heavenly Father, has the same tender heart toward all. One may do greater deeds and may bring more glory to the Father, but the one whose name is least in the kingdom of heaven is as much God's child as the one who stands among the King's mighty men. This thought should comfort us as we come to God in prayer, saying, "Our Father."

Yet while this may comfort us, let us not rest contented with weak faith. Instead, ask, like the apostles, to gain more faith. However feeble our faith may be, if it is real faith in Christ, we will get to heaven. Yet our weak faith will not honor our Master very much along the way—and it will not give us much joy. So if you want to live for Christ's glory and be happy in his service, seek to be filled with the spirit of adoption more and more completely, until perfect love drives away all fear.

March 19

Strengthened in his faith.
(Romans 4:20)

Christian, take good care of your faith. Remember that faith is the only way you can obtain blessings. If we want blessings from God, nothing except faith can acquire them. Prayer cannot draw down answers from God's throne, unless it is the earnest prayer of one who believes. Faith is the angelic messenger between our souls and the Lord Jesus. If that angel is taken away, we can neither send up prayers nor receive answers. Faith is the telegraph wire that links earth and heaven. God's messages of love fly so fast that he answers us even before we call. But if that wire snaps, how can we receive his promises?

If I am in trouble, faith helps me find help. If I am afflicted by the enemy, my soul leans by faith on God's refuge. But if faith is taken away, my cries to God are in vain; there is no road between my soul and heaven. Faith is the road on which we travel. Without faith, the road is blockaded.

Faith links me with God. Faith clothes me with his power. Faith puts the divine power at my disposal. Faith calls every attribute of God to my defense. It helps me defeat the hosts of hell. With faith, I march in triumph over my enemies. But without faith, how can I receive anything from the Lord?

The one who wavers, "like a wave of the sea" (James 1:6), must not expect to get anything from the Lord. But with faith, fellow Christian, you can gain everything, however poor you may be.

March 20

My beloved!
(Song of Songs 2:8 KJV)

In her most joyous moments, this was a name the ancient church gave to the Lord's Anointed One. When "the season of singing has come," and "the cooing of doves is heard in our land" (Song of Songs 2:12), her songs of love are sweeter than either, as she sings, "My beloved is mine and I am his!" (v. 16).

In this Song of Songs, she is always calling him by that delightful name—"My beloved!" Even in the long winter, when idolatry had withered the Lord's garden, her prophets found an opportunity to lay aside their burdens for a while and say, as Isaiah did, "I will sing to the one I love a song about his vineyard" (Isaiah 5:1). Though he had not yet taken on humanity and had not lived among us, though those Old Testament saints had never seen his face, still he was the comfort of Israel, the hope and joy of all the chosen, the "beloved" of all those who honored the Most High God.

Now in the summer days of the church, we often speak of Christ as our souls' beloved. He is very precious to us, "outstanding among ten thousand . . . altogether lovely" (Song of Songs 5:10, 16). The love between Jesus and the church is so strong that the apostle dares to defy the whole universe to separate her from Christ's love. Persecutions cannot do this. Neither can trouble nor hardship nor famine nor danger. "No," he boasts, "in all these things we are more than conquerors through him who loved us" (Romans 8:35, 37).

O precious Lord, we long to know more of you. We pray with the hymn writer,

> My sole possession is thy love
> I have no other store.
> And though with fervent suit I pray
> I ask thee nothing more.

March 21

You will be scattered, each to his own home.
You will leave me all alone. (John 16:32)

Few knew the sorrows of Gethsemane. Most of Jesus' followers were not sufficiently advanced in grace to be allowed to witness the mysteries of Christ's agony. They were probably occupied with the Passover feast at their own houses. They represent the many who live by the letter of the law, but are mere babes when it comes to the spirit of the gospel.

Only twelve—no, only eleven—were given the privilege to enter Gethsemane. Out of these eleven, eight were left at a distance. They were participating with Christ, in a way, but not to the same extent as the three specially beloved disciples. Only Peter, James, and John could approach the veil of our Lord's mysterious sorrow. Even these could not intrude within the veil. They were left a stone's throw away. Jesus had to go through this experience alone.

Those three apostles we may consider "fathers." They are like a few others through the church's history, and in our own churches, who have been especially close to Christ. Having navigated great seas with him, they can to some extent deal with the huge Atlantic waves of the Redeemer's passion. Some selected souls, for their own strengthening and that of others, are allowed to enter the inner circle and hear the pleadings of the suffering High Priest. They know "the fellowship of sharing in his sufferings, becoming like him in his death" (Philippians 3:10). But even these cannot penetrate the secret places of the Savior's grief.

The Greek liturgy has a remarkable expression: "Thine unknown sufferings." There *was* an inner chamber in our Master's grief, shut out from human fellowship. There Jesus is "left alone." Isaac Watts is right when he sings, "All the unknown joys he gives, were bought with agonies unknown."

March 22

Going a little farther, he fell with his face to the ground and prayed. (Matthew 26:39)

There are several instructive features in our Savior's prayer during his time of trial. First, it was *lonely* prayer. He withdrew even from his three favorite disciples. Believer, you too should withdraw into solitary prayer, especially in times of trial. Family prayer, social prayer, church prayer are all very precious, but they are not enough. The best incense rises from your personal prayers, where no ear hears but God's.

It was *humble* prayer. Luke says he knelt, but Matthew adds that he "fell with his face to the ground." If *he* did this, what then is *your* place as a humble servant of your great Master? What dust and ashes should cover your head? Humility gives us a good foothold in prayer. There is no hope of finding favor with God unless we humble ourselves—so that he may eventually exalt us.

It was *filial* prayer. That is, he was praying as a Son to his Father. And we too can claim adoption as God's children in our times of trial. We have no rights as citizens; we lost them by the treason we committed. But nothing can forfeit a child's right to a father's protection. So we must never be afraid to say, "Abba, Father, hear my cry."

Note that it was also *persevering* prayer. He prayed three times. Do not stop until you prevail. Be like the persistent widow, whose continual pleading won her what her first request could not (Luke 18:1–8). Keep praying and keep thanking God for what he provides.

It was also a prayer of *resignation*. "Yet not as I will," he prayed, "but as you will" (Matthew 26:39). Yield to God, and he yields to you. Let God do his will, and he will do what is best for you. Leave your prayer in his hands. He knows when to give, how to give, what to give, and what to withhold.

March 23

His sweat was like drops of blood falling to the ground. (Luke 22:44)

The mental pressure arising from our Lord's struggle with temptation forced him into such a state that his pores exuded great drops of blood. This shows how great the weight of sin must have been. It was already crushing our Lord.

It also shows the mighty power of his love. Botanists have observed that the sap which comes forth from the tree without cutting is always the sweetest. Jesus shed his precious blood as he was whipped and pierced and nailed on the cross. But here he is already shedding blood, of his own accord.

So we also see the voluntary nature of Christ's sufferings. The blood flowed freely without any wound inflicted. When most of us go through trying times, our blood rushes *to* the heart. Our cheeks go pale, we feel faint, the blood goes inward to nourish the center of our bodies and strengthen us for the conflict. But what happens to our Savior? He is so utterly oblivious to himself that his agony drives his blood outward, not inward. Instead of rushing inside to nourish his own heart, his blood pushes outward to nourish the hearts of others. This shows us the fullness of the sacrifice he made for us.

Don't you see how intense his inner wrestling was? Doesn't that say something to you? "In your struggle against sin, you have not yet resisted to the point of shedding your blood" (Hebrews 12:4). As we resist temptation, we can learn from the intensity of our Lord.

March 24

He was heard because of his reverent submission.
(Hebrews 5:7)

This "reverent submission" is what the Bible often calls "the fear of the Lord." It is a healthy fear that leads to obedience.

But imagine the fears that Satan must have used to attack our Lord, fears that would have led him away from obedience, had he heeded them. The devil must have suggested to Jesus that he was all alone, utterly forsaken. As Jesus prayed in the garden, this would have been a potentially powerful fear.

"See," Satan would have said, "you have no friends anywhere. Your Father has discontinued his mercies toward you. Not an angel in his courts will reach out to help you. All of heaven is alienated from you, and you are left alone. You have a few disciples over there, but what are they worth? James, John, Peter—see how those cowards are sleeping while you suffer. No, you have no true friends in heaven or on earth.

"And all of hell is against you. I have stirred up my infernal den. I have sent messages throughout my regions, summoning every prince of darkness to attack you tonight. We will spare no arrows. We will overwhelm you. What can you do to stop us?"

Yet Jesus did not fall for the fears of Satan. An angel did come to strengthen him. Heaven was with him. He went three times to see if his disciples were truly sleeping, but he may have gained some comfort that it was not a sleep of disinterest, but of sorrow. The spirit was willing, but the flesh was weak.

Jesus had a choice as he prayed in the garden: fear the Lord and yield in obedience to him or fear everything else that Satan might throw at him. He chose to fear the Lord, in reverent submission. So should we.

March 25

Judas, are you betraying the Son of Man with a kiss?
(Luke 22:48)

"The kisses of an enemy are deceitful" (Proverbs 27:6 KJV). Be on guard when the world puts on a loving face. It will, if possible, betray you, as it did your Master, with a kiss. Whenever someone is about to stab religion, he usually professes great reverence for it. Beware of the sleek-faced hypocrisy that brings heresy right behind it. We need to be wise as serpents to detect and avoid the enemy's tricks. The young man in Proverbs, lacking understanding, was led astray by the kiss of the strange woman (Proverbs 7). We should all learn from this, so that all the world's fair speech will not sway us. Holy Spirit, do not let me, frail as I am, be betrayed with a kiss!

But what if I am guilty of the same sin as Judas, the son of perdition? I have been baptized into the name of the Lord Jesus. I am a member of his visible church. I sit at the communion table. All of these are like kisses, expressions of love and affection. Am I sincere in them? If not, I am a low-down traitor.

Do I live in the world as carelessly as others do and yet profess to follow Jesus? Then I am exposing my religion to ridicule and leading people to disparage the holy name I claim. In that case, I am a Judas.

O Lord, keep me clear in this matter. Make me sincere and true. Never let me betray my Savior. I do love you, Jesus. I know I often grieve you, but I want to be faithful to you all my life.

March 26

If you are looking for me, then let these men go.
(John 18:8)

See how much care Jesus showed for his disciples even in his hour of trial. Jesus surrenders himself to the enemy but speaks forcefully to set his friends free. For himself, "as a sheep before her shearers is silent, so he did not open his mouth" (Isaiah 53:7). But for his disciples' sake he speaks with Almighty energy.

Here is love—constant, self-forgetting, faithful love. But isn't there much more we can find here beneath the surface? Don't we have the very soul and spirit of atonement in these words? The Good Shepherd "lays down his life for the sheep" (John 10:11) and pleads that they must go free. The payment has been made for them. Justice demands that the ones in whose place he stands as a substitute should be "let go."

In the midst of Egypt's bondage, that voice rings out in power: "Let my people go!" Out of slavery to sin, the redeemed must come forth. In every cell of the dungeons of despair, the sound echoes, "Let them go!" And those who have been held captive by depression or fear come out. Satan hears the well-known voice and lifts his foot from the neck of the fallen one. Death hears it, and the grave opens her gates to let the dead arise.

God's children are "let go," and where do they go? On to holiness, triumph, glory. No lion will frighten them off the path. No ravenous beast will bar their way. The storm has already raged upon the cross of Calvary, and now we pilgrims do not need to fear those vengeful thunderbolts. Rejoice in this blessed immunity, this glorious freedom. And praise his name all day.

March 27

Then all the disciples deserted him and fled.
(Matthew 26:56)

He never deserted them. But they, fearing for their lives, fled from him as his sufferings just began. This is just one example of how frail we believers are on our own. At best, we are sheep—and we run off when the wolf comes.

Jesus' disciples had been warned of the danger. They had all promised to die with their Master rather than leave him. Yet they panicked, when the time came, and took to their heels.

This happens to me, too. Sometimes, as the day starts, I brace myself for some challenge. I determine to bear a certain trial for the Lord's sake. I fully intend to be faithful to him. But it is one thing to promise and another to perform.

If those disciples had stood bravely with Jesus, they would have been honored forever. But they fled from honor. Where could they have been any safer than next to their Master, who could call for twelve legions of angels at any time? They fled from true safety. May we all learn this lesson well. Fleeing from the Lord when times get tough is not only cowardly; it is foolish.

Yet God's grace can make the coward brave. These same apostles who ran like scared rabbits grew to be bold as lions once the Spirit had come upon them. And the same Spirit can make my timid spirit brave enough to confess my allegiance to the Lord.

What anguish must have filled Jesus' heart as he saw his friends run off! This was an especially bitter taste in his cup of sorrows. But he has drained that cup dry; I don't want to put any more drops in it. O Spirit, keep me from forsaking my beloved Savior.

March 28

This love that surpasses knowledge. (Ephesians 3:19)

The love of Christ goes beyond human comprehension. Where can we find the words to describe its sweetness, greatness, and faithfulness? It is so vast that all our adjectives just skim the surface—as a swallow skims the water, but will not dive into its depths. Immeasurable depths of love lie beneath us. None of us deserves to swim in this endless sea.

To begin to get an idea of Jesus' love, we must understand the glory he came from—and how far he came to pour himself out in shame upon the earth. But who can tell us how great his majesty was? When he was enthroned in the highest heavens, he was "very God of very God." By him were the heavens made and all the heavenly hosts. His own almighty arm upheld the spheres. The praises of cherubim and seraphim surrounded him. An eternal "Hallelujah Chorus" flowed to the foot of his throne. He reigned supreme over all creatures, God over all, blessed forever.

And who can tell how low he descended? To be a man—that was something. To be a "man of sorrows"—that was far more. To bleed, to die, to suffer—these were unthinkable for the very Son of God. To suffer such unparalleled agony, to endure a death of shame and desertion by his Father—this is a depth of love our minds cannot begin to grasp.

This is love. Love that "surpasses knowledge." Let this love fill your heart with adoring gratitude and lead you to some practical manifestations of its power.

March 29

Although he was a son, he learned obedience
from what he suffered. (Hebrews 5:8)

The Captain of our salvation was "made perfect" through suffering. Might that mean that we who are sinful—and far from perfect—must go through suffering, too? Should the head be crowned with thorns and the rest of the body coddled on the dainty lap of ease? If Christ must pass through a sea of his own blood to win the crown, can we expect to walk to heaven in silver slippers, without getting our feet wet?

No, our Master's experience teaches us that suffering is necessary. The true-born child of God should not try to escape it—even if he could. But there is one very comforting thought in the fact of Christ's being "made perfect through suffering." He can sympathize fully with us. "For we do not have a high priest who is unable to sympathize with our weaknesses" (Hebrews 4:15). We can draw a sustaining power from Christ's sympathy.

One of the early martyrs said, "I can bear it all, for Jesus suffered; and He suffers in me now; He sympathizes with me, and this makes me strong." Believer, grab onto this thought in your times of agony. Let the thought of Jesus strengthen you as you follow in his steps. Find a sweet support in his sympathy.

Remember that suffering is an honorable thing. To suffer for Christ is glory. The apostles rejoiced that they were considered worthy enough to do this. The jewels of a Christian are his afflictions. So let's not shun this honor. Let's not give up this glory. Griefs exalt us, and troubles lift us up. "If we suffer, we shall also reign with him" (2 Timothy 2:12 KJV).

March 30

He . . . was numbered with the transgressors.
(Isaiah 53:12)

Why did Jesus allow himself to be counted among sinners? There were many reasons. First, by doing so, he could better serve as their advocate. In some trials there is an identification of the lawyer with the client. The law treats them as the same person. Now when the sinner is brought to court, Jesus appears there on his behalf. *Jesus* stands to answer the accusation. He points to his hands, his side, and his feet and challenges the prosecution to bring any further charge against the sinner he represents. He pleads his blood. Because he has been numbered with the sinners, his pleading is powerful. The Judge proclaims, "Let them go their way. We need not hand them over for punishment, since their ransom has been paid."

Our Lord Jesus was also numbered with the transgressors so that their hearts might be drawn toward him. Who can be afraid of someone who is "one of us"? We can come boldly to him and confess our guilt. He who is numbered with us cannot condemn us.

Wasn't Jesus also listed on the roll of sinners so that we might be listed in the roll of saints? He was holy and was recorded as being holy. We were guilty and listed as guilty. He transfers his name from that list to ours and our names are taken from the guilty roll and added to the roll of acceptance. There is a complete transfer between Jesus and his people. Jesus has taken our situation upon himself, and all that Jesus possesses is now ours. His righteousness, his blood—this is our dowry.

Enjoy your new position, numbered among the saints. Live a life that shows you belong there.

March 31

By his wounds we are healed.
(Isaiah 53:5)

Pilate handed Jesus over to his soldiers to be scourged. The Roman scourge was a very dreadful instrument of torture. It was made of the sinews of oxen, and sharp bones were twisted in here and there. Every time the lash came down on a victim's back, the bones cut into the flesh and tore it away. Our Savior was, no doubt, tied to a column and beaten in this way. He had been beaten before, but this Roman scourging was probably the most severe. We may weep as we imagine the blows upon his precious body.

Jesus stands before you, believer, as a mirror of agonizing love. Can you look at him without tears? In innocence, he is as fair as a lily, but he is now red as a rose, the color of his own blood. Feel the healing that his wounds have brought to your life—doesn't your heart melt with love and grief? If we have ever loved our Lord Jesus, that love must be growing now as we consider his agony—the pain he went through for us.

It's enough to make you want to spend the rest of the day in your room crying. But there is work to do. We must attend to our business today. So instead ask your beloved Lord to imprint the image of his bleeding self on the tablets of your heart today—all day. Tonight we may return to commune with him some more, and our hearts will be full of love and gratitude. It is our sin that has cost him so much.

April 1

Let him kiss me with the kisses of his mouth.
(Song of Songs 1:2)

For several days now, we have been considering Christ's passion, and we will continue to do so. But as we start a new month, let's try to stir some of our own passion for the Lord by looking at this love song between Christ and his church.

See how she leaps to him right away. No lengthy preface; she doesn't even name him yet; immediately she presents her theme. She speaks of "him" who was the only "him" in the world to her. Notice how bold her love is. With rich love, Mary sat at Jesus' feet to learn of him. With humble love, the woman anointed Jesus' feet with perfume. But this is strong, fervent love, demanding even closer expressions of fellowship. Esther trembled before Xerxes the king, but this spouse, in the joyful liberty of perfect love, knows no fear.

We can share her spirit. The "kisses" we receive are the various manifestations of Christ's love for us. The kiss of *reconciliation* came at our conversion. It was sweet as honey. The kiss of *acceptance* is still warm on our brow, since we know that God accepts us through his grace. The kiss of ongoing *communion* with him is one we long for each day, until we enjoy the kiss of *reception*, which removes our souls from earth, and the kiss of *consummation*, which fills us with the joy of heaven.

We walk by faith, but we rest in Christ's fellowship. Faith is the road, but communion with Jesus is the well from which we drink.

O lover of our souls, come close to us. Let the lips of your blessing meet the lips of our asking. Let the lips of your fullness touch the lips of our need.

April 2

But Jesus made no reply, not even to a single charge.
(Matthew 27:14)

Jesus had never been slow to speak when he was blessing others, but here he does not say a word in his own defense. The temple guards had declared, "No one ever spoke the way this man does" (John 7:46). But no one was ever silent as he was, either.

This silence shows us the nature of *his perfect self-sacrifice*. He would not utter a word to stay his own execution. That was being offered up for our atonement. His silence also depicts *the defenselessness of sin*. Nothing can be said to excuse human guilt. Therefore, he who bore the weight of our sin stood speechless before his judge.

By his silence, Jesus also demonstrated *the best reply to a hostile world*. Calm endurance answers some questions far more conclusively than the loftiest eloquence. The best apologists for Christianity, in its early days, were its martyrs. The anvil breaks a host of hammers by quietly bearing their blows.

The silent Lamb of God also gave us *a grand example of wisdom*. Every word was being pounced on as "blasphemous" by those who were being blasphemous themselves. It was best to keep from fueling this sinful fire. The ambiguous and false, the unworthy and mean, will eventually confute themselves. So the truth can afford to be quiet.

Finally, our Lord, by his silence, furnished *a remarkable fulfillment of prophecy*. "He was led like a lamb to the slaughter," Isaiah had predicted, "and as a sheep before her shearers is silent, so he did not open his mouth" (Isaiah 53:7). By his quiet, Jesus conclusively proved himself to be the true Lamb of God.

Be with us, Jesus, and in the silence of our hearts, let us hear the voice of your love.

April 3

So the soldiers took charge of Jesus.
(John 19:16)

He had been in agony all night. He had spent the early morning in the hall of Caiaphas. He had been hurried from Caiaphas to Pilate, from Pilate to Herod, and from Herod back again to Pilate. He had little strength left, yet they offered him no refreshment or rest. They were eager for his blood and therefore led him out to die, weighed down with the cross. As you see this scene, weep with the daughters of Jerusalem.

This scene brings out the truth of that Old Testament ritual of the scapegoat (Leviticus 16). The high priest would put both hands on the goat's head, confess the sins of the people, symbolically laying those sins on the goat's head. Then a man "took charge" of the goat and led him away into the desert—taking the people's sin away in the process.

Now it is Jesus who is brought before the priests and rulers and pronounced guilty. "The Lord has laid on him the iniquity of us all" (Isaiah 53:6). Bearing our sin, in the form of that cross, our great Scapegoat is led away by appointed officers of justice.

Is that *your* sin he is carrying with him? There is only one way to know for sure. Have you confessed your sin and trusted in him? If so, then your sin has been transferred to Christ. He bears it on his shoulder as he trudges toward Calvary.

Don't let this picture vanish until you have rejoiced in your own deliverance and adored the loving Redeemer who took your sins upon himself.

April 4

God made him who had no sin to be sin for us, so that in him we might become the righteousness of God.
(2 Corinthians 5:21)

Do you feel guilty about your sinfulness? Look to your perfect Lord and remember: You are complete in him. In God's sight you are as perfect as if you had never sinned. Even more than that—the Lord Our Righteousness has put a divine garment on you, so that you have more than mere human righteousness. *You have the righteousness of God!* If you are mourning the fact that you sin so naturally, remember that none of your sins can condemn you. You have learned to hate sin; but you have also learned that your sin is no longer yours—it was laid on Christ's head. Your position with God is not your own—it is *in Christ*.

You know that someday you will stand before God's throne, and he will declare you righteous through Christ. But you are accepted just as thoroughly *today*, even with all your sinfulness. Grab on to this thought: You are perfect in Christ. Wearing his garment, you are as holy as the Holy One. "Who is he that condemns? Christ Jesus, who died—more than that, who was raised to life—is at the right hand of God and is also interceding for us" (Romans 8:34).

Christian, let your heart rejoice! What do you have to fear? Let your face wear a smile. Live close to your Master. Soon, when your time has come, you will rise up where Jesus sits and reign at his right hand—and all this because "God made him who had no sin to be sin for us, so that in him we might become the righteousness of God."

April 5

They seized Simon . . . and put the cross on him and made him carry it behind Jesus. (Luke 23:26)

We see here a picture of the church: She follows Jesus, bearing the cross. Note that Jesus did not suffer to keep you from suffering. He bears the cross not for you to escape it, but for you to endure it. Christ exempts you from sin, but not from sorrow. Remember that and expect to suffer.

But we can comfort ourselves with this thought: As with Simon, *it is not our cross, but Christ's cross that we carry*. When you are mocked for your devotion to Jesus, remember it is *his* cross.

You carry the cross after him. You have blessed company. Your path is marked with the footprints of your Lord. The mark of his blood-red shoulder is on the very wood. He goes before you as a shepherd goes before his sheep. Take up that cross daily and follow him.

But don't forget that *you bear this cross in partnership*. Some have suggested that Simon only carried one end of the cross, not all of it. That is very possible. Christ may have carried the heavier part, the crossbeam, and Simon may have borne the lighter end. Certainly it is the same way with you. You only carry the lighter end of the cross, while Christ carries its weight.

One more thing: *Simon carried the cross for a short time, but it gave him lasting honor*. In the same way, we carry the cross for a little while at most, but then we will receive a crown of glory.

We should love the cross. Instead of shrinking from it, we should consider it very precious. "For our light and momentary troubles are achieving for us an eternal glory that far outweighs them all" (2 Corinthians 4:17).

April 6

Let us, then, go to him outside the camp.
(Hebrews 13:13)

Jesus, bearing his cross, went to suffer outside the city. The Christian also goes "outside the camp" of this world's sin, not because we want to be peculiar, but because Jesus did so, and we must follow him. Christ was "not of the world." His life and teaching were a constant protest against conformity with the world. He had unmatchable affection for humanity, but he was still separate from sinners.

In the same way, Christ's people must "go to him outside the camp." We must be prepared to tread the straight and narrow path. We must have bold, unflinching, lionlike hearts, loving Christ and his truth far more than we love the world.

You cannot grow very much in grace while you are conformed to the world. The life of separation may be a path of sorrow, but it is the highway of safety. It may hurt some, making every day a battle, yet it is ultimately a happy life. Jesus gives such sweet refreshment that the warrior feels more calm and peace in his daily strife than others do in their times of rest. The highway of holiness is the highway of communion with Christ.

Remember that the crown of glory will follow the cross of separation. A moment's shame will be rewarded with eternal honor.

April 7

How long, O men, will you turn my glory into shame?
(Psalm 4:2)

One writer has noted the mocking "honors" that the blinded people of Israel gave to Jesus, their King.

1. They gave him a *procession of honor*, including Roman legionaries, Jewish priests, and the common men and women. Jesus carried his cross. This is the ovation they gave the one who came to overthrow humanity's worst foes—derisive shouts and cruel taunts instead of paeans of praise.

2. They gave him the *wine of honor*. Instead of a golden cup of fine wine, they offered the criminal's numbing death drink. He refused it, because he wanted to taste death with his senses unimpaired. Later, when he cried, "I thirst!" they gave him vinegar mixed with gall, thrust to his mouth on a sponge. What wretched hospitality shown to their King!

3. He was provided with a *guard of honor*, who showed their esteem by gambling over his garments.

4. A *throne of honor* was found for him on the bloody tree. That was the best these rebels would offer their Lord. The cross was, in fact, the full expression of the world's feeling toward him.

5. The *title of honor* was written as "King of the Jews," but those blinded Jewish leaders even disputed that. They preferred to consider him the "king of thieves," choosing the release of Barabbas and placing Jesus between two common robbers.

In each case, men turned Jesus' glory into shame, but it eternally gladdens the eyes of saints and angels.

April 8

For if men do these things when the tree is green, what will happen when it is dry? (Luke 23:31)

There are many interpretations for this intriguing question. Here is a good one. "If I, the innocent substitute for sinners, suffer like this, what will happen when the sinner himself—the dry tree—falls into the hands of an angry God?"

When God saw Jesus in the sinner's place, he did not spare him. And when he finds unrepentant sinners without Christ, he will not spare *them*. Jesus was led away by his enemies; so will sinners be dragged by devils to their place of punishment. Jesus was deserted by God. If this happened to him, who was only bearing other people's sin, it will happen even worse to you—if you have not let Jesus save you.

With an awful shriek, Jesus cried, "My God! My God! Why have you forsaken me?" When you cry that same question, the answer may come back: "Since you ignored all my advice and would not accept my rebuke, I in turn will laugh at your disaster; I will mock when calamity overtakes you" (Proverbs 1:25–26). What will your cry be then?

If God did not spare his own Son, how much less will he spare you? You rich, high-living, self-righteous sinners—what kind of life will you have when God finally judges you? We cannot sum up in one word all the sorrows that came upon Jesus, who died for us. So it is impossible to say what streams, what oceans of grief must come upon your soul if you die without Christ. By the agonies of Christ, by his wounds, and by his blood, do not bring on yourselves God's wrath. Trust in the Son of God, and you will never die.

April 9

A large number of people followed him, including women who mourned and wailed for him. (Luke 23:27)

Amid the contentious crowd that hounded the Redeemer to his doom, there were some gracious souls who vented their anguish with wailing and lamentation. This was fit music to accompany that woeful march. When my soul imagines that scene, it joins those godly women and weeps with them. Indeed, there is good reason to grieve—more than those women realized.

They bewailed innocence mistreated, goodness persecuted, love bleeding, and meekness about to die, but my heart has a deeper reason to mourn. My sins were the whips that tore those blessed shoulders. My sins were the thorns that penetrated his bleeding brow. My sins cried, "Crucify him! Crucify him!" and laid the cross on his gracious back. Just seeing him led forth to die causes sorrow enough for an eternity; but realizing that I was his murderer—that brings infinitely more grief, more than one poor fountain of tears can express.

Those women had their reasons to love Christ and weep, but so do I. Perhaps one was the widow of Nain, who saw her son brought back to life. But I have also been raised to newness of life. Perhaps another was Peter's mother-in-law, cured of a fever. But I have been cured of a greater disease: sin itself. Surely Mary Magdalene was there, from whom Christ had cast seven devils. But he cast a whole legion of evil out of me. Mary and Martha were favored with visits. But he dwells with me. Jesus' mother bore him in her womb. But in my soul Jesus is formed again, the hope of glory.

So since I owe as much to my Savior as these women did, let me join them in gratitude and grief.

April 10

The place, which is called Calvary.
(Luke 23:33 KJV)

Calvary is the hill of our comfort. The house of our consolation is built with the wood of the cross. The temple of heavenly blessing is founded on that riven rock—riven by the spear that pierced his side. No scene in sacred history gladdens the soul like Calvary's tragedy.

Is it not strange, the darkest hour
  That ever dawned on sinful earth,
Should touch the heart with softer power,
  For comfort, than an angel's mirth?
That to the Cross the mourner's eye should turn,
Sooner than where the stars of Bethlehem burn?

Light springs from the midday midnight of Golgotha, and every herb of the field blooms sweetly beneath the shadow of the once-cursed tree. In that place of thirst, grace has dug a fountain that gushes forth with crystal-pure waters—each drop can cure the ills of humanity.

If you have had times of conflict, you can testify that the Mount of Olives was not where you found comfort, or Mount Sinai or Tabor. But Gethsemane, Gabbatha, and Golgotha have helped you. The bitter herbs of Gethsemane have often taken away the bitter taste of life. The whipping post of Gabbatha has often scared away your cares; and the groans of Golgotha have calmed your other groans.

So Calvary's comfort is rare and rich. We would never have known Christ's love in all its heights and depths if he had not died. If you want to know love, come to Calvary, and see the Man of Sorrows die.

April 11

I am poured out like water, and all my bones are out of joint. (Psalm 22:14)

Was there ever a sadder spectacle? In soul and body, our Lord felt himself to be weak as water poured on the ground. When the cross was placed in its socket, he was shaken violently, his ligaments strained, nerves pained, bones dislocated. Burdened with his own weight, our royal sufferer felt the strain increasing every moment of those six long hours. In his own consciousness, overpowered by faintness, he must have become nothing but a mass of misery.

Daniel described his sensation, seeing an overpowering vision: "I had no strength left, my face turned deathly pale and I was helpless" (Daniel 10:8). How much more faint must this greater Prophet have felt when he saw the dreadful vision of God's wrath—and felt it in his own soul! To us, such sensations would be unbearable; unconsciousness would kindly come to our rescue. But in his case, he was wounded and *felt* the sword. He drained his cup of sorrow and *tasted* every drop.

As we kneel before the throne of our ascended Savior, let us drink of the cup of his strength so that we may be ready for our time of trial. Every part of his body suffered, but he came through it all, into his power and glory, uninjured. Even so shall his spiritual body, the church, come through the furnace with not so much as the smell of fire upon it.

April 12

My heart has turned to wax; it has melted away within me. (Psalm 22:14)

Our Lord experienced a terrible sinking and melting of his soul. "A man's spirit sustains him in sickness, but a crushed spirit who can bear?" (Proverbs 18:14). Deep depression is the worst of all trials. Everything else is little compared to this. Imagine how the suffering Savior longed for God to be close to him, for this is the time a man needs God the most—when his heart is melting within him.

Believer, come to the cross this morning and humbly adore the King of Glory. Realize that he was once brought far lower, in mental distress and inward anguish, than any of us. See how well he qualifies to be our High Priest—for he has felt our infirmities.

If you feel far away from God, if you lack a sense of his love, then—*especially* then—come to the cross and find communion with Jesus. He passed through this despair himself. Our souls may sometimes shudder to behold the glory of our Savior, because he is so far beyond us, but we must remember that he sympathizes fully with our situation.

Our drops of sorrow may be forgotten in the ocean of his griefs, but how high our love ought to rise! Let that strong, deep love of Jesus flow into your soul like a stream flooding its banks. Let it flood all your faculties, drown all your sins, wash away your cares, lift up your earthbound soul, and float it right to the Lord's feet. Rest there, a broken shell on the beach. But as he bends his ear to you, he hears faint echoes of the vast waves of his own love.

April 13

My lover is to me a sachet of myrrh.
(Song of Songs 1:13)

Why myrrh? It may be used here as a type of Jesus—on account of its preciousness, its perfume, its pleasantness, its healing, preserving, disinfecting qualities, and its connection with sacrifice. But why a whole *sachet* of myrrh?

First, the amount. He is not just a drop of myrrh; he's a whole bundle. There is enough in Christ for all my needs—I should not be slow to avail myself of this resource.

Second, for variety. Christ does not only meet a single need, but "in Christ all the fullness of the Deity lives in bodily form" (Colossians 2:9). Everything we need is here. He is Prophet, Priest, King, Husband, Friend, and Shepherd. Consider him in life, death, resurrection, ascension, and second coming. See him in his virtue, gentleness, courage, self-denial, love, faithfulness, truth, and righteousness. In every way, he is a bundle of preciousness.

Third, for preservation. He is not a bit of loose myrrh that might drop on the floor, but myrrh gathered into a sachet. Similarly, we must value him as our best treasure. We must prize his words, keeping our thoughts of him under lock and key, lest the devil steal them.

Finally, the sachet is set apart for a special purpose. So Jesus was set apart for his people. He gives his perfume only to those who enter into communion with him, who come close to his presence. How blessed we are to enjoy this secret scent! He has set himself apart for us.

April 14

All who see me mock me; they hurl insults,
shaking their heads. (Psalm 22:7)

Mockery was a major ingredient in our Lord's sorrows. Judas mocked him in the garden; the chief priests and scribes laughed him to scorn; Herod despised him; the servants and the soldiers jeered at him and brutally insulted him; Pilate and his guards ridiculed his royalty; and on the tree all sorts of horrid jests and hideous taunts were hurled at him. Ridicule is always hard to bear, but when we are in intense pain it is especially cruel—it cuts us to the quick.

Imagine the Savior crucified, racked with anguish beyond all human apprehension. Then picture the motley multitude, all wagging their heads or thrusting out their lips in bitter contempt of one poor suffering victim. Why was this mixed crowd so unanimous in their contempt? Could it be that evil itself was confessing, in this moment of apparent triumph, that it could do no more than mock Christ's victorious goodness?

O Jesus, "despised and rejected by men" (Isaiah 53:3), how could you die for people who treated you so poorly? Here is love amazing, love divine, yes, love beyond degree. We, too, have despised you in the past, and even since our rebirth we have given the world first place in our hearts. Yet you are bleeding to heal our wounds. You are dying to give us life. I wish we could set you on a glorious throne in everyone's heart. We would ring out your praises over land and sea, until your adoration is as unanimous as your rejection once was.

April 15

My God, my God, why have you forsaken me?
(Psalm 22:1)

Here we see the Savior in the depth of his sorrows. No other place shows us his griefs as Calvary does, and no other moment at Calvary is so full of agony as this one, when his cry rips through the air: "My God, my God, why have you forsaken me?"

At this moment, physical weakness was united with acute mental torture from the shame he had to go through. To top it all, he suffered inexpressible spiritual agony, resulting from the departure of his Father's presence. This was the dark midnight of his horror. This was when he descended the abyss of suffering.

None of us can enter into the full meaning of these words. Sometimes we think we could cry, "My God, my God, why have you forsaken me?" There are seasons when the brightness of our Father's smile is eclipsed by clouds and darkness. But we must remember that God never does really forsake us—it only seems that way. With Christ, it was a *real* forsaking. We moan at a little withdrawal of our Father's love, but the full turning away of God's face from his Son, who can calculate the depth of that agony?

In our case, our cries often come from unbelief. In Christ's case, it was a statement of dreadful fact—for God really had turned away from him. If you are a poor, distressed soul, who once lived in the sunshine of God's face, but are now in darkness, remember that he has not really forsaken you. God in the clouds is just as much our God as when he shines forth in all the luster of his grace.

April 16

The precious blood of Christ.
(1 Peter 1:19)

Standing at the foot of the cross, we see hands, feet, and side, all pouring out crimson streams of precious blood. Why is it "precious"? Because it *redeems* us. By this blood, the sins of Christ's people are atoned for. We are redeemed from under the law. We are reconciled to God, made one with him.

Christ's blood is also precious in its *cleansing power*—it "purifies us from all sin" (1 John 1:7). "Though your sins are like scarlet, they shall be as white as snow" (Isaiah 1:18). Because of Jesus' blood, there is not a spot left on any believer, no wrinkle or anything like that. Although we have rebelled against our God, this blood allows us to stand before him, accepted.

The blood of Christ is also precious in its *preserving power*. Under the sprinkled blood, we are safe from the destroying angel (Exodus 12:23). Remember that the reason we are spared is that *God sees* the blood. This should comfort us in those times when our eyes of faith are dim. God's eye never dims.

The precious blood of Christ also *sanctifies* us. It not only takes away our sin, but also awakens our new nature and leads us on to follow God's commands. There is no motive for holiness any greater than that which streams from the veins of Jesus.

Ultimately, the blood is precious because of its *overcoming power*. "They overcame . . . by the blood of the Lamb" (Revelation 12:11). Can it be any other way? He who fights with the precious blood of Jesus fights with a weapon that cannot know defeat.

The blood of Jesus! Sin dies in its presence; death is no longer death; heaven's gates are opened.

April 17

The sprinkled blood that speaks a better word than the blood of Abel. (Hebrews 12:24)

Have you come to this sprinkled blood? I'm not asking whether you have come to a knowledge of doctrine or the observance of ceremonies or some special experience, but *have you come to the blood of Jesus?*

The blood of Jesus gives life to godliness. If you have truly come to Jesus, the Holy Spirit has brought you, with no merit of your own. Guilty, lost, helpless, you came to take that blood as your eternal hope. With a trembling and aching heart, you came to the cross of Christ. How precious it was to hear the voice of his blood! To the repentant people of earth, the shedding of Christ's blood is the music of heaven.

We are full of sin, but as we gaze on the Savior's wounds, each drop of blood, as it falls, cries, "It is finished! I have put an end to sin!"

What sweet language this is! If you have come to that blood once, you will come constantly. You will fix your eyes on Jesus (Hebrews 12:2). You will feel your need to come to him every day. It is a joy and privilege to wash in that fountain.

Past experiences are doubtful food for Christians. But to come to Christ *in the present* gives us joy and comfort. This morning, let's sprinkle our doorpost fresh with blood and then feast on the Lamb, with the steady assurance that the destroying angel will pass over us.

April 18

And she tied the scarlet cord in the window.
(Joshua 2:21)

Rahab put her life in the hands of the spies. To her, they were representatives of the God of Israel. Her faith was simple and firm, but it was very obedient. Tying the scarlet cord in the window was a very trivial act in itself, but she dared not forget it.

Isn't there a lesson here for us? Have you paid attention to *all* of the Lord's will, even though some of his commands may seem unimportant? Have you observed the ordinances of baptism and the Lord's Supper? If not, that shows some disobedience in your life. Try to be blameless in everything—even to the tying of a thread, if that's what God commands.

But there is a more solemn lesson in Rahab's simple act. Am I implicitly trusting in the precious blood of Jesus? Have I tied the scarlet cord permanently, as with a Gordian knot, in my window? Or can I look out toward the Dead Sea of my sins or the Jerusalem of my hopes and forget about the blood?

The passersby can easily see a cord of such a conspicuous color hanging from a window. I should be making the reality of my salvation just as conspicuous to the people I meet. What is there to be ashamed of? Let people stare; I don't care. Christ's blood is my boast and my song.

There is One who sees that scarlet line even when I lack the faith to see it myself. My Lord will see it and preserve me from his judgment. Jericho's walls fell flat, but Rahab's house stood (even though it was on the wall!). My nature may be built into the wall of humanity, but when destruction comes, I will be secure.

April 19

At that moment the curtain of the temple was torn in two from top to bottom. (Matthew 27:51)

This was no small miracle—the tearing of such a thick veil—but it was not intended merely as a display of power. It was a great object lesson for us.

The old law was put aside, like a worn-out garment. When Jesus died, the sacrifices were all finished. They were all fulfilled in him. So it made sense that the place where the sacrifices were presented would become obsolete.

The tearing also *revealed all the hidden things of the old system*. The mercy seat could now be seen, and God's glory gleamed above it. Jesus' death gives us a clear revelation of God. Life and immortality now come to light.

The annual ceremony of atonement was abolished. The atoning blood had been sprinkled once a year behind the veil, but now the great High Priest offered his blood *once for all*. The blood of bullocks and lambs was no longer needed.

Access to God is now available to every believer in Christ Jesus. This is not some small peephole, through which we may peer at the mercy seat. No, this veil has been ripped apart, from top to bottom. We may come boldly to the throne of heavenly grace.

The opening of the Holy of Holies in this way also *gave us a picture of the opening of heaven's gates*. Our suffering Lord has the key of heaven. What he opens for us, no one can shut. Let us go in with him to our heavenly home and sit with him until all our common enemies become his footstool.

April 20

So that by his death he might destroy him who holds the power of death. (Hebrews 2:14)

Death has lost its sting, because the devil's power over it is destroyed. Then why are you afraid to die?

Ask God to give you such a deep awareness of your Redeemer's death that you will be strengthened for that final hour. Living near the cross of Calvary, you may think of death with pleasure and welcome it with intense delight when it comes.

It is sweet to die in the Lord. It is a covenant blessing to "fall asleep" in Jesus. Death is no longer a banishment; it is a *return* from exile, a going home to the "many mansions" where our loved ones already live.

The distance between the glorified spirits in heaven and the militant saints on earth may seem great, but it's not really. We are not far from home—we're just a moment away. The sail is spread, the soul is launched upon the sea—how long will the voyage be? How long will the soul be tossed on the waves before it comes to the stormless sea? Listen to the answer: "absent from the body . . . present with the Lord" (2 Corinthians 5:8 KJV). The ship just departed, but already it has reached its haven. Like that storm-tossed ship on the Sea of Galilee—Jesus said, "Peace, be still," and *immediately* it came to land.

No, don't expect a long period between the moment of death and the eternity of glory. When the eyes close on earth, they open in heaven. So what is there for you to fear? The curse of death has been destroyed by our Lord. It is now only a "Jacob's ladder," with its foot in the dark grave, but its top reaching to eternal glory.

April 21

I know that my Redeemer lives.
(Job 19:25)

The marrow of Job's comfort lies in that little word *my*—"*my* Redeemer"—and in the fact that his Redeemer *lives*. Oh, to get hold of a living Christ!

First, we must have a claim on him. What good is gold in a mine to me? It is gold in my purse that buys me what I need. So a Redeemer who does not redeem *me* and an avenger who will not pursue *my* interests, what good are these? Do not rest until you can say, by faith, "Yes, I throw myself upon my living Lord, and he is mine."

It may be that you hold him with a feeble grip. You may think it presumptuous to say, "He is *my* Redeemer." But remember that faith entitles you to say that—even if your faith is as small as a mustard seed.

Yet there is another word here that expresses Job's strong confidence: "I *know*." It is easy to say, "I hope so, I trust that . . ." And there are thousands of Christians who never get much further. But to reach the essence of Christ's comfort, you must say, "I know."

Ifs, *buts*, and *maybes* are murderers of peace and comfort. Doubts are dreary things in times of sorrow. Like wasps, they sting the soul. If I have any suspicion that Christ is not mine, then there is vinegar mixed with the gall of death. But if I know that Jesus lives for me, then darkness is not dark. Even the night lights up around me.

Certainly if Job, in those ages before the coming of Christ, could say, "I know," we should not speak any less positively. A living Redeemer, truly mine, is joy unspeakable.

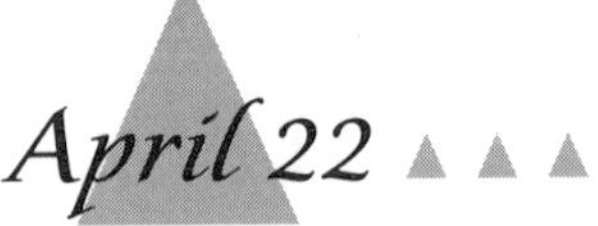

April 22

God exalted him.
(Acts 5:31)

Jesus our Lord, once crucified, dead, and buried, now sits on the throne of glory. He has an undisputed right to the highest place that heaven affords.

It is sweet to remember that the exaltation of Christ in heaven is a *representative exaltation*. He is exalted at the Father's right hand. Certainly the Father has glories far beyond his creatures, but Jesus is the Mediator, so his honors are shared with all the saints. Consider the union of Christ with his people. We are actually one with him. We are members of his body. His exaltation is our exaltation. As he has been given a heavenly throne, so he will give us thrones. He has a crown, but he gives us crowns, too.

Look up, believer, look to Jesus. Let the eye of your faith see him with all his crowns, and remember that you will one day be like him. You will not be as great as he is, you will not be so divine, but you will, in some measure, share his honors and enjoy the same happiness and dignity that he has.

So be content to live unknown for now, and to walk your weary way through the fields of poverty or up the hills of affliction. Someday you will reign with Christ, for he has made us "kings and priests," and we will reign forever.

What a wonderful thought! We have Christ as our glorious representative in heaven's courts *now*, and soon he will come and receive us to himself, to be with him there, to behold his glory, to share his joy.

April 23

No, in all these things we are more than conquerors through him who loved us. (Romans 8:37)

We go to Christ for forgiveness, but all too often we look to the law for the power to fight our sins. Paul would rebuke us: "You foolish Galatians! Who has bewitched you? . . . Did you receive the Spirit by observing the law, or by believing what you heard? Are you so foolish? After beginning with the Spirit, are you now trying to attain your goal by human effort?" (Galatians 3:1–3).

Take your sins to Christ's cross, for our old nature can only be crucified there: We are crucified *with him*. The only weapon to fight sin with is the spear that pierced the side of Jesus.

To give an illustration: You want to overcome an angry temper: how do you do it? It is very possible that you have never tried the right way of going to Jesus with it. How did I get salvation? I came to Jesus just as I was, and I trusted him to save me. I must kill my angry temper in the same way. I must go to the cross with it and say to Jesus, "Lord, I trust you to deliver me from it." This is the only way to give it a death blow.

Are you covetous? Do you feel the world entangling you? You may struggle against such things as long as you please, but you will never be delivered from them except by the blood of Jesus.

Take it to Christ. Tell him, "Lord, I have trusted you, and your name is Jesus—for you save your people from their sins. Lord, this is one of my sins. Save me from it!"

Your prayers, your repentances, your tears—all of them put together—are worth nothing apart from him. You must be conquerors through him who has loved you, if you will be conquerors at all.

April 24

And because of all this we make a sure covenant.
(Nehemiah 9:38 KJV)

There are many times when we may renew our covenant with God. After *recovery from sickness*, we may do this, thanking God, like Hezekiah, for our new lease on life. After *deliverance from trouble*, when our joys are budding forth again, we may return to the foot of the cross and renew our consecration.

We should especially do this after any *sin that has grieved the Holy Spirit*. We must look to that blood that makes us whiter than snow and offer ourselves again to the Lord.

But we should not only confirm our dedication in troubled times. We should also come to him in *times of prosperity*. If he has crowned us with joy, we ought to crown him again as our God. Let us bring out all the jewels from the treasure chest of our hearts and let our God sit on the throne of our love, arrayed in his royal robes.

If we would learn to profit from our prosperity, we would not need so much adversity. Have you recently received some blessing you didn't expect? Can you sing of the mercies God has blessed you with? Then this is the day to come to the altar, put yourself on it, and say, "I am yours, O Lord, fully and completely."

We need to be reminded regularly of God's promises to us. In the same way, we should renew our old vows, praying for God's strength to be true to them. This is a good time now. For the last month we have been considering Christ's sufferings. With gratitude, then, let us renew our "sure covenant" with the Lord.

April 25

Arise, my darling, my beautiful one, and come with me. (Song of Songs 2:10)

Listen! I hear the voice of my Beloved! He is speaking to *me*! Fair weather is smiling on the earth, and he doesn't want me spiritually asleep while nature is waking from her winter's rest.

"Arise," he says. I have been lying long enough amid the pots of worldliness. He is risen, and I am risen with him. Why then should I stay in the dust? From my lower loves, desires, pursuits, and aspirations, I rise to him.

He calls me "darling" and considers me "beautiful." This is also a good argument for rising. If he exalts me like this, if he thinks I am so comely, how can I linger where I am, away from him?

"Come with me," he beckons. Farther and farther from everything selfish, groveling, worldly, and sinful, he calls me. From that outwardly religious world that does not truly know him, he calls me. "Come with me!" The sound is not harsh at all. What possible reason would I have for staying in this wilderness of vanity and sin?

Lord, I want to come with you, but I am caught in these thorns and can't get away. If it were possible, I would like to have no heart for sin, no eyes or ears for sin. I want to follow your melodious call: "Come with me." To come to you is to come home from exile, to come out of a raging storm, to come to the goal of my desires and the summit of my wishes. But Lord, how can a stone rise? How can a lump of clay crawl out of the horrible pit? Raise me. Draw me. Your grace can do it. Send your Spirit to kindle sacred flames of love in my heart, and I will continue to rise until I leave life and time behind me and come to you.

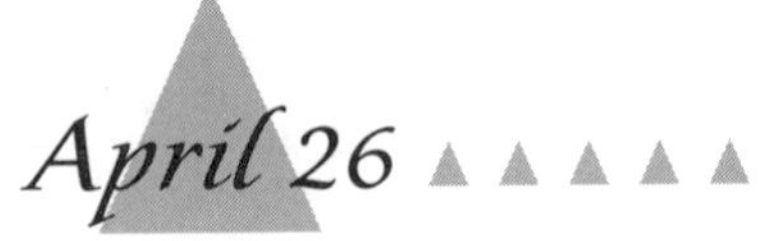

April 26

Do this in remembrance of me.
(1 Corinthians 11:24)

It would seem, from this verse, that Christians could forget Christ! There would be no need for this loving exhortation, unless we suppose that our memories might betray us. This is confirmed in our experience, not as a possibility but as a lamentable fact.

How can those who have been redeemed by the blood of the dying Lamb and loved with an everlasting love ever forget their gracious Savior? Forget him who never forgot us? Forget him who poured out his blood for our sins? Forget him who loved us, even to the death? Can it be possible?

Yes. Our consciences confess that it is a problem with all of us. We invite him into our lives as a temporary visitor, when he should be a permanent tenant. You would think our memories would linger at the cross, but this cross is desecrated by the feet of forgetfulness.

So what does your conscience say? Is this true of you? Do you find yourself forgetting Jesus? Some other person or possession steals your heart, and you neglect the one who ought to have all your affection. Some earthly business engrosses your attention when you should fix your eyes steadily on the cross. The incessant turmoil of the world and the constant attraction of earthly things take the soul away from Christ. Memory preserves the poisonous weeds and lets the Rose of Sharon wither.

Let's bind a heavenly forget-me-not around our hearts for Jesus, our Beloved. Whatever else we may forget, let's hold fast to him.

April 27

God, our God, will bless us.
(Psalm 67:6)

It is strange how little use we make of the spiritual blessings God gives us, but stranger how little use we make of God himself. He is "our God," but we pay little attention to him and ask him few favors.

We seldom even ask him for advice. We go about our own business. In our troubles, we try to bear our own burdens, instead of casting them on the Lord. And it is not as if the Lord doesn't want to be bothered. No! He says to us, "I am yours. Come and make use of me as you want. Use my resources freely and as often as you like." It is our own fault if we fail to take advantage of our Lord's riches.

Since you have him as your friend and since he invites you, draw from him daily. Don't suffer need when you have a God to provide for you. Don't be afraid when you have a God to comfort you. Go to your treasure chest and take what you need—there is all you could ever want.

Learn the divine skill of making God everything to you. He can supply you with all things, but better yet, he can *be* all things to you. Make use of your God *in prayer*. Go to him often, tell him your wants. This is such a great privilege. Use him *by faith*. If your future looks cloudy, use God as your "sun." If some enemy is attacking you, use God as your "shield." He has promised to be sun and shield to his people. If you have lost your way in the mazes of life, use him as a "guide." He will direct you. Whatever you are, wherever you are, remember God is there when you need him; he is *what you need* and he is *everything* you need.

April 28

Remember your word to your servant, for you have given me hope. (Psalm 119:49)

Whatever your special need may be, you will find some promise in the Bible suited to it. Do you feel weary because your life is so difficult? Here is the promise: "He gives strength to the weary and increases the power of the weak" (Isaiah 40:29). When you read a promise like this, take it back to the Great Promiser and ask him to keep his word.

Are you seeking after Christ, thirsting for a closer communion with him? Then this promise shines like a star upon you: "Blessed are those who hunger and thirst for righteousness, for they will be filled" (Matthew 5:6). Take this promise to the throne regularly. Don't ask for anything else, just go to God over and over again with this: "Lord, you have said it. Do what you have promised."

Are you distressed about your sin, weighed down with a heavy load of guilt? Listen to these words: "I, even I, am he who blots out your transgressions, for my own sake, and remembers your sins no more" (Isaiah 43:25). You have no merit of your own on which to demand forgiveness, but if you ask on the basis of what he has put in writing, he will fulfill his word.

Are you afraid that you will not be able to hold on to the end? Are you afraid that, after considering yourself a child of God, you will abandon the faith? If so, then take this word to God's throne: "Though the mountains be shaken and the hills be removed, yet my unfailing love for you will not be shaken" (Isaiah 54:10).

Feast on God's own word. Whatever your fears or wants, go to the bank of faith with your Father's handwritten check and say, "Remember your word to your servant, for you have given me hope."

April 29

You are my refuge in the day of disaster.
(Jeremiah 17:17)

The path of the Christian is not always bright with sunshine. We have times of darkness and storm. True, it is written in God's Word, "Her ways are pleasant ways, and all her paths are peace" (Proverbs 3:17), and it is true that our religion is designed to give us happiness below as well as eternal bliss above. But experience tells us that, even if the life of the righteous is "like the first gleam of dawn, shining ever brighter till the full light of day" (Proverbs 4:18), even *that* light is sometimes eclipsed. At certain times clouds cover the believer's sun, and he walks in darkness.

There are many who have rejoiced in the presence of God for a time. They have basked in the early stages of their Christian lives. They have walked along the "green pastures," by the side of the "still waters." But suddenly they find the glorious sky has clouded over; they are walking in a desert. Instead of sweet waters, they find turbulent streams, bitter to the taste, and they say, "If I were really a child of God, this would not be happening."

But that's not true. Even the best of God's saints must bear the cross. No Christian enjoys constant prosperity. Perhaps the Lord gave you a smooth, bright path at first because you were weak and timid. But now that you are stronger in your spiritual life, you must encounter the riper, rougher experience of God's full-grown children.

We need "disasters" to exercise our faith, to prune away the rotten branch of self-dependence and root us more firmly in Christ. The day of disaster shows us the full value of our glorious refuge.

April 30

All the Israelites grumbled.
(Numbers 14:2)

There are grumblers among Christians now, just as there were in Israel's camp. There are those who cry out when God's rod of discipline falls on them. They ask, "Why am I being tormented like this? What have I done to be disciplined in this way?"

Let me have a word with you, grumbler. What gives you the right to complain against our Lord's treatment of you? Can he treat you any more harshly than you deserve? Consider what a rebel you were—and he has pardoned you! Certainly, if he in his wisdom now decides to discipline you, you should not complain.

Consider the corruption inside you—and still you wonder why God needs to punish you? Weigh yourself, see how much dross is mixed with your gold. And then do you dare to wonder why God's refining fire is so hot?

Doesn't even your proud, rebellious spirit prove that your heart is not completely sanctified? Aren't your grumbles themselves contrary to the submissive nature of God's children? Doesn't that in itself show that you need correction?

But if you insist on grumbling, watch out. God always chastises his children twice, if they do not learn from the first stroke. But know this: "He does not willingly bring affliction or grief to the children of men" (Lamentations 3:33). All his corrections are performed in love, to purify you, to draw you closer to himself.

Certainly it should help you to deal with the chastening if you recognize your Father's hand in it, "because the Lord disciplines those he loves, and he punishes everyone he accepts as a son. Endure hardship as discipline; God is treating you as sons" (Hebrews 12:6–7).

May 1

His cheeks are as a bed of spices, as sweet flowers.
(Song of Songs 5:13 KJV)

The month of flowers is here. March winds and April showers have done their work, and the earth is bedecked with beauty. Now let us go and gather garlands of heavenly thoughts.

We know exactly where to go, because we have spent time in "the beds of spices" and have smelled "the sweet flowers." We are going to our beloved Savior, to find all loveliness and joy in him.

That cheek, which was once so harshly beaten, moistened with tears and then defiled with spittle—that cheek, as it smiles with mercy, brings rich fragrance to my heart. Those cheeks were furrowed by the plow of grief and reddened with lines of blood from his thorn-crowned temples. Such marks of love charm my soul even more than perfume.

If I cannot see his whole face, at least let me see his cheeks, for even this glimpse of him refreshes my spirit and yields a variety of delights. In Jesus I find not only one flower, but a whole garden. He is my rose and lily. When he is with me, it is May all year long. My soul washes its happy face in the morning dew of his grace and finds comfort as the birds sing his promises.

Precious Lord Jesus, let me know the blessedness that comes from abiding in unbroken fellowship with you. I am poor and worthless, yet you stoop to kiss my cheek. Let me kiss you in return.

May 2

My prayer is not that you take them out of the world but that you protect them from the evil one. (John 17:15)

At some point, when God chooses, every believer will go home to be with Jesus. The Lord's soldiers, now fighting "the good fight of faith" (1 Timothy 6:12), will be finished with conflict and will enter the joy of their Lord.

Here we read of Christ praying that his people would *eventually* be with him, but he does not ask that they be taken from the earth right away. He wants them to stay here.

How often do we weary pilgrims cry out, "Oh, that I had the wings of a dove! I would fly away and be at rest" (Psalm 55:6)? But Christ does not pray like that. He leaves us in his Father's hands, until, like sheaves of corn that have ripened, we will be gathered into our Father's storehouse.

Jesus does not plead for our instant removal by death, because our life on earth is important for others, if not for ourselves. Christians often want to die when they face any trouble. Ask them why, and they tell you, "Because we would be with the Lord." But I suspect that it is not so much their longing to be with the Lord as it is their desire to get rid of their troubles. Otherwise, they would feel the same wish to die when things are going well. They want to go home, not so much for the Savior's company, but to be at rest.

Now it is quite all right to want to depart if we can do it in the same spirit that Paul did (Philippians 1:21–26), because to be with Christ is "far better," but the wish to escape from trouble is a selfish one. Instead, let your desire be to glorify God by your life *here*, as long as he pleases, even if it does involve toil, conflict, and suffering. Let him say when it is enough.

May 3

In this world you will have trouble.
(John 16:33)

Do you wonder why this is? Look *upward* to your heavenly Father and see how pure and holy he is. Do you know that one day you will be like him? Do you think that will happen easily? Won't it take a great deal of refining in the furnace of affliction to purify you?

Next, Christian, turn your eyes *downward*. Do you realize what foes you have beneath your feet? You were once a servant of Satan, and no king likes to lose his subjects. Do you think that Satan will leave you alone? No, he will be always at you. After all, he "prowls around like a roaring lion looking for someone to devour" (1 Peter 5:8).

Then look *around you*. Where are you? In enemy territory. You are a stranger, a wanderer. The world is not your friend. Then you can be sure you will find enemies everywhere. When you sleep, you are resting on a battlefield. When you walk, expect an ambush in every hedge. It is said that mosquitoes bite strangers more than natives; in the same way, the trials of earth will be sharpest to you.

Finally, look *within you*, into your own heart. *Sin* and *self* are still inside you. If you had no devil to tempt you, no enemies to fight you, no world to entrap you, you would still have enough evil in yourself to trouble you. For "the heart is deceitful above all things" (Jeremiah 17:9).

You should expect trouble, then. But don't despair, God is with you to help and strengthen you. He has said, "I will be with you in trouble, I will deliver you and honor you" (see Psalm 91:15).

May 4

Do men make their own gods? Yes, but they are not gods! (Jeremiah 16:20)

One of the great besetting sins of Israel was idolatry, and the church—the spiritual Israel—is tempted in the same way. Remphan's star does not shine for us, and women no longer weep for Tammuz, but Mammon still puts up his golden calf, and the shrines of pride are well-kept. Self in various forms struggles to make believers slaves, and the flesh sets up altars wherever it can find space.

Favorite children are often a cause of sin in Christian families. The Lord is grieved when he sees us doting on them too much. They will become as great a curse as Absalom was to David, or they will be taken from us, leaving our homes desolate.

Jeremiah says, "They are not gods!" He is right. The objects of our foolish love are dubious blessings. The solace they offer us now is dangerous for us, and they give us little help in times of trouble. Why, then, are we so bewitched by these things? We pity the poor heathen who adores a god of stone, yet we worship a god of gold. Is it any better to worship a god of our own flesh than a god of wood? The principle is the same in both cases, only our crime is worse, because we should know better. The heathen bows to a false deity, but he has never known the true God. We are committing two evils, forsaking the living God, and turning to idols. May the Lord purge us all from the worship of our modern idols.

May 5

I will be their God, and they will be my people.
(2 Corinthians 6:16)

How much meaning is couched in these two words: "my people"! Here we find *specialness*. The whole world is God's: the heaven, even the heaven of heaven, belongs to him, and he reigns over all people. But he says something special about his chosen ones, the ones he has purchased: They are "my people."

In these words there is also the idea of *proprietorship*. "For the Lord's portion is his people, Jacob his allotted inheritance" (Deuteronomy 32:9). All the nations on earth are his. The whole world is in his power. Yet his people, his chosen ones, are his possession in a special way. He has done more for them than for others. He has bought them with his own blood. He has brought them close to himself. He has loved them with an eternal love, a love that many waters cannot quench and that the revolutions of time will never lessen.

Now can you see yourself as one of those chosen ones? Can you look up to heaven and say, "My Lord and my God, you are mine because of the *relationship* you have established, entitling me to call you my Father; and you are mine by that holy *fellowship* we have when you reveal yourself to me and I delight in your presence"?

Can you read the Book God has inspired and read the adoption papers for yourself? Can you read where it was signed in blood? If you can, then God says of you, and others like you, "My people." For if God is your God, then the Lord loves you in a special way.

May 6

We live in him.
(1 John 4:13)

Do you want a house for your soul? You may ask, "What is the purchase price?" It is less than proud human nature would like to pay. It is without money, without price.

Ah! So you say you still want to pay a respectable rent. You want to do something to earn the right to live in Christ. Well, then you can't have this house, for it is "without price" (Isaiah 55:1 KJV).

Will you take it on these terms? An eternal lease, nothing to pay, just the upkeep of loving and serving him? Will you take Jesus and "live in him"?

Look, this house is furnished with everything you could want. It is filled with riches, more than you could spend as long as you live. Here you can have intimate communion with Christ and feast on his love. When weary, you can rest here with Jesus. From this house, you can look out and see heaven itself.

Do you want the house? If you are homeless, you might say, "Sure I want it, but can I have it?" Yes, here is the key: "Come to Jesus."

You may still protest. "But I am too shabby for such a house." Never mind that; there are clothes for you inside. If you feel guilty, condemned, come in. Yes, the house is too good for you, but Christ will eventually make you good enough for the house.

Believer, you have three great blessings in a house like this. Not only is it a perfect house, it is also a "strong habitation" (Psalm 71:3 KJV) in which you are always safe. And it is also eternal. When this world melts like a dream, this house will live, sturdier than granite, for it is God himself.

May 7

Many followed him, and he healed all their sick.
(Matthew 12:15)

What a mass of hideous sickness must have come before Jesus! Yet he was not disgusted by it. Instead, he waited on each sufferer. What sickening ulcers and putrefying sores must have paraded before him. Yet he was ready for every new shape of the monster evil, and he proved himself the victor. Let the arrows fly from any quarter, he would quench their fiery power. The heat of fever, the chill of dropsy, the lethargy of palsy, the rage of madness, the filth of leprosy, and the darkness of blindness—all knew the power of his word and fled at his command.

In every corner of the field, he was triumphant over evil and received the acclaim of delivered captives. He came, he saw, and he conquered everywhere.

The same is true this morning. Whatever my own case may be, the beloved Physician can heal me. Whatever may be the state of the others I am praying for, I have hope in Jesus that he will be able to heal them of their sins.

However severe my struggle with sins and sicknesses, I can still rejoice. He who walked among the sick on earth still dispenses his grace, and he still works wonders among us. I can go to him with my need.

I praise him this morning as I remember how he brought the spiritual healing he is most famous for. He took our infirmities on himself. "By his wounds we are healed" (Isaiah 53:5). The church on earth is full of souls healed by our beloved Physician. Then let us proclaim his grace far and wide.

May 8

The man who was healed had no idea who it was.
(John 5:13)

Years are short to the happy and healthy, but thirty-eight years of disease must have dragged, seeming long and slow, for this disabled man. So when Jesus healed him with a simple word, as he lay at the pool of Bethesda, he was delightfully *aware of a change*. In the same way, the sinner who is paralyzed for weeks and months by despair, who wearily sighs for salvation, is very conscious of the change when the Lord Jesus says the word and gives him joy and peace. The evil removed is so great that we have to notice it. The new life we receive is so remarkable that we must enjoy it immediately.

Yet the poor man was *unaware of his healer*. He knew nothing about Jesus' holiness, his divine identity, or his mission. A great deal of ignorance of Jesus may remain in hearts that have felt his power. We should not condemn people for their lack of knowledge: If they have faith in Christ, we must assume salvation has been bestowed. The Holy Spirit makes people confessors long before he makes them professors. The person who believes what he knows will soon know more clearly what he believes.

However, there is still danger in ignorance. This man was *tantalized by the Pharisees* and was unable to cope with them. It is good to be able to answer our critics, but we cannot do so unless we know the Lord Jesus well. But this man found a cure for his ignorance: He was *visited by the Lord*, and later he was *found testifying* that "it was Jesus who had made him well" (v. 15).

May 9

Who has blessed us . . . with every spiritual blessing in Christ. (Ephesians 1:3)

All the goodness of the past, present, and future—this is what Christ gives his people. In the mysterious ages of the past, the Lord Jesus was chosen by his Father; and we have a share in this choosing, because "he chose us in him before the creation of the world" (Ephesians 1:4). From all eternity, Jesus had the privileges of Sonship; and he has, by his gracious adoption and regeneration, elevated us to sonship as well, giving us "the right to become children of God" (John 1:12).

The eternal covenant, confirmed by God's oath, is ours, too. In his predestinating wisdom, the Lord Jesus has always had his eye on us. We may rest assured that we are safe in him.

The great betrothal of the Prince of Glory is also ours, because we are his intended bride. Before too long, we will enjoy the wedding feast before the assembled universe. The marvelous incarnation of the God of heaven, in all its humble love, is ours, too. The bloody sweat, the brutal whipping, the cross, are all ours forever.

We also have the blessings that come from perfect obedience, finished atonement, resurrection, ascension, and intercession. He has given us these things himself. On his breastplate he wears our names. In his pleas before his Father's throne, he remembers our needs.

May 10

But Christ has indeed been raised from the dead.
(1 Corinthians 15:20)

The whole system of Christianity rests on the fact that Christ has been raised from the dead. For, "if Christ has not been raised, your faith is futile; you are still in your sins" (1 Corinthians 15:17).

The *divinity* of Christ finds its fullest proof in the resurrection. Jesus was "declared with power to be the Son of God by his resurrection from the dead" (Romans 1:4).

Christ's *sovereignty* also depends on his resurrection. "For this very reason, Christ died and returned to life so that he might be the Lord of both the dead and the living" (Romans 14:9).

Our *justification* is also linked with Christ's triumph over death and the grave. "He was delivered over to death for our sins and was raised to life for our justification" (Romans 4:25). Even more, our *regeneration* is connected with his rising, for "he has given us new birth into a living hope through the resurrection of Jesus Christ from the dead" (1 Peter 1:3).

Finally, our *ultimate resurrection* rests here, for, "if the Spirit of him who raised Jesus from the dead is living in you, he who raised Christ from the dead will also give life to your mortal bodies through his Spirit, who lives in you" (Romans 8:11).

So the silver thread of resurrection runs through all the believer's blessings, from his regeneration to his eternal glory, and it binds them all together. What a glorious fact it is that "Christ has indeed been raised from the dead"!

May 11

I am with you always.
(Matthew 28:20)

There is Someone who is always the same and always with us. There is one stable Rock amid the turbulent waves of the sea of life. O my soul, why do you set your affections on rusting, moth-eaten, decaying treasures? Set your heart on the One who is always faithful to you. Do not build your house on the shifting quicksand of a deceitful world, but found your hopes upon this Rock, which stands firm despite pounding rain and roaring floods.

I charge you to store your treasure in the only secure cabinet there is. Hide your jewels where you can never lose them. Put your all in Christ. Set all your affections on his person, all your hope in his merit, all your trust in his atoning blood, all your joy in his presence. If you do this, you can laugh at loss and defy destruction.

Remember that all the flowers in the world's garden eventually fade, and the day is coming when there will be nothing left but cold, black soil. Death will soon blow out your candle. But, oh, how sweet to have sunlight when the candle is gone. The dark flood will soon roll between you and everything you have. So fix your heart on the One who will never leave you. Trust yourself to the One who will go with you through the surging current of death's stream and land you safely on the celestial shore.

Go ahead—if you are suffering, tell your secrets to the Friend who sticks closer than a brother. Entrust all your concerns to him who can never be taken from you, who will never leave you, and who will never let you leave him.

May 12

I . . . will love him and show myself to him.
(John 14:21)

The Lord Jesus gives special revelations of himself to his people. Even if Scripture did not tell us this, there are many of God's children who could testify to it from their own experience. In the biographies of great saints, you will find many instances recorded where Jesus spoke to their souls, unfolding the wonders of his person. In some cases, their souls were so steeped in happiness through this experience that they thought they were in heaven. Of course they weren't; but they were close, because when Jesus reveals himself to his people, it is heaven on earth, it is paradise in embryo, it is bliss begun.

Such manifestations of Christ have a holy influence on the believer's heart. One effect is *humility*. If someone says, "I have had such-and-such a spiritual experience, so I am a great Christian," he has never had any communion with Jesus at all. For the Lord "looks upon the lowly, but the proud he knows *from afar*" (Psalm 138:6, *italics added*). That is, he doesn't need to come near them; he will not visit them with his love.

Another effect is *happiness*. In God's presence there are eternal pleasures. *Holiness* is sure to follow. A person without holiness has never had such a special revelation of Christ. Some may claim a great deal, but we must not believe them until we see that their deeds match their words. "Do not be deceived: God cannot be mocked" (Galatians 6:7). He will not bestow his favors on the wicked.

So we see three results of being near to Jesus—humility, happiness, and holiness. May God give them to you!

May 13

Weeping may remain for a night, but rejoicing comes in the morning. (Psalm 30:5)

If you are in a night of trial, think of tomorrow. Cheer up your heart with the thought of the Lord's coming. Be patient! The Farmer is waiting to reap his harvest.

Be patient! For you know that he has said, "Behold, I am coming soon! My reward is with me, and I will give to everyone according to what he has done" (Revelation 22:12).

Your head may be crowned with thorny troubles now, but before long it will be wearing a starry crown. Your hand may be filled with cares, but soon it will be sweeping the strings of a heavenly harp. Your clothes may be soiled and dusty now, but they will be white as snow. Wait a little longer.

Think how trivial our troubles will seem when we look back on them! As we look at them now, they seem immense, but when we get to heaven, our trials will seem like light and momentary afflictions.

So let us move on boldly. Even if the night is darker than it has ever been, the morning is coming. That's more than they can say in the darkness of hell. Do you know how to anticipate the joys of heaven, to live in expectation? It is a comforting hope. It may be dark now, but the morning brings light. Our weeping will turn to rejoicing.

May 14

Heirs of God and co-heirs with Christ.
(Romans 8:17)

The unlimited realms of the Father's universe belong to Christ. As God's Son, he is the heir to this fortune, the sole proprietor of the vast creation. He has allowed us to claim the whole estate as ours, too, since we have officially been named as "co-heirs" with him.

The golden streets of paradise, the pearly gates, the river of life, the transcendent joy, the unspeakable glory have all been signed over to us eternally by our blessed Lord. All that he has he shares with his people. He has placed the royal crown on the head of his church, appointing her as a "kingdom" and calling her sons a "royal priesthood," a generation of priests and kings (1 Peter 2:9; Revelation 1:6).

He put down his own crown for a time, so that we might have a glorious coronation. He would not sit on his own throne until he had procured a place on it for his people. Crown the head, and the whole body shares the honor.

Here is the reward of every Christian conqueror! Christ's throne, crown, scepter, palace, treasure, robes, and heritage are yours. Why settle for jealousy, selfishness, and greed—which never share their wealth anyway—when Christ is longing for you to join in his happiness?

"I have given them the glory that you gave me" Jesus prayed (John 17:22). The smiles of his Father were all the sweeter to him because his people were sharing them. The honors of his kingdom are more pleasing, because his people will appear with him in glory. His conquests are more valuable, because they have taught his people to overcome. He delights in his throne, because there is a place on it for them.

May 15

Everyone who believes is justified.
(Acts 13:39)

A person who believes in Christ receives a *present* justification. Faith produces this fruit *now*, not at some distant time. Justification is given to the soul at the moment when it accepts Christ as its all in all. Those who stand before God's throne are justified, yes, but so are we. We are just as righteous in God's eyes as those who "walk in white" and sing melodious praises on celestial harps.

The thief on the cross was justified the moment he turned his eyes in faith to Jesus. After years of service, Paul, the aged saint, was no more justified than this thief, who believed moments before he died.

Today we are absolved from sin. *Today* we are acquitted in God's court. Certainly there are some clusters from heaven's vines that we will not gather until we enter heaven. But this justification is a branch that hangs over the wall. It is not the "corn of the land," which we cannot eat until we cross the Jordan. But it is part of the "manna in the desert," a portion of our daily nutrition, which God supplies us as we journey.

Now we are pardoned. *Now* our sins are put away. *Now* we stand accepted before God, as if we had never been guilty. "Therefore, there is *now* no condemnation for those who are in Christ Jesus" (Romans 8:1, *italics added*). There is not a single sin in God's Book, even *now*, against any of God's people. Who dares to accuse them?

Let our present privilege awaken us to present duty. *Now*, while life lasts, let us spend and be spent for our sweet Lord Jesus.

May 16

God . . . richly provides us with everything for our enjoyment.
(1 Timothy 6:17)

Our Lord Jesus is always giving to us. As long as there is a vessel of grace that is not yet full to the brim, he will not stop pouring the oil of his blessing. He is an ever-shining sun. He is manna that is constantly falling around the camp. He is a rock in the desert, always sending out streams of life from his smitten side. The rain of his grace is always pouring down; the river of his blessing flows on and on; and the wellspring of his love overflows endlessly.

Daily we pluck his fruit, and daily his branches bend down to our hands. There are seven feast days in his weeks, and every day of the year has a special banquet. Who has ever returned from his door unblessed? Who has ever risen from his table unsatisfied? Who has left his side without the joy of paradise?

His mercies are new every morning and fresh every evening. Who can count all his benefits? Every sand that drops through the hourglass is only a tardy follower of a myriad of mercies. The wings of our hours are covered with the silver of his kindness and the bright gold of his affection. The countless stars are like flag bearers, each leading a huge army of blessings.

How can my soul ever praise him enough for all his benefits? He crowns us daily with loving-kindness. Oh that my praise could be as rich as his bounty. O my tongue, how can you be silent! Wake up and sing his praises. "Awake, harp and lyre! I will awaken the dawn" (Psalm 108:2).

May 17

Whoever claims to live in him must walk as Jesus did.
(1 John 2:6)

Why should Christians imitate Christ? They should do it *for their own sakes*. If they want their souls to be healthy, if they want to avoid the sickness of sin and enjoy the vigor of growing grace, they should let Jesus be their model. For their own happiness, if they want the finest in life, if they want to enjoy holy and happy communion with Jesus, if they want to be lifted above the cares and troubles of this world, then let them walk as Jesus walked.

There is no better way to walk quickly toward heaven than to wear the image of Jesus on your heart and let it guide your motions. When you are enabled, by the Holy Spirit, to walk in the very footsteps of Jesus, you are as happy as you can be, and you show yourself to be a child of God. To stand far off, like Peter at Christ's trial, is both unsafe and uneasy.

Next, try to live like Jesus *for religion's sake*. Religion has received plenty of attacks from its foes, but those wounds are only half as serious as the wounds from its friends. Who has wounded the fair hand of godliness like this? The professor, using the dagger of hypocrisy. The pretender, who enters the fold as a wolf in sheep's clothing and worries the flock even more than the lion outside. There is no weapon half so deadly as the Judas kiss.

But especially, *for Christ's own sake*, follow his example. Do you love your Savior? Is his name precious to you? Do you want him to be glorified? Are you longing for souls to be won to him? If so, imitate Jesus. Be a letter from Christ that is "known and read by everybody" (2 Corinthians 3:2–3).

May 18

For in Christ all the fullness of the Deity lives in bodily form, and you have been given fullness in Christ. (Colossians 2:9–10)

All the attributes of Christ, as God and man, are at our disposal. All the fullness of the Deity, whatever that marvelous term may include, is ours to make us complete. He cannot endow us with the attributes of deity. But he has done all that can be done, for he made his divine power subservient to our salvation. His omnipotence, omniscience, omnipresence, immutability, and infallibility are all combined for our defense.

Look and see the Lord Jesus harnessing all of his divinity to the chariot of salvation! How vast is his grace, how firm his faithfulness, how infinite his power! All of these become the pillars of the temple of salvation. And all of them, without lessening them, have been promised to us as our eternal inheritance.

The fathomless love of the Savior's heart is ours—every drop. Every sinew in his mighty arm, every jewel in his crown, the immensity of divine knowledge and the sternness of divine justice are all ours and will be used on our behalf.

All of Christ, in his adorable character as the Son of God, is granted to us for our enjoyment. His wisdom directs us, his knowledge instructs us, his power protects us, his justice upholds us, and his love comforts us. He holds nothing back but opens the recesses of the mountain of God and invites us to dig in its mines for buried treasure. "All, all, all are yours," he says. "Be satisfied with my grace and be full of my goodness."

May 19

I have seen slaves on horseback, while princes go on foot like slaves. (Ecclesiastes 10:7)

Upstarts often grab the highest honors, while the truly great languish in obscurity. This is a riddle whose answer will one day satisfy us. But in the meantime, it is so common that we should not complain if it happens to us.

When our Lord was on the earth, although he was the Prince of the kings of the earth, yet he walked the paths of weariness and service—a Servant of servants. We should not be surprised if his followers, who are princes by his blood, should also be looked down upon as contemptible people. The world is upside down, so the first are last and the last first.

See how the proud sons of Satan lord it over others on earth. Haman is in the king's court, while Mordecai sits at the city gate. David wanders in the desert, while Saul rules the nation. Elijah complains in his cave, while Jezebel boasts in her palace. But who would wish to take the place of these proud rebels? When the wheel turns, those who are lowest rise, and the highest sink. Have patience. Eternity will right the wrongs of time.

We must not let our passions and carnal appetites ride in triumph, while our nobler instincts walk in the dust. Grace must reign in our lives as a prince, making the members of our bodies its servants. We were not created to allow our passions to rule over us, but so that we, as kings, might reign with Christ over our spirits, souls, and bodies, to the glory of God the Father.

May 20

Show the wonder of your great love.
(Psalm 17:7)

When we give our offerings, do we also give our hearts? We often fail in this respect, but the Lord never does. His favors always come to us with the love of his heart. He does not send us the leftovers and crumbs from his dining table, but he dips our morsel in his own dish and seasons our meals with the spices of his fragrant affection.

When he puts the gold tokens of grace in our palms, he accompanies the gift with such a warm pressure on our hands that the way in which he gives is as precious as the gift itself. On his errands of kindness, he enters our homes and does not act like some distant visitor in a poor man's cottage. No, he sits by our sides, not despising our poverty for a moment.

And what a smile he has! What golden sentences drop from his gracious lips! What embraces of affection he gives us! It is impossible to doubt the sincerity of his charity, for there is a bleeding heart stamped upon everything he gives us. He gives freely, and there is no hint that we are a burden to him, not one cold look. He rejoices in his mercy and presses us close to him as he pours out his life for us.

There is a fragrance in his spikenard that nothing but his heart could produce. There is a sweetness in his honeycomb that would not be there unless the essence of his soul's affection were mixed in with it all. What a special communion this is: May we continually taste it and know its blessedness.

May 21

If . . . ye have tasted that the Lord is gracious.
(1 Peter 2:3 KJV)

If"—then this is not a matter to be taken for granted about everyone in the human race. "If"—then there is a possibility, even a probability, that some may not have tasted that the Lord is gracious. "If"—then we need to consider we know the grace of God through personal experience.

While this should be a matter of earnest and prayerful inquiry, no one ought to be content as long as there is an "if" about his having tasted that the Lord is gracious. A zealous and holy distrust of self may create a momentary doubt in the believer's heart, but the *continuing* of such a doubt would be an awful thing. We must not rest without a desperate struggle to clasp our Savior in the arms of faith and say, "I know whom I have believed, and am convinced that he is able to guard what I have entrusted to him" (2 Timothy 1:12).

Do not rest, believer, until you have a full assurance of where you stand with Jesus. Do not let anything satisfy you, until, as the Holy Spirit bears witness with your spirit, you are convinced that you are a child of God. Don't be satisfied with *perhaps* or *if* or *maybe*. Build on eternal sureties and build on them surely.

Advance beyond these dreary *ifs*. Do not wander any longer in the wilderness of doubts and fears. Cross the Jordan of doubt and enter the Canaan of peace—where there may be some enemies, but where the land never stops flowing with milk and honey.

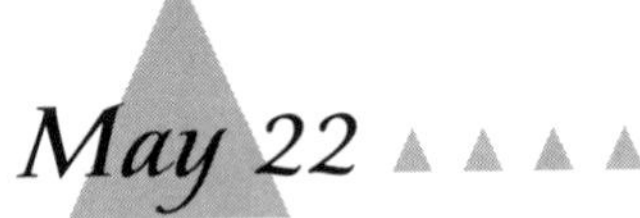

May 22

He led them by a straight way.
(Psalm 107:7)

Experiencing great changes, the anxious believer might sometimes ask, "Why am I going through this?" I looked for light, but there was only darkness. I wanted peace, but found trouble. I said in my heart, I am standing firm on my mountain of faith—I will not be moved. But Lord, you hide your face for a moment, and I am troubled. Just yesterday I was sure of my position with you, but today I have lost the evidence, my hopes are clouded. Yesterday I could climb to the top of Mount Pisgah and look with confidence toward the Promised Land. But today my spirit has no hopes, but many fears; no joys, but much distress.

Is this part of God's plan for me? Is this any way for God to bring me toward heaven? Yes, it is. The eclipse of your faith, the darkness of your mind, the fainting of your hope—all these things are just parts of God's method of making you ripe for the great inheritance you will soon receive. These trials are for the testing and strengthening of your faith. They are waves that wash you farther up on the rock of safety. They are winds that waft your ship more swiftly toward your desired haven.

By honor and dishonor, by slander and praise, by plenty and poverty, by joy and distress, by persecution and peace—by all these things is the life of your soul maintained. Each of these helps you on your way. "We must go through many hardships to enter the kingdom of God" (Acts 14:22). So learn to "consider it pure joy" (James 1:2).

May 23

The Lord will fulfill his purpose for me.
(Psalm 138:8)

Clearly, the confidence the psalmist was expressing here was a *divine confidence*. He did not say, "*I* have grace enough to fulfill God's purposes for me. *My* faith is so steady that it will never stagger. *My* love is so warm that it will never grow cold. *My* resolution is so firm that nothing can shake it." No, his dependence was on the Lord alone.

If we indulge in any confidence that is not grounded on the Rock of Ages, our confidence is worse than a dream—it will fall on us and cover us with its ruins, causing sorrow and confusion. The psalmist was wise. He rested on nothing short of the *Lord's* work. It is the Lord who has begun a good work in us, and he has carried it on. If *he* does not finish it, no one will. If there is one stitch in the celestial robe of righteousness that we have to insert ourselves, then we are lost. But this is our confidence: The Lord who began it will complete it. He *has* done it all, *must* do it all, and *will* do it all. Our confidence must not be in what we have done or in what we have resolved to do, but entirely in what *the Lord* will do.

Unbelief insinuates, "You will never be able to stand. Look at the evil in your heart. You can never conquer sin. Look at all the sinful pleasures and temptations of the world that are all around you. You will certainly be led astray."

Ah, yes. We would certainly fail, if left to our own strength. But thanks be to God, he will fulfill his purposes for us. We can never be too confident when we confide in him alone.

May 24

Praise be to God, who has not rejected my prayer.
(Psalm 66:20)

If we honestly looked at the character of our prayers, we would be surprised that God ever answers them. Some may think that their prayers are worthy of acceptance—like the Pharisees. But the true Christian looks more humbly at his prayers, and if he could retrace his steps, would want to learn how to pray more earnestly.

Remember, Christian, how *cold* your prayers have been. In your prayer closet, you should have been wrestling as Jacob did. But instead your requests have been faint and few, far removed from that persevering faith that cries, "I will not let you go unless you bless me!" (Genesis 32:26). Yet strange as it may seem, God has heard these cold prayers of yours—and not only heard, but answered them.

Consider also how *infrequent* your prayers have been, except when you're in trouble. *Then* you rush to the mercy seat. But when your deliverance comes, where are your prayers then? But even though you may have stopped praying as you once did, God has not stopped blessing.

It is strange and wonderful that God should pay attention to these intermittent spasms of prayer that come and go according to our immediate needs. What a God he is, to hear the prayers of those who come to him when they have pressing wants, but neglect him once they have received mercy. They approach him when they are forced to, but they almost forget to speak to him at all when mercies are plentiful and sorrows are few. Oh, may our hearts be touched by his gracious kindness, so that we may "pray in the Spirit on all occasions, with all kinds of prayers and requests" (Ephesians 6:18).

May 25

O Lord, do not forsake me.
(Psalm 38:21)

We often pray that God will not forsake us in our times of trial and temptation, but we forget that we need to pray like this *at all times*. There is no moment of our lives, however holy, in which we can do without his constant upholding. In light or darkness, in communion or temptation, we always need to pray, "O Lord, do not forsake me."

A little child, learning to walk, always needs a steadying hand. The ship left by its pilot immediately drifts from its course. We cannot do without continued aid from above.

So let this be your prayer today: "Do not forsake me, Lord. Father, do not forsake your child, lest I fall to the enemy. Shepherd, do not forsake your lamb, lest I wander from the safety of the fold. Great Gardener, do not forsake your plant, lest I wither and die. Do not forsake me now or at any moment of my life. Forsake me not in my joys, lest they absorb my heart. Forsake me not in my sorrows, lest I complain against you. Forsake me not in my moment of repentance, lest I lose the hope of pardon and fall into despair. Forsake me not in the time when my faith is strongest, lest faith degenerate into presumption. Without you, Lord, I am weak. With you, I am strong. Do not forsake me, for my path is dangerous. I cannot do without your guidance. As the hen will not forsake her brood, so cover me forever with your feathers, let me find refuge under your wings."

"Do not be far from me, for trouble is near and there is no one to help" (Psalm 22:11).

May 26

Cast your cares on the Lord and he will sustain you.
(Psalm 55:22)

Care can be sinful—even when we are caring about legitimate things—if it is carried to extremes. Our Savior regularly taught that we should avoid anxious concern. The apostles repeated this. We cannot ignore this teaching without falling into sin.

The very essence of anxious care is imagining that we are wiser than God. When we worry, we put ourselves in his place and try to do for him what he intends to do for us. We try to think of some detail he might have forgotten. We struggle to bear our burden, as if he were unable or unwilling to carry it for us.

This disobedience to his teaching, this unbelief in his Word, this presumption as we intrude on his responsibilities—it is all sinful. But beyond this, anxiety often leads to acts of sin. The one who cannot calmly leave his affairs in God's hands, but insists on carrying his own burden, is very likely to be tempted to use wrong means to help himself. This sin leads people to forsake God as their counselor, resorting to human wisdom instead. It is a matter of going to the "broken cistern" rather than the "spring of living water"—a sin that Israel was once accused of (Jeremiah 2:13).

Anxiety makes us doubt God's loving-kindness, and so our love for him grows cold. We feel mistrust, and so we grieve the Holy Spirit. As a result, our prayers are hindered, our consistent example is marred, and our lives become self-seeking.

But if, through simple faith in his promise, we cast each burden upon him, we will remain close to him, strengthened against temptation. "You will keep in perfect peace him whose mind is steadfast, because he trusts in you" (Isaiah 26:3).

May 27

And Mephibosheth lived in Jerusalem, because he always ate at the king's table, and he was crippled in both feet. (2 Samuel 9:13)

Mephibosheth was no great ornament to a royal table, yet he had a regular place in David's home, because the king could see in his face the features of his dear friend Jonathan. Like Mephibosheth, we may cry unto the King of Glory, "What is your servant, that you should notice a dead dog like me?" (2 Samuel 9:8). But still the Lord blesses us with his friendship, because he sees in us the righteousness of his dearly beloved Jesus.

This is the kind of love the Father has for his only begotten Son, that for his sake he raises his lowly brothers from poverty and banishment to noble rank and royal provisions. Their deformity does not rob them of their privileges. Lameness is no bar to sonship. Our "might" may limp, but our "right" does not. A king's table is a noble hiding place for lame legs, and at the Lord's feast we learn to glory in our infirmities, because the power of Christ rests upon us.

It is true that even the best-loved saints may suffer some grievous disability. Mephibosheth here was so lame in both feet that he could not flee the city with David. As a result he was insulted by the servant Ziba. Saints whose faith is weak and whose knowledge is slender are great losers. They fall prey to many enemies and cannot always follow the king where he goes.

And as with Mephibosheth, this problem often results from a fall. Bad nursing in spiritual infancy often causes converts to fall into a despondency from which they never recover.

Lord, help the lame to leap like a deer. Satisfy all your people with the bread of your table!

May 28

Those he justified, he also glorified.
(Romans 8:30)

Here is a precious truth for you, believer. You may be poor or suffering, but it may encourage you to review your "calling" and the consequences that flow from it. As surely as you are God's child, your trials will soon end, and you will bask in his riches. Wait a while, and your weary head will wear a crown of glory, your laboring hand will grab the palm branch of victory.

Do not lament your troubles, but rejoice! Before long you will be where "there will be no more death or mourning or crying or pain" (Revelation 21:4). The chariots of fire are at your door, and they will carry you to glory in a moment. The eternal song is almost on your lips. The gates of heaven stand open for you.

Nothing can go wrong. If he has called you, nothing can divide you from his love. Distress cannot sever the bond. The fire of persecution cannot burn the ropes that bind you to him. The hammer of hell cannot break the chain. You are secure. The voice that first called you will call you again from earth to heaven, from death's dark gloom to the unuttered splendors of immortality. Rest assured, the heart of your Justifier beats with an infinite love for you. Soon you will be with the glorified. You are only waiting here to prepare for your inheritance. When that is done, the wings of angels will waft you far away, to the mountain of peace, joy, and blessedness.

May 29

You . . . hate wickedness.
(Psalm 45:7)

There can hardly be any goodness in a person if he does not hate wickedness. If he loves truth, he must despise every false way. How our Lord Jesus hated it when the temptation came! Three times it attacked him in different forms, but he always met it with "Get behind me, Satan!"

He hated evil in others, even though he showed it more often in tears of pity than in words of rebuke. Yet what language could be sterner, more Elijah-like, than "Woe to you, teachers of the law and Pharisees, you hypocrites! You devour widows' houses and for a show make lengthy prayers" (Matthew 23:13–14)?

He hated wickedness so much that he bled in order to deal it a deathblow. He died so that it might die. He was buried so that he might bury it in his tomb. And he rose so that he might trample it under his feet.

Wickedness dresses up in fine clothes and imitates the language of holiness. But the teachings of Jesus, like his famous whip of small cords, chase it out of the temple—and will not tolerate it in the church. So, too, in the heart where Jesus reigns, the war rages between Christ and Satan. When our Redeemer comes in judgment, he will reveal his eternal abhorrence of iniquity with the words "Depart from me, you who are cursed!" As warm as his love is toward sinners, so hot is his hatred for sin.

May 30

Catch for us the foxes, the little foxes that ruin the vineyards.
(Song of Songs 2:15)

A little thorn may cause much suffering. A little cloud may hide the sun. Little foxes ruin the vineyards. And little sins do mischief to the tender heart.

These little sins burrow in the soul, filling it with things that Christ hates, so that he cannot have comfortable fellowship with us. A great sin cannot destroy a Christian, but a little sin can make him miserable. Jesus will not walk with his people unless they drive out every known sin. He says, "If you obey my commands, you will remain in my love, just as I have obeyed my Father's commands and remain in his love" (John 15:10). Sadly, some Christians seldom enjoy their Savior's presence.

Why do they let this happen? Surely it must be a problem for a tender child to be separated from his father. But you are a child of God! And are you satisfied to live day by day without seeing your Father's face? You are the bride of Christ, and can you be content without his company? If so, then you have fallen into a sad state.

So think about it. What has driven Christ away from you? He hides his face behind the wall of your sins. That wall may be built of *little* pebbles. The sea that divides you from Christ may be filled with the drops of your little sins.

If you want to live with Christ, watch out for "the little foxes that ruin the vineyards." But Jesus can "catch" them. Like Samson, he can round them up easily. Go and help him hunt them.

May 31

The king also crossed the Kidron Valley.
(2 Samuel 15:23)

David crossed the gloomy brook of Kidron while fleeing from his traitor son. This "man after God's own heart" was not exempt from trouble. No, his life was full of it. He was both the Lord's Anointed and the Lord's Afflicted. Why then should we expect to escape? Even the noblest of our race have encountered sorrow. Why do we complain as if some strange thing were happening to us?

The King of Kings himself was not favored with a road that was any more cheerful or royal. He crossed the filthy ditch of Kidron, through which the refuse of Jerusalem flowed. God had one Son without sin, but he would not spare the rod for any of his children.

It should comfort us to know that Jesus has been tempted in every way that we are. What is our Kidron this morning? Is it a treacherous friend, a sad bereavement, a slanderous attack, a dark sense of foreboding? The King has gone through all of these. Is it bodily pain, poverty, persecution, or contempt? The King has crossed each of these Kidrons before us. We must banish once and for all the idea that our afflictions are unique, because Jesus has been through it all.

Despite his humiliating flight, David returned in triumph to his city. And David's Lord arose victorious from the grave. Let us be of good courage, too, for we will also win the day. We will still draw water from the wells of salvation, even though now we must pass briefly through the noxious streams of sin and sorrow. Courage, soldiers of the cross, the King himself triumphed after going through Kidron, and so will you.

June 1

And there was evening, and there was morning—the first day.
(Genesis 1:5)

Was it true even from the beginning? Did light and darkness divide the realm of time in the first day? Then it is little wonder that my life also changes between the sunshine of prosperity and the midnight of adversity. There will not always be the blaze of noon in my soul. At times I must expect to mourn the loss of previous joys and to seek my Beloved in the night.

I am not alone in this. All the Lord's beloved ones have had to sing the mingled song of judgment and mercy, of trial and deliverance, of mourning and delight. It is one of the arrangements of divine providence: Day and night will continue in both the spiritual and natural creation, until we reach that land where "there will be no more night" (Revelation 22:5).

What then should I do? First, learn to be content with this divine order. Be willing, with Job, to receive evil from the Lord's hand as well as good.

Second, learn to rejoice in these changes. Praise the Lord for the sun of joy when it rises and for the gloom of evening as it falls. There is beauty in both sunrise and sunset. Sing of it and glorify the Lord. Like the nightingale, ring out your notes at all hours.

Then believe that the night is as useful as the day. The dews of grace fall heavily in the night of sorrow. The stars of promise shine gloriously in the darkness of grief.

Continue your service through it all. Work in the day and watch in the night. Every hour has its duty, so continue in your calling as the Lord's servant until he suddenly appears in his glory.

June 2

For the sinful nature desires what is contrary to the Spirit, and the Spirit what is contrary to the sinful nature. (Galatians 5:17)

In every believer's heart there is a constant struggle between the old nature and the new. The old nature is very active and takes every opportunity to wield the weapons of its deadly armory against newborn grace. On the other hand, the new nature is always on the watch, seeking to resist and destroy its enemy. Grace within us uses prayer and faith and hope and love to battle against evil. It puts on "the whole armor of God" and wrestles earnestly.

These two opposing natures will keep struggling as long as we are in this world. The enemy is so securely entrenched within us that he can never be driven out while we are in this body. But although the battle is often fierce, we have a mighty helper—Jesus, the captain of our salvation. He is always with us, and he assures us that we will end up as "more than conquerors" through him. With assistance like this, our newborn nature is more than a match for its foes.

Are you fighting with the enemy today? Have Satan, the world, and your sinful nature all lined up against you? Do not be discouraged or dismayed. Keep fighting! For God himself is with you. He is your battle flag. He is the healer of your wounds. So do not be afraid. Who can defeat the All-powerful One? You will overcome. Keep fighting, "looking unto Jesus." The conflict may be long and intense, but the victory will be sweet, and the promised reward is glorious.

June 3

These were potters, and those that dwelt among plants and hedges: there they dwelt with the king for his work.
(1 Chronicles 4:23 KJV)

Potters were not the very highest grade of workers, but "the king" needed potters, and therefore they were in the royal service, although the material they worked with was nothing but clay. We, too, may be engaged in the most menial part of the Lord's work, but it is a great privilege to do anything for "the king."

The text also tells us of those who "dwelt among plants and hedges," having rough hedging and digging work to do. They might have preferred to live in the city, in the middle of all its life, society, and refinement, but they stayed where they were, because they were also doing the king's work.

We are what we are. We should not let whims or fancies move us this way or that, but we should seek to serve the Lord where we are, by being a blessing to those around us. These potters and gardeners had royal company—they lived "with the king"—and though their work was with hedges and plants, they lived with the king there. No legitimate place of residence or occupation will keep us from communion with our Lord. We may visit crowded tenements, rundown shacks, busy factories, or even jails—and go with the king.

You unknown workers who are busy for your Lord in the middle of the dirt and misery of the lowest of the low, rejoice! Earthen pots get filled with heavenly treasure. Stay close to the king in whatever work you do, and when he writes his chronicles, your name will be recorded.

June 4

The kindness and love of God our Savior.
(Titus 3:4)

There is nothing more delightful than seeing the Savior communing with his people. When we consider the history of the Redeemer's love, we recall a thousand enchanting acts of affection. Each of these weaves our hearts with Christ's, twisting together the thoughts and emotions of our renewed souls with the mind of Jesus. When we meditate on this amazing love, we may even faint with joy. To consider that great Benefactor of the church endowing her with all his wealth—who can comprehend such weighty love?

The Holy Spirit sometimes gives us a partial sense of the magnitude of divine love, but our souls even have a hard time containing that! How staggering it would be to see its fullness!

Someday our souls will be able to understand all the Savior has given us. We will have wisdom to grasp it all and time to meditate on it, in the world to come. There our fellowship with Jesus will be even closer than it is now, and who can imagine the sweetness of that fellowship?

That must be one of the things that "no mind has conceived" but that "God has prepared for those who love him" (1 Corinthians 2:9). By faith we see, as if through a dark mirror, the reflection of his limitless treasures, but when we actually see the treasures themselves, our souls will bathe in the deep stream of fellowship. Until then, our loudest sonnets will be reserved for our loving Benefactor, Jesus Christ our Lord, whose love for us is wonderful, beyond anything we have ever known.

June 5

Then the Lord shut him in.
(Genesis 7:16)

Noah was shut in, away from the world, by the hand of divine love. God intentionally separates us from the world, which lies in the domain of the evil one. We are not of the world, just as our Lord Jesus was not of the world. We cannot follow the sinful pursuits of the multitude. We cannot play in the streets of Vanity Fair with the children of darkness, because our heavenly Father has shut us in.

Noah was shut in with his God. All the chosen ones live in God, and he lives in them. It is a joyous thing to be enclosed in the same circle with Father, Son, and Spirit. We must not be inattentive to his gracious call: "Go, my people, enter your rooms and shut the doors behind you; hide yourselves for a little while until his wrath has passed by" (Isaiah 26:20).

Noah was shut in so that no evil could reach him. The floods only lifted him toward heaven, and the winds only carried him on his way. Outside the ark, it was all ruined, but inside there was rest and peace. Without Christ, we perish. But in Christ Jesus there is perfect safety.

Noah was shut in so that he could not even desire to come out. So those who are in Christ Jesus are in him forever. Eternal faithfulness has shut them in, and no amount of devilish malice can drag them out. What the Lord shuts, no man can open.

Lord, shut me in by your grace.

June 6

I am unworthy.
(Job 40:4)

This is actually a comforting thought for the humble sinner. You may think that you cannot approach God because you are so unworthy, but there is not a saint on earth who has not felt unworthy. If Job and Isaiah and Paul were all obliged to say they were unworthy, will you be ashamed to join in the same confession?

If God's grace does not eradicate all sin from the soul of the believer, how can you hope to do it yourself? And if God loves his people when they are unworthy, do you think *your* unworthiness will prevent him from loving *you*? Put your faith in Jesus! Jesus wants you just as you are. "I have not come to call the righteous, but sinners to repentance," he said (Luke 5:32).

Say it now: "Lord, you died for sinners. I am a sinner. Sprinkle your blood on me." If you confess your sin, you will find forgiveness. If with all your heart you say, "I am unworthy, wash me," you will be washed.

You may have awakened this morning with every sin that a human being ever committed weighing down on you, but you will rest tonight accepted by God himself. You may have been degraded with the rags of sin, but you will be dressed in a robe of righteousness, as white as the angels'. "Now"—note that—"*now* is the time of God's favor, *now* is the day of salvation" (2 Corinthians 6:2). If you "trust God who justifies the wicked" (see Romans 4:5), you will be saved. Oh, may the Holy Spirit give you a saving faith in the One who welcomes the unworthy.

June 7

Let those who love the Lord hate evil.
(Psalm 97:10)

You have good reason to "hate evil." Consider what harm it has already done to you. What a world of mischief sin has brought into your heart! Sin blinded you so that you could not see the Savior's beauty. It made you deaf so that you could not hear his tender invitations. Sin directed your feet into the pathway of death and poisoned the very fountain of your being. It tainted your heart, making it "deceitful above all things" (Jeremiah 17:9). Oh, what a creature you were when evil had done its utmost with you, before God's grace intervened. You were an heir of God's wrath.

So were all of us. "But," Paul reminds us, "you were washed, you were sanctified, you were justified in the name of the Lord Jesus Christ and by the Spirit of our God" (1 Corinthians 6:11).

We have good reason for hating evil when we look back and trace its deadly ways. Our souls would have been lost, if God's all-powerful love had not stepped in. Even now, evil is an active enemy, always trying to hurt us, to drag us into treachery.

So, "hate evil," Christian, unless you like trouble. If you want to sprinkle thorns in your path and put briars on your pillow, then you can forget this. But if you want to live a happy life and die a peaceful death, then walk in all the ways of holiness, hating evil, all your life. If you truly love your Savior and want to honor him, then "hate evil."

How? There is no better cure for the love of evil in a Christian than intimate fellowship with the Lord Jesus. Live close to him, and it will be impossible for you to be at peace with sin.

June 8

Many others fell slain, because the battle was God's.
(1 Chronicles 5:22)

If you are fighting under the banner of the Lord Jesus, then read this verse with holy joy. As it was in those days of old, so it is now: If the battle is God's, the victory is sure.

The Reubenites, the Gadites, and the half tribe of Manasseh could barely muster 45,000 fighting men, yet in their war with the Hagarites, they took 100,000 captives. Why? "Because they cried out to him during the battle. He answered their prayers because they trusted in him" (1 Chronicles 5:20).

The Lord doesn't care how many are in the army. We must go forth in the Lord's name even if we are only a handful of warriors, because the Lord himself, our Captain, goes with us. The biblical fighters carried shields, swords, and bows, but they did not put their trust in these weapons. In the same way, we must use all proper methods in our struggles, but our confidence must rest in God alone. He is the sword and shield of his people.

The major reason for the extraordinary success of the Reubenites and the others was the fact that "the battle was God's." Friends, as we fight against sin, in our lives and in society, against errors both doctrinal and practical, against spiritual wickedness in high places and low, we are waging God's battle! We need not fear defeat. Do not shrink before superior forces, do not be cowed by difficulties, do not flinch at wounds or even death. Attack with the two-edged sword of the Spirit, and you will prevail. The Lord will deliver our enemies into our hands. With steadfast feet, a strong hand, a fearless heart, and flaming zeal, rush into battle, and the hosts of evil will fly like chaff in the wind.

June 9

The Lord has done great things for us,
and we are filled with joy. (Psalm 126:3)

Some Christians are sadly prone to look on the dark side of everything. They dwell more on what they have gone through than on what God has done for them. Ask for their impression of the Christian life, and they will describe their continual conflicts, their deep troubles, and the sinfulness of their hearts—without any allusion to the mercy and help that God provides them.

But a Christian whose soul is in a healthy state will come forward joyously and say, "Let me tell you what the Lord has done in my life. 'He lifted me out of the slimy pit, out of the mud and mire; he set my feet on a rock and gave me a firm place to stand. He put a new song in my mouth, a hymn of praise to our God'" (Psalm 40:2–3).

This kind of summary of our experience is the best that any child of God can present. It *is* true that we endure trials, but it is just as true that we are delivered out of them. It *is* true that we have sins that we are sorry for, but we also have an all-sufficient Savior who overcomes these sins and keeps us out of their power.

It would be wrong to deny that we have problems. But it would be just as wrong to forget that we come *through* our problems, thanks to our Almighty Helper. The deeper our troubles, the louder our thanks to God, who has kept us safe. Our griefs cannot mar the melody of our praise. They are merely the bass line of our life's song: "The Lord has done great things for us, and we are filled with joy."

June 10

We live to the Lord.
(Romans 14:8)

If God wanted it, each of us might have entered heaven at the moment of our conversion. It was not absolutely necessary for us to remain on earth in order to prepare us for heaven. A person can be taken to heaven almost immediately, even if he has just believed in Jesus, and he will still be worthy to partake "in the inheritance of the saints in the kingdom of light" (Colossians 1:12).

It is true that our sanctification is a long process, and we will not be perfected until we lay aside our bodies and enter glory. But still, if the Lord wanted to, he could have changed us immediately from imperfection to perfection and taken us to heaven right away.

Why then are we still here? Would God keep his children out of paradise for a single moment longer than was necessary? Why do his children still wander around, as in a maze, when a single word from his lips would bring them to the center of their hopes in heaven?

The answer is: We are here so that we may "live to the Lord" and bring others to know his love. We remain on earth as sowers to scatter good seed, as plowmen to break up the fallow ground, as messengers to proclaim salvation. We are here as "the salt of the earth," to be a blessing to the world. We are here to glorify Christ in our daily lives. We are here as workers for him, and as workers together with him.

Let us make sure our lives fulfill their purpose. Let us live earnest, useful, holy lives, to the praise of the glory of his grace.

June 11

We love because he first loved us.
(1 John 4:19)

There is no light in a planet except that which is reflected from the sun, and there is no true love in our hearts except that which comes from Jesus. All our love flows from this overflowing fountain of the infinite love of God.

This is a remarkable truth: We love God for no other reason than because he first loved us.

Of course, our love for God is a natural outgrowth of his love for us. Anyone can have a cold admiration, when studying God's works, but the warmth of love is kindled in our hearts only by God's Spirit.

It is incredible that we could ever be brought to love Jesus at all. We rebelled against him—it is amazing that he would want to draw us back. We would not have had a grain of love toward God at all if his sweet seed of love had not been planted in our hearts.

But even after God's love is born in our hearts, it must be nourished by him. Love is an exotic plant; it does not grow naturally in human soil. It must be specially watered from above. Love for Jesus is a flower of a delicate nature. If it receives no nourishment except what it can draw from our rocky hearts, it will soon wither. It requires heavenly nourishment. It cannot exist in the wilderness unless it receives God's manna. Love must feed on love. The very soul and life of our love for God is his love for us.

June 12

You have been weighed on the scales and found wanting. (Daniel 5:27)

We should frequently weigh ourselves on the scale of God's Word. You may find it helpful to read a psalm and, as you meditate on each verse, ask yourself, "Can I say this? Have I felt as the psalmist felt? Has my heart ever been broken over my sin, as his was in his penitential psalms? Has my soul been confident in the midst of difficulty, as David's was when he sang of God's mercies in the desert caves? Do I lift up the cup of salvation and call on the name of the Lord?" (Psalm 116:13).

Then turn to the life of Christ. As you read, ask yourself how closely you conform to his image. Determine whether you have the meekness, the humility, the loving spirit that he constantly displayed.

Then take the epistles and see whether you can go along with what the apostle says about his experience. Have you ever cried out, as Paul did, "What a wretched man I am! Who will rescue me from this body of death?" (Romans 7:24)? Have you ever felt his humility? Do you consider yourself the "worst" of sinners (1 Timothy 1:15) and "less than the least of all God's people" (Ephesians 3:8)? Have you experienced anything similar to his devotion? Could you join him in saying, "For to me, to live is Christ and to die is gain" (Philippians 1:21)?

If we read God's Word in this way as a test of our spiritual condition, we may stop every so often and say, "Lord, I feel that I haven't yet been here. Bring me here! Give me true repentance, real faith, warmer zeal, more fervent love—as I read about here. Make me more like Jesus. I don't want to be 'found wanting' anymore."

June 13

And whoever wishes, let him take the free gift of the water of life. (Revelation 22:17)

Jesus says, "Take freely." He wants no payment. He seeks no special favors. If you are willing, you are invited. So come!

If you have no belief and no repentance—come to him anyway. He will give them to you. Come just as you are and take this "free gift," without money and without price. He gives himself to those who need him. Drinking fountains in public places are valuable institutions. We can hardly imagine anyone so foolish as to stand before one of these, look through his wallet, and say, "I'd love to have a drink of water here, but I just can't afford it." However poor this man is, the fountain is there for him. He may drink from it just as he is. Thirsty people may stop by and drink whether they are dressed in the finest suits or the rattiest rags. They may drink from the fountain freely, just because it is there. They need to acquire no special license to do so.

Actually, the only ones who need to go thirsty in a place with a water fountain are those ladies and gentlemen who pass by in all their finery. They may be very thirsty, but they cannot think of being so vulgar as to stoop down and sip from a public fountain. That would demean them, they think. So they pass by with parched lips.

How many are there who are rich in their own good works and therefore will not come to Christ? "I refuse to be saved," they say, "in the same way as prostitutes and garbage collectors."

But is there any other pathway to glory except the path that led the dying thief there? No. No one will be saved in any other way. Such proud boasters may remain without the living water, but "whoever wishes, let him take the free gift of the water of life."

June 14

Delight yourself in the Lord.
(Psalm 37:4)

These words may seem surprising to one who is a stranger to vibrant godliness. But to the sincere believer, they capsulize a crucial truth. The believer's life is described here as a *delight* in God, so we are reminded that true religion overflows with happiness and joy. Ungodly people and those who merely profess the faith never look on religion as a joyful thing. To them it is service, duty, necessity, but never pleasure or delight. If they observe religion at all, it is either in the hope of getting some gain from it or because they dare not do otherwise.

The thought of delight in religion is so strange to most people that they probably can't think of two words that are further apart in meaning than *holiness* and *delight*. But believers who know Christ understand that delight and faith are united. Nothing can separate the two. Those who love God with all their hearts find that his ways are ways of pleasantness and all his paths are peace. The saints find such joys, such brimming delights, such overflowing blessedness in the Lord that serving him is no mere custom—they would follow him even if the whole world despised their faith. And we don't fear God out of compulsion. Our faith is no fetter; our commitment is not bondage; we are not pushed into holiness or driven to duty. No, our piety is our pleasure; our hope is our happiness; our duty is our delight.

Delight and true religion belong together like root and flower, like truth and certainty, like two precious jewels glittering side by side in a setting of gold.

June 15

Sarah said, "God brought me laughter, and everyone who hears about this will laugh with me." (Genesis 21:6)

It was far beyond the laws of nature that the aged Sarah should be honored with a son. In the same way, it is beyond all ordinary rules that I, a poor, helpless, undone sinner, should bear in my soul the Spirit of Jesus—I, who once was full of despair—and rightly so, for my nature was dry, withered, barren, cursed as a howling desert. Yet I have been enabled to bring forth fruit unto holiness. Yes, my mouth should be filled with joyous laughter, because of this surprising grace that I have received from the Lord. I have found Jesus, the promised seed, and he is mine forever.

Today I lift up psalms of triumph to the Lord. "My heart rejoices in the Lord; in the Lord my horn is lifted high. My mouth boasts over my enemies, for I delight in your deliverance" (1 Samuel 2:1).

I want everyone who hears of my great deliverance from hell and my new relationship with God, to laugh for joy with me. I want to surprise my family with abundant peace. I want to delight my friends with my ever-increasing happiness. I want to build up the church with my grateful confessions of faith and even impress the world with the cheerfulness of my daily life.

The Lord Jesus is a deep sea of joy. My soul will dive into it and will be swallowed up in the delights of his companionship. Sarah looked on her Isaac and laughed with her overwhelming emotion, and all her friends laughed with her. When my soul looks at Jesus, I want heaven and earth to unite in joy unspeakable.

June 16

I give them eternal life, and they shall never perish.
(John 10:28)

The Christian should never take doubt lightly. For a child of God to mistrust his Father's love, truth, and faithfulness must be greatly displeasing to the Lord. How could we ever doubt his upholding grace? It is contrary to every promise of God's precious Word that we should ever be forgotten or left to perish. Remember, he has said, "'Can a mother forget the baby at her breast and have no compassion on the child she has borne? Though she may forget, I will not forget you!'" (Isaiah 49:15).

Consider the value of this promise: "Though the mountains be shaken and the hills be removed, yet my unfailing love for you will not be shaken" (Isaiah 54:10).

Christ himself said, "I give them eternal life, and they shall never perish; no one can snatch them out of my hand" (John 10:28).

If his love could fail, these promises would be false. All the doctrines of God's grace would be disproved if one child of God perished. God could no longer claim to be true, honorable, all-powerful, gracious, and promise keeping if any of those for whom Christ has died and who have put their trust in him should be cast away.

Banish those doubting fears that dishonor God. Get up, shake off the dust, and put on your beautiful garments of faith. Do not sin any more by doubting God's Word—and his promise that you will never perish. Let the eternal life within you express itself in constant rejoicing.

June 17

Help, Lord.
(Psalm 12:1)

This prayer itself is remarkable, for it is *short*, but *seasonable*. It expresses the deep *sentiments* of the psalmist, and it *suggests* that the Lord is strong enough to help.

David was mourning the fact that there were so few faithful people around, so he lifted up his heart in prayer. When God's creatures failed him, he went to the Creator. Apparently he felt his own weakness, too, or he wouldn't have cried for help. But at the same time, he was working hard for the cause of truth—because the word *help* doesn't really apply when we ourselves are doing nothing.

These two words are *direct*, *clear*, and *distinctive*. They say much more than many of us do in our rambling outpourings. The psalmist runs straight to God. He knows what he wants and where to get it. Lord, teach us to pray like this.

We can find many occasions to use this simple prayer. When our faith is tested, it is suitable for us to cry out to God when all our human helpers fail us. Students who encounter doctrinal difficulties may often find aid by lifting up this cry of "Help, Lord" to the Holy Spirit, the great Teacher. Spiritual warriors facing inward conflicts may use this prayer to ask God's throne for reinforcements.

Those who are working hard for the Lord may ask for grace in time of need. Of course, sinners who are seeking the Lord may launch this same prayer at their crisis moments. In fact, at all times and in all places, this prayer can serve needy souls.

The answer to this prayer is certain, if the prayer is sincerely offered through Jesus. The Lord has promised that he will not leave his people. He guarantees his aid: "Do not fear, I will help you" (Isaiah 41:13).

June 18

Your redeemer.
(Isaiah 54:5)

Jesus, our Redeemer, is thoroughly ours—and he is ours forever. All the offices of Christ are held on our behalf. He is King for us, Priest for us, and Prophet for us. Whenever we read a new title of the Redeemer, we can assume that he performs that role for us as well. The shepherd's staff, the father's rod, the captain's sword, the priest's censer, the prince's scepter, the prophet's mantle—all are ours. Jesus has no dignity that he will not share with us, no privilege that he will not use to help us. The fullness of his divinity is our inexhaustible treasure house.

But his humanity is also ours, in all its perfection. Our gracious Lord offers to us the spotless virtue of his stainless character. He gives us the reward he won for his obedient submission and loyal service. The unsullied garment of his life covers us with beauty. The glittering virtues of his character are our jewels. And the superhuman meekness of his death is our boast and glory.

He bequeaths us his manger, so we can learn how God came down to man, and his cross, to teach us how man can go up to God. All his thoughts, emotions, actions, sayings, miracles, and prayers were for us. He walked the road of sorrow on our behalf and has given us the results of all his labors as our legacy.

He is not ashamed to be called "*our* Lord Jesus Christ," though he is the King of kings and Lord of lords. Christ is in every way *our* Christ, for us to enjoy richly forever.

June 19

All of them were filled with the Holy Spirit.
(Acts 2:4)

The blessings of this day were rich. It is impossible to estimate the full consequences of this sacred filling of the soul. Life, comfort, light, purity, power, peace, and many other precious blessings—all these go along with the Spirit's presence. As sacred *oil*, he anoints the head of the believer, setting him apart for the priesthood of the saints and giving him the grace he needs to perform that office. As the only truly purifying *water*, he cleanses us from the power of sin and sanctifies us to holiness, working in us "to will and to act according to his good purpose" (Philippians 2:13).

As the *light*, he first showed us how lost we were, and now he reveals the Lord Jesus to us and in us. He also guides us in the way of righteousness. Enlightened by his pure heavenly rays, we are no longer darkness, but light in the Lord. As *fire*, he purges away our impurities and sets a holy fire inside us. He is the sacrificial flame, enabling us to offer our whole selves as a living sacrifice to God.

As heavenly *dew*, he relieves our drought and fertilizes our lives. Morning dew from the Spirit is a great beginning for each day. As the *dove*, he broods over our souls with wings of peaceful love. As a Comforter, he dispels the cares and doubts that mar our peace. He descends upon his chosen ones as he fell upon Jesus in the Jordan and testifies that they are God's children by developing within them a spirit to cry, "Abba, Father." As the *wind*, he breathes life into people, blowing where he wants to, animating and sustaining all creation.

May we feel his presence today and every day.

June 20

For I will give the command, and I will shake the house of Israel among all the nations as grain is shaken in a sieve, and not a pebble will reach the ground. (Amos 9:9)

Every sifting comes by divine command or permission. Satan had to get God's approval before he could lay a finger on Job. But beyond that, sometimes our siftings are directly God's doing. As the text says, "*I* will shake the house of Israel." Satan, like a menial servant, may hold the sieve, hoping to destroy the corn. But the overruling hand of the Master is purifying the grain in the very same process that the enemy intends as a destructive measure. If you feel like grain on the Lord's floor that has been sifted again and again, take comfort from the fact that the Lord is ultimately in charge of the sieve. He is using it for his glory and for your eternal profit.

The Lord must work further to divide the precious from the vile. The heap of grain on the floor is not yet ready for consumption—it must be winnowed. But the Lord's "winnowing fork is in his hand" (Matthew 3:12), and he will use it. Husks and chaff with no substance will fly in the wind, and only solid grain will remain.

But observe the complete safety of God's grain. Even the smallest "pebble" has a promise of preservation. Every individual believer is precious in the Lord's sight. A shepherd would not want to lose a single sheep, nor a jeweler one diamond, nor a mother one child, nor a man one limb of his body. In the same way, the Lord will not lose one of his redeemed people. However little we may be, if we are the Lord's, we may rejoice that we are preserved in Christ Jesus.

June 21

You are the most excellent of men.
(Psalm 45:2)

The entire person of Jesus is like a single jewel. He is complete, not only in his various aspects, but as a gracious, all-glorious whole. His character is not a mass of colors mixed in a confusing way or a heap of precious stones tossed carelessly together. He is, in total, a picture of beauty. In him, all his praiseworthy attributes are in their proper places—they assist in adorning each other. Not one feature of his glorious person attracts attention at the expense of others. He is perfectly and altogether lovely.

O Jesus! Your power, your grace, your justice, your tenderness, your truth, your majesty, and your immutability combine to make up such a man—or rather such a "God-man"—that neither heaven nor earth have seen elsewhere. Your infancy, your eternity, your sufferings, your triumphs, your death, and your immortality are all woven into one gorgeous tapestry, without seam or tear. You are music without discord. You are many, but not divided. As all the colors blend into one resplendent rainbow, so all the glories of heaven and earth meet in you and unite so wondrously that there is no one to compare with you. You are the mirror of all perfection. You have been anointed with the holy oil of myrrh and cassia, which God has reserved for you alone. Your fragrance is a holy scent that the best perfumer could never match. Each spice is fragrant, but the compound is divine.

June 22

It is he who will build the temple of the Lord, and he will be clothed with majesty. (Zechariah 6:13)

Christ himself is the builder of his spiritual temple, and he has built it on the mountains of his unchanging affection, his omnipotent grace, and his infallible truthfulness. But just as in Solomon's temple, the materials still need to be prepared. There are the "cedars of Lebanon," but they need to be cut down and shaped, made into planks whose rich cedar scent will be a delight. There are also the rough stones still in the quarry. These must be cut out and squared. All of this is Christ's own work. Each individual believer is being prepared and polished, made ready for his place in the temple. Afflictions themselves cannot sanctify us—only when they are used by Christ to do so. Our prayers and efforts cannot make us ready for heaven, apart from the hand of Jesus, who is fashioning our hearts the way he wants them.

In the building of Solomon's temple, "no hammer, chisel or any other iron tool was heard at the temple site" (1 Kings 6:7), because every stone was brought perfectly fitted to the spot it was to occupy. So it is with the temple Jesus builds. The preparation is all done on earth. When we reach heaven, there will be no sanctifying of us there, no squaring us with affliction, no planing us with suffering. No, we must be prepared here—and Christ will do all of that. Once he has done it, we will be ferried by a loving hand across the stream of death and brought to heavenly Jerusalem, where we will remain as eternal pillars in the temple of our Lord.

June 23

Ephraim is a flat cake not turned over.
(Hosea 7:8)

A cake not turned is uncooked on one side. And so Ephraim was, in many respects, untouched by God's grace. Though there was partial obedience, there was much rebellion as well. Each of us should consider whether this is our own case. Are we thoroughly devoted to God? Has grace gone through the very center of our being? Do we feel its divine working in all our actions, words, and thoughts? To be sanctified—spirit, soul, and body—should be what we are praying for. While there is always a long way to grow, we should be growing evenly. If there is holiness in one part of our lives while sin reigns in another, then we are also a "flat cake not turned over."

A cake not turned is soon burnt on the side nearest the fire. Although no one can have too much religion, there are some who seem burnt black with bigoted zeal for one part of the truth that they have received, while neglecting others. Or they are charred to a cinder with a boastful, Pharisaic display of the religious actions that suit their liking. But the appearance of superior sanctity is often accompanied by a total absence of all vital godliness. The saint in public is a devil in private. He deals in flour by day and in soot by night. The cake is burnt on one side and doughy on the other.

If this is the way I am, Lord, please turn me! Turn my unsanctified nature to the fire of your love. Let it feel the sacred glow and let my burnt side cool a little while I learn my own weakness. I want to come completely under the influence of your reigning grace.

June 24

A woman in the crowd called out, "Blessed is the mother who gave you birth and nursed you." He replied, "Blessed rather are those who hear the word of God and obey it." (Luke 11:27–28)

Some people fondly imagine that it must have involved very special privileges to have been the mother of our Lord, because they suppose that she had the benefit of looking into his very heart in a way that we cannot hope to do. That idea may seem to carry some plausibility, but not much. We don't know that Mary knew more than others. What she did know, she properly stored up in her heart. But nothing we read in the Gospels indicates that she was better instructed than any other of Christ's disciples. Everything that she knew we may discover, too.

Does this seem surprising to you? Consider this text: "The Lord confides in those who fear him; he makes his covenant known to them" (Psalm 25:14). And remember the Master's words: "I no longer call you servants, because a servant does not know his master's business. Instead, I have called you friends, for everything that I learned from my Father I have made known to you" (John 15:15).

This divine Revealer of Secrets tells us everything that is in his heart, everything that we need to know. He assures us, "If it were not so, I would have told you" (John 14:2). Even today he is revealing himself to you. So you don't need to cry out, "Blessed is the woman who bore you!" Instead, you can bless the Lord for giving you the privilege of hearing his Word and obeying it. That gives us just as close a relationship with Jesus and just as thorough a knowledge as Mary would have had.

June 25

Go up on a high mountain.
(Isaiah 40:9)

Our knowledge of Christ is something like climbing a mountain, at least one of the mountains we find here in Wales. When you are at the base, you only see a little bit. The mountain itself seems to be about half as high as it really is. Confined in a little valley, you find hardly anything except the rippling brooks as they descend into the stream at the foot of the mountain.

Climb the first rising knoll, and the valley lengthens and widens beneath your feet. Go higher, and you see the country for four or five miles around—and the widening vista is delightful. Keep climbing, and the scene enlarges, until at last you are on the summit. Then look east, west, north, and south, and you see almost all of England lying before you.

In the distance you see a forest from some far county, perhaps two hundred miles away. Here's the sea and there's a shining river and the smoking chimneys of a manufacturing town or the masts of the ships in a busy port. All these things please and delight you, and you say, "I never realized I could see so much at this elevation."

Now the Christian life is of the same order. When we first believe in Christ, we only see a bit of him. The higher we climb, the more we discover of his beauties. The gray-haired Paul, shivering in a dungeon in Rome, could say, "I know whom I have believed" (2 Timothy 1:12), for each of his experiences was like the climbing of a hill, and his approaching death was like reaching the top. From there he could see the entire panorama of the faithfulness and love of the one to whom he had committed his soul.

June 26

You have become like us.
(Isaiah 14:10)

Consider the tragedy of the person who professes Christianity but doesn't truly believe. When his naked soul appears before God, how will he react to that voice that says, "Depart from me, you who are cursed. You have rejected me, and I reject you. I have banished you from my presence and will not have mercy on you"? Imagine the shame of this poor soul on that last great day, unmasked before the assembled multitudes. See the profane ones, the sinners who never professed religion at all, lifting themselves up from their beds of fire to point at him.

"There he is," says one. "Will he preach the gospel in hell?"

"There he is," says another. "He rebuked me for cursing—and he was a hypocrite himself!"

"Aha!" says a third. "Here comes a psalm-singing 'Christian'—one who was always going to church. He boasted about always being sure of eternal life—and here he is!"

No greater eagerness will ever be seen among the tormentors of hell than when devils drag a hypocrite's soul down to destruction. John Bunyan wrote about the "back door" to hell. Watch out for that. "Examine yourselves to see whether you are in the faith" (2 Corinthians 13:5). Look deeply at your situation. Are you in Christ? It is the easiest thing in the world to give a lenient verdict when you are putting yourself on trial. But be fair and true here. If your house is not built on the rock, it will fall, and its fall will be great.

May the Lord give you sincerity, consistency, and firm commitment.

June 27

But you must not go very far.
(Exodus 8:28)

This is a crafty word from the lips of that arch-tyrant Pharaoh. If the poor, enslaved Israelites must leave Egypt, he bargains with them to keep the distance short. In that case, they will not be far enough away to escape the observation of his spies or the range of his troops.

In the same way, the world does not appreciate the nonconformity of nonconformity, or the dissidence of dissent. The world wants us to be more compromising and not to take our faith to an extreme. The ideas of "dying to the world" and "being buried with Christ" seem ridiculous to carnal minds. Worldly wisdom speaks of "moderation." According to this principle, purity may be desirable, but let's not get too precise about it. Of course, they say, truth should be followed, but one should never denounce error too severely.

"Yes," says the world, "be spiritually minded, if you wish. But don't deny yourself a little revelry here and there. How can you preach against something when everybody's doing it?"

Millions of those who merely profess the faith have followed this cunning advice—to their own eternal ruin. If we want to follow the Lord thoroughly, we must depart immediately for the wilderness of separation, leaving the Egypt of the carnal world behind us. We must leave its maxims, its pleasures, and its religion, too. When a town is on fire, you are glad when your house is far from the flames. The farther you are from a deadly viper, the better. The same is true of worldly conformity—stay away! Let the trumpet call be sounded to all true believers: "Therefore come out from them and be separate" (2 Corinthians 6:17).

June 28

Let us fix our eyes on Jesus.
(Hebrews 12:2)

The Holy Spirit is always working to turn our eyes from ourselves to Jesus. But Satan's work is just the opposite: he is always trying to get us to think of ourselves instead of Christ. He insinuates, "Your sins are too great to be forgiven. You have no faith. You do not confess your sins enough. You will never be able to remain faithful to the end. You do not have the joy that true children of God have. Your hold on Jesus is shaky."

All of these are thoughts about ourselves, and we will never find comfort or assurance by looking within.

Yet the Holy Spirit turns our eyes entirely away from self. He tells us that we are nothing, but "Christ is all in all." Remember, it is not your hold on Christ that saves you—it is Christ. It is not your joy in Christ that saves you—it is Christ. It is not even faith in Christ, though that is the instrument of salvation—it is Christ's blood and his merit.

So don't look at your own hand trying to grasp Christ. Look to Christ. Don't look to your own hope, but to Jesus, the source of your hope. Don't look at your faith, but to Jesus, the "author and perfecter of our faith" (Hebrews 12:2).

We will never find happiness by looking at our prayers, our doings, our feelings. It is what *Jesus* is, not what we are, that gives rest to the soul. If we really want to overcome Satan and have peace with God, we must "fix our eyes on Jesus." Let his death, his suffering, his glories, and his intercession be fresh on your mind. When you first wake up, look to him. When you go to bed, look to him. Don't let your hopes and fears come between you and Jesus. Follow him closely, and he will never fail you.

June 29

God will bring with Jesus those who have fallen asleep in him.
(1 Thessalonians 4:14)

We must not imagine that the soul sleeps without any sensation. As Jesus said to the thief on the cross, "Today you will be with me in paradise" (Luke 23:43). He says the same to every dying saint. They "sleep in Jesus," but their souls are before the throne of God, praising him day and night in his temple, singing hallelujahs to the One whose blood washed their sins away. The body sleeps in its lonely bed of earth, beneath the coverlet of grass. But what is this sleep?

The idea connected with sleep is "rest," and that is the idea the Spirit wants to convey to us. Sleep makes each night a Sabbath for the day. Sleep shuts the door of the soul and keeps all visitors out for a while, so that the inner life may enjoy its garden of ease. The hardworking believer sleeps quietly, as does the weary child on its mother's breast. In the same way, those who die in the Lord are happy. They rest from their labors, and their works follow them. Their quiet repose will never be broken until God rouses them to give them their full reward. Guarded by watching angels, curtained by eternal mysteries, they sleep on, the heirs of glory, until the "fullness of time" brings their full redemption.

And imagine their awakening! Weary and worn, they were laid to rest, with furrowed brow and wasted features, but they will wake up in beauty and glory. The shriveled seed rises from the dust as a beautiful flower. The winter of the grave gives way to the spring of redemption and the summer of glory.

June 30

I have given them the glory that you gave me.
(John 17:22)

How great is the generosity of Jesus! He has given us his all. Even if he only donated a tenth of his possessions to our cause, it would make us rich beyond belief. But he was not content until he had given everything. If he had merely allowed us to eat the crumbs of blessing that fell from the table of his mercy, that would be amazing grace. But he will do nothing by halves. He invites us to sit with him and share the feast.

If he had arranged some small pension from his royal coffers—that would give us reason to love him eternally. But no, he wants his bride as rich as himself. He makes us joint heirs with himself. He has emptied his entire estate into the coffers of the church and shares all things in common with the redeemed.

There is not one room in his house that we have not been given the key to. He gives us full liberty to take anything he has as our own. "Feel free to take any treasure you see," he says. "Grab all you can carry." The boundless depth of his all-sufficiency is as free to the believer as the air we breathe. Christ has lifted the goblet of love and grace to our lips and asks us to drink. We can keep drinking forever. We will never exhaust the supply. What greater proof of God's love and care for us could there be?

July 1

On that day living water will flow . . . in summer and in winter. (Zechariah 14:8)

The streams of living water that flow from Jerusalem are not dried up by the parching heat of the sultry summer, nor are they frozen by the blustery winds of winter. The seasons change—and you change—but your Lord is always the same. The streams of his love are as deep, as broad, as full as ever.

The heat of my business worries and my scorching trials makes me rush to the cool river of his grace. At any time I can go and drink from this inexhaustible fountain—it pours forth its blessings in summer and winter. Elijah found the brook of Cherith dried up (1 Kings 17:7), but Yahweh was still the God of providence. Job said his friends were like intermittent brooks (Job 6:15), but he found that his God was an overflowing river of comfort. The Nile is the pride of Egypt, but its flow varies; our Lord is always steady. By turning the course of the Euphrates, Cyrus took the city of Babylon, but no power, human or infernal, can divert the current of divine grace. The beds of ancient rivers have been found, all dry and desolate, but the streams that flow from the mountains of divine sovereignty and infinite love will always be full to the brim. Generations melt away, but the course of grace is unaltered.

How blessed we are to be led beside such still waters! Why would we want to wander to any other stream?

July 2

In him our hearts rejoice.
(Psalm 33:21)

Christians can rejoice even in the deepest distress. Though trouble may surround them, they still sing. As with many birds, they sing best in their cages. The waves may roll over them, but their souls soon rise to the surface and see the light of God's face. They have a buoyancy about them that keeps their heads above water and helps them to sing in the middle of the storm, "God is with me still!"

Who should get the credit for this? Jesus, of course. It is all Jesus' doing. Trouble does not necessarily bring comfort along with it; it is the presence of the Son of God in the fiery furnace with him that fills the believer's heart with joy. The Christian may be sick and suffering, but Jesus visits him and makes his bed. He may be dying, the cold waters of the Jordan rising to his neck, but Jesus puts his arms around him and reassures him: "Do not be afraid, my friend. It is a blessed thing to die in my arms. These waters spring from the fountain of heaven. They are not bitter, but sweet as nectar, for they flow from the throne of God." As the departing saint wades through that stream, as the water envelopes him, as his heart and flesh finally fail him, the same voice comes to his ears: "Do not fear, for I am with you; do not be dismayed, for I am your God" (Isaiah 41:10). As he nears the borders of the infinite unknown and is almost afraid to enter the realm of the shadows, Jesus says, "Do not be afraid, . . . for your Father has been pleased to give you the kingdom" (Luke 12:32). Thus strengthened and consoled, the believer is not afraid to die. No, he is even willing to depart. He has seen Jesus as the morning star, and he longs to gaze upon him as the sun in all his strength. Truly, the presence of Jesus is all the heaven we desire.

July 3

And the cows that were ugly and gaunt ate up the seven sleek, fat cows. (Genesis 41:4)

Pharaoh's dream has too often been my waking experience. My days of laziness have destroyed all that I achieved in times of hard work. My seasons of coldness have frozen all the genial glow of my periods of fervency and enthusiasm. My fits of worldliness have thrown me back from my advances in my walk with God.

I need to beware of "ugly and gaunt" prayers, praises, duties, and experiences. They will eat up the fat of my comfort and peace. If I neglect prayer for even a short time, I lose all the spirituality I had attained. If I draw no fresh supplies from heaven, the old corn in my silo is soon consumed by the famine in my soul. When the caterpillars of indifference, the cankerworms of worldliness, and the palmerworms of self-indulgence completely desolate my heart, all my previous fruitfulness as a Christian does me no good.

If I journey every day toward the goal of my desires, I will reach it. But backsliding leaves me still very far from the "prize of my high calling" (see Philippians 3:14). The only way all my days can be "sleek and fat" is to feed them in the right meadow, that is, to spend these days with the Lord, in his service, in his company, in his way.

Why shouldn't every day be richer than the day before—in love, in usefulness, in joy? O Lord, keep my soul from being "ugly and gaunt," lean and poorly fed. But may I be well-fed and nourished in your house, so that I may praise your name.

July 4

Sanctify them by the truth.
(John 17:17)

Sanctification begins in regeneration. The Spirit of God infuses into a person the new living principle that makes him a "new creation" (2 Corinthians 5:17) in Christ Jesus. This work goes on in two ways—mortification, subduing the lusts of the flesh; and vivification, allowing the life of God to well up within us. This process is carried on every day in what we call "perseverance," as the Christian is preserved in God's grace. The Spirit helps the Christian to abound in good works, for the glory of God. This culminates when the soul is caught up to dwell with the holy ones at the right hand of the Majesty on high.

But while the Spirit of God is clearly the author of sanctification, there is another factor involved as well. "Sanctify them," Jesus prayed, "by the *truth*; your word is truth." Many passages of Scripture indicate that the instrument of our sanctification is the Word of God. The Spirit of God brings to our minds the precepts and doctrines of truth, and applies them with power. We hear this with our ears and receive them in our hearts, where they work in us ". . . to will and to act according to his good purpose" (Philippians 2:13).

The truth is our sanctifier. If we do not hear or read it, we will not grow in sanctification. We only progress in sound living as we progress in sound understanding. "Your word is a lamp to my feet and a light for my path" (Psalm 119:105). Do not make light of any error because it is merely an error in thinking. Bad judgment leads to bad practice. Hold tightly to the truth; in this way you will be sanctified by the Spirit of God.

July 5

Called to be saints.
(Romans 1:7)

We tend to regard the apostles as if they were "saints" in some special way, more than the other children of God. Each person whom God has called by his grace and sanctified by his Spirit is a saint, but we usually look on the apostles as extraordinary beings, hardly subject to the same weaknesses and temptations as ourselves.

Yet in so doing, we forget an important truth, that the closer a person is to God, the more intensely he mourns over his own evil heart. The more the Master honors a person in his service, the more his own desires will vex and tease him. The fact is, if we had seen the apostle Paul, we would have considered him remarkably similar to the rest of the chosen family. If we had an opportunity to talk with him, we would say later, "His experience and ours are much the same. He is more faithful, more holy, and more deeply taught than we are, but he has the same trials to endure. No, in some ways he is even more sharply tested than we are."

So do not look on the ancient saints as being exempt from weakness or sin. Do not regard them with that mystic reverence that almost makes us idolaters. Their holiness is something that we, too, can attain. We are "called to be saints" by the same voice that called them. It is a Christian's duty to force his way into the inner circle of saintship. If these saints accomplished more than we have—and they did—then let's follow them, let's emulate their ardor and holiness. They lived *with* Jesus, they lived *for* Jesus, and so they grew to be *like* Jesus. Let us live by the same Spirit as they did, "looking unto Jesus" (Hebrews 12:2 KJV), and our sainthood will soon be apparent.

July 6

Whoever listens to me will live in safety and be at ease, without fear of harm. (Proverbs 1:33)

God's love shines most clearly in the midst of judgment. Like the single star that smiles between the thunderclouds, like the oasis that blooms in a wilderness of sand, so fair and bright is love in the midst of wrath.

When the Israelites provoked God by their continued idolatry, he punished them by withholding both dew and rain, but he also took care of his chosen ones. If all other brooks are dry, there is always one reserved for Elijah. And when that fails, God will still provide for him. Besides Elijah, God had a group of faithful people, hidden by fifties in two caves. Though the whole land was subject to famine, yet these faithful ones were fed—and even fed from the king's table, through the prophet Obadiah (1 Kings 18:1–15).

We may conclude that God's people are safe. Let convulsions shake the solid earth, let the skies themselves be torn in two, yet amid the wreck of worlds the believer will be as secure as in the calmest hour of rest. If God does not save his people *under* heaven, he will save them *in* heaven. If the world becomes too hot to hold them, then heaven will welcome them and protect them.

So be confident when you hear of wars and rumors of wars. Do not be distressed or agitated. Whatever happens on this earth, you will be secure under the broad wings of Jehovah. Trust in his faithfulness. You can laugh at the bleakest prospects for the future, for it cannot hurt you. Your sole concern should be to show the world how blessed it is to listen to the voice of wisdom.

July 7

Brothers, pray for us.
(1 Thessalonians 5:25)

Allow me this morning to repeat the apostle's request. Pray for us. Pray for all Christian ministers.

Friends, our work is so momentous, involving the well-being of thousands. We conduct an eternal business with people's souls; and our words are either the sweet taste of life, leading them to life, or the stench of death, which they reject on their way to death. A very heavy responsibility rests on us. As officers in Christ's army, we are especially attacked by our enemies, both human and demonic. They watch for us to slip and then try to grab us by the heels.

Our sacred calling brings us temptations that nonministers never see. Above all, it draws us away from our personal enjoyment of truth, into a ministerial and official consideration of it. We deal with many knotty cases that baffle us. We see some people backslide, and that wounds our hearts. We see millions perishing, and our spirits sink.

We want you to profit from our preaching. We want to bring blessing to your children. We want to be useful to both saints and sinners. So dear friends, intercede for us with our God.

We will be miserable if your prayers are not backing us up. But we will be very happy if you are supporting us. It's true, you do not look to us for spiritual blessings, but to our Master. Yet how many times has he provided those blessings through his ministers? Pray then that we may be the "earthen vessels" (2 Corinthians 4:7 KJV) into which God may put the treasure of his gospel.

July 8

Tell me the secret of your great strength.
(Judges 16:6)

What is the secret of the strength of faith? It rests in the food it feeds on.

First, faith considers *what the promise is*. God's promises are emanations of divine grace, overflowings from his great heart. Faith says, "My God could not have given this promise apart from love and grace. So it is quite certain that his Word will be fulfilled."

Then faith asks, "*Who gave this promise*?" Now it's not the greatness of the promise itself, but of its author. It is God, who cannot lie—God all-powerful, God unchanging. Therefore, faith concludes that the promise must be fulfilled.

Third, faith remembers *why the promise was given*—namely, for God's glory. Faith feels perfectly sure that God's glory is safe, that he will never stain his own reputation, so the promise must and will stand.

Then faith considers the amazing *work of Christ* as being a clear proof of the Father's intention to fulfill his Word. "He who did not spare his own Son, but gave him up for us all—how will he not also . . . graciously give us all things?" (Romans 8:32).

Faith also looks back to *the past*, over all the battles that have been won and the courage that has been given. God has never failed us in the past. In times of great peril, deliverance is there. In hours of awful need, God gives strength.

So faith concludes, "God will not change his ways and leave me now. He has helped me so far, and he will continue to help me." Faith views each promise in connection with the Promise Giver, and says with assurance, "Surely goodness and love will follow me all the days of my life" (Psalm 23:6).

July 9

Forget not all his benefits.
(Psalm 103:2)

It is delightful and profitable to trace the hand of God in the lives of the saints of old, to observe his goodness in delivering them, his mercy in pardoning them, and his faithfulness in keeping his covenant with them. But wouldn't it be even more interesting and profitable for us to trace the hand of God in our own lives? Shouldn't we look at our own lives as being just as full of God as the lives of any previous saints?

We do our Lord an injustice when we think that he performed all his mighty acts in olden days and does not show off his strength for saints who are currently on the earth. Let's look at our own lives. Certainly we will find some incidents that have blessed us and glorified God.

Have you had any deliverances? Have you passed through any rivers, supported by God's presence? Have you walked through any fires unharmed? Have you had any moments when God has uniquely revealed his nature to you? Have you had any special blessings?

The God who gave Solomon the desires of his heart, has he ever listened to you and answered your requests? The God of great riches, the One "who satisfies your desires with good things," as David sang (Psalm 103:5), has he ever met *your* desires? Have you ever been made to lie down in green pastures? Have you ever been led beside the still waters?

Surely the goodness of God has been just the same to us as it was to the saints of old. So let us weave his mercies into a song. Let us take the pure gold of thankfulness and the jewels of praise and make them into another crown for Jesus' head. Let our souls burst forth with music as sweet and as exhilarating as that of David's harp, while we praise the Lord, "whose mercy endures forever."

July 10

Fellow citizens with God's people.
(Ephesians 2:19)

What does it mean to be a citizen of heaven? It means that *we are under heaven's government*. Christ the king of heaven reigns in our hearts. Our daily prayer is, "Your will be done on earth as it is in heaven." We welcome the proclamations issued from the throne of glory. We cheerfully obey the decrees of the Great King.

As citizens of the New Jerusalem, *we share heaven's honors*. The glory that belongs to the honored saints belongs to us as well, for we are already the children of God, princes and princesses of imperial blood. Already we wear the spotless robe of Jesus' righteousness. Already we have angels as our servants, saints as our companions, Christ as our Brother, God as our Father, and an eternal crown as our reward. We share the honors of citizenship, for we have joined the assembly of those whose names are written in heaven.

As citizens, *we have rights to all the property of heaven*. Its pearly gates and chrysolite walls belong to us. The azure light of the city that needs no candle or sunlight, the river of the water of life, the twelve kinds of fruit that grow on the trees along the banks of that river—all of this is ours as well.

Also, as citizens of heaven, *we enjoy its delights*. In heaven they rejoice over sinners who repent, prodigals who have returned—and so do we. In heaven they chant the glories of triumphant grace—and so do we. They cast their crowns at Jesus' feet, exult in his smile, and long for his second coming. We do, too.

So then, if we are citizens of heaven, let our actions be consistent with this high position.

July 11

Christ, after you have suffered a little while, will himself restore you and make you strong, firm and steadfast.
(1 Peter 5:10)

You have seen a rainbow as it spans the plains. Glorious are its colors and rare its hues. It is beautiful, but it passes away. The fair colors give way to fleecy clouds, and the sky is no longer brilliant with the tints of heaven.

The rainbow is not firm or steadfast. How could it be? A glorious display made up of transitory sunbeams and passing raindrops, how could it remain?

But the virtues of Christian character must not resemble the rainbow in its transitory beauty. On the contrary, they must be established, settled, and abiding. Every good quality you possess should be an enduring quality. May your character be, not a writing on the sand, but an inscription on a rock. May you be rooted and grounded in love (Ephesians 3:17). May your convictions be deep, your love real, and your desires earnest. May your whole life be so firm and steadfast that all the blasts of hell and all the storms of earth will never be able to knock you down.

But notice how this steadfastness comes. The apostle mentions suffering as the vehicle. It is no use to hope that we will be well rooted if no rough winds blow around us. Look at an old oak tree. Those old gnarlings on its roots, the strange twistings of its branches—these tell of the many storms that swept over it. They also indicate how deeply the roots have grown. So the Christian is made strong and firmly rooted by all the trials and storms of life. So do not shrink from the rough winds, but take comfort. God is using them to make you firm.

July 12

Sanctified by God the Father. (Jude 1 KJV)
Sanctified in Christ Jesus. (1 Corinthians 1:2)
Through the sanctifying work of the Spirit. (1 Peter 1:2)

Note the unity of the Three Divine Persons in their gracious acts. Often believers will show a preference for one particular member of the Trinity. They may think of Jesus as the embodiment of everything lovely and gracious, while they see the Father as severely just and devoid of kindness. This is foolish. These believers are just as wrong as those who magnify the Father's decrees and the Son's atonement, but make little of the Spirit's work.

In deeds of grace, none of the Persons of the Trinity acts apart from the rest. They are as united in their actions as they are in their essence. They are one in their love for us and undivided in the actions that flow from that great love.

We may honestly speak of sanctification as the work of the Spirit, but we must be careful not to imply that the Father and Son have no part in it. It is correct to speak of sanctification as the work of the Father, of the Son, and of the Spirit. It is as if God is still saying, "Let *us* make man in our image, in our likeness" (Genesis 1:26, *italics added*).

See the value that God places on real holiness, since the Three Persons of the Trinity work together to produce a church "without stain or wrinkle or any other blemish" (Ephesians 5:27). As a follower of Christ, you should also prize holiness. Value the blood of Christ as the foundation of your hope, but never speak disparagingly of the work of the Spirit. That is what prepares you for your inheritance.

July 13

But God said to Jonah, "Do you have a right to be angry?" (Jonah 4:9)

Anger is not necessarily sinful, but it has such a tendency to run wild that, whenever it displays itself, we should be quick to question its character. This question may help us: "Do you have a right to be angry?"

It may be that we could answer, "Yes!" Anger is often the madman's torch, but it is sometimes Elijah's fire from heaven. We *should* be angry at sin, because of the way it hurts our good and gracious God. We can be angry with ourselves when we remain so foolish after so much divine instruction. We may even be legitimately angry at others, when the sole cause of anger is the evil that they do. He who is not angry at sin becomes a partaker in it. Sin is a loathsome thing. God himself is angry with the wicked every day. As it is written, "Let those who love the Lord hate evil" (Psalm 97:10).

But it is far more common that our anger is not justifiable. When we ask, "Do you have a right to be angry?" we must answer, "No." Why should we lash out at our children, our coworkers, or our friends? Does such anger speak well of our Christian faith? Does it glorify God? Isn't the old evil heart trying to gain dominion, and shouldn't we resist it? Many who profess Christianity let their tempers flare as if it were impossible to resist. But we must be conquerors of all things through Christ—even our tempers.

Our natural tendencies are no excuse for sin. We must hurry to the cross and ask the Lord to crucify our tempers and renew us in gentleness and meekness, after his own image.

July 14

If you make an altar of stones for me . . . you will defile it if you use a tool on it. (Exodus 20:25)

God's altar was to be built of unhewn stones, so that no trace of human skill or labor would be seen on it. Human wisdom loves to trim and arrange the doctrines of the cross into a system that's more congenial to our fallen nature and its depraved tastes. But instead of improving the gospel, our carnal wisdom defiles it, until it becomes a very different gospel and not the truth of God at all. All alterations and amendments of the Lord's own Word are defilements and pollutions.

The proud human heart is anxious to have a hand in the justification of the soul before God. We dream up ways that we'll prepare ourselves for Christ, elaborate shows of humility and repentance, all the good works we will do. We trust in our own ability to approach God. But this is all just an effort to take human tools to God's altar. We must remember that we cannot perfect the Savior's work. The Lord alone must be exalted in our atonement, and not a single mark of human chisels or hammers will be allowed.

There is an inherent blasphemy in seeking to add to the act that Jesus himself said was "finished" in his dying moments. Put your tools away and fall on your knees in humble prayer. Let the Lord Jesus be your altar of atonement and rest in him alone.

Today's text also warns us about the doctrines we accept. Christians today have too much desire to square and reconcile the truths of revelation. This is a form of irreverence and unbelief. Let's receive the truth as we find it, rejoicing that the doctrines of the Word are unhewn stones.

July 15

The fire must be kept burning on the altar continuously; it must not go out. (Leviticus 6:13)

Keep the altar of *private prayer* burning. This is the lifeline of holiness. The altars of church and family borrow their flames from this fire, so let your private altar burn well. Personal devotion is the very essence, evidence, and barometer of vital and experimental religion.

Burn the fat of your sacrifices here. Let these times in your "prayer closet" be regular, frequent, and undisturbed. Such prayer is "powerful and effective" (James 5:16). Do you have nothing to pray for? Let me suggest these: the church, your minister, your own spiritual growth, your children, other relatives, your neighbors, your country, and the cause of God throughout the world.

Let us examine ourselves on this important matter. Are we lukewarm in our private devotions? Is the fire burning dimly in our hearts? If so, we should be alarmed. Let us go, weeping, to the Spirit and ask for grace. We should set aside special times for extra prayer. If our fires should be smothered by our desire to conform to the world, it will dim the fires on the family altars as well and lessen our influence both in the church and in the world.

God loves to see the hearts of his people glowing. Let us give to God our hearts, all blazing with love. Let us ask him to keep the fire burning. Many enemies will try to extinguish it, but if God's unseen hand keeps fueling it, the fire will blaze higher and higher. We can use texts of Scripture as coals for the fire. We should be listening to sermons that fan the flame, but above all, we should be spending time alone with Jesus.

July 16

Each morning everyone gathered as much as he needed.
(Exodus 16:21)

Try to maintain a sense of your entire dependence on the Lord for the things you enjoy each day. Never try to live on the old manna. Don't go back to Egypt for help. It all must come from Jesus.

Old anointings will not supply unction to your spirit. Your head must have fresh oil poured upon it from the golden horn of the sanctuary. Today you may be on the summit of God's mountain, but the One who put you there must keep you there. Otherwise you will slide down that mountain faster than you would dream possible. Your mountain only stands firm because he has settled it in its place. But if he hides his face, you will be in trouble.

If the Savior wanted to, he could darken any of the windows through which you see the light of heaven. Joshua made the sun stand still, but Jesus can shroud it in total darkness. He can take away the joy of your heart, the light of your eyes, and the strength of your life. All your comforts lie in his hand.

Our Lord wants us to feel this hourly dependence on him. For instance, he asks us to pray for our "daily bread," and promises, "Your strength will equal your days" (Deuteronomy 33:25). Isn't this best for us, so that we may often go to his throne and be reminded of his love? His rich grace supplies us continually and does not hold back even when we are ungrateful.

O Lord Jesus, we bow at your feet, conscious of our utter inability to do anything without you. We adore your blessed name and acknowledge your inexhaustible love.

July 17

For we know, brothers loved by God, that he has chosen you. (1 Thessalonians 1:4)

Many people want to know, even before they look to Christ, whether they are chosen. But that is something that can only be discovered by "looking unto Jesus." If you wanted to assure yourself of your election, try this.

Do you feel that you are a lost, guilty sinner? Go immediately to the cross of Christ and tell this to Jesus. Tell him you have read in the Bible, "Whoever comes to me I will never drive away" (John 6:37). Remind him that he has said, "Here is a trustworthy saying that deserves full acceptance: Christ Jesus came into the world to save sinners" (1 Timothy 1:15).

Look to Jesus and believe on him. Then you will know you are chosen. For if you believe, you are chosen. If you give yourself wholly to Christ and trust him, then you are one of the elect. But if you stop and say, "I want to know first whether I am elect," you don't know what you're talking about. Go to Jesus, however guilty you are. Forget all this wondering about election. Go straight to Christ and hide in his wounds. The assurance of the Holy Spirit will be given to you, so that you will be able to say, "I know whom I have believed, and am convinced that he is able to guard what I have entrusted to him" (2 Timothy 1:12).

Christ was at the everlasting council. He can tell you whether you were chosen or not. But you can't find out any other way. Go put your trust in him, and his answer will be: "I have loved you with an everlasting love; I have drawn you with lovingkindness" (Jeremiah 31:3). There will be no doubt about his having chosen *you*, when you have chosen *him*.

July 18

They will set out last, under their standards.
(Numbers 2:31)

The tribe of Dan brought up the rear when the armies of Israel were on the march. But what did their position matter, since they were as much a part of the nation as the tribes that went first? They followed the same bright cloud, they ate of the same manna, they drank from the same miraculous rock, and they journeyed toward the same inheritance.

So cheer up, if you feel that you are last and least. It is a privilege merely to be in this army. Someone has to be last in honor and esteem; someone must do the menial work for Jesus. Whether you are serving the Lord in a poor village, among untrained peasants, or among the down-and-out on back streets of some city, work on and carry your standards high.

The Danites occupied a very useful place. Stragglers have to be picked up during a march, and lost property has to be gathered from the field. There may be some fiery souls who dash ahead over untrodden paths to learn fresh truth and win more souls to Jesus. But some, of a more conservative spirit, may legitimately spend their energies reminding the church of her ancient faith and restoring those believers who have strayed. Every position has its duties, and the slowly moving children of God will find that they, too, can be a blessing to the whole group.

The rear guard is also a place of danger. There are foes behind us as well as before us. The experienced Christian will keep his weapons busy in helping those poor wavering souls. These must not be neglected.

July 19

The Lord our God has shown us his glory.
(Deuteronomy 5:24)

God's great design in all his works is the manifestation of his own glory. Any aim less than this would be unworthy of him. But how can his glory be revealed to fallen human beings? The human eye is never clearly focused. We are always glancing sideways at our own benefit and overestimating our own power. We are not qualified to behold the glory of the Lord.

Clearly, then, our "self" must stand out of the way, so that we may have room to exalt God. This is why he often brings his people into difficult times. When we become aware of our own weakness, we are more prepared to see God's majesty as he comes to deliver us. The person whose life is smooth and carefree will see little of God's glory, for he has had few moments of self-emptying. Those who navigate small streams and shallow creeks don't know much about the God of tempests. But those who go "out on the sea in ships" can see "the works of the Lord, his wonderful deeds in the deep" (Psalm 107:23–24).

So thank God if you have had to travel a rough road. This has allowed you to experience God's greatness and mercy. Your troubles have enriched you with a wealth of knowledge you could not have gained in any other way. Your trials have been the "cleft of the rock" into which God has set you, as he did Moses, so that you might see his glory as it passed by (Exodus 33:18–23). Praise God that you have not been left in the ignorance of prosperity, but that through your afflictions you have been prepared to see God's glory shine.

July 20

A deposit guaranteeing our inheritance.
(Ephesians 1:14)

What a delightful thing it is to feed on Jesus! Yet our experience of Jesus is imperfect at best—it is only a taste of the goodness he has. We have tasted "that the Lord is good" (Psalm 34:8), but we don't yet know *how* good he is. We only know that his sweetness makes us long for more.

We have enjoyed the firstfruits of the Spirit, and these have made us hunger and thirst for the fullness of the heavenly crop. We groan within ourselves and wait for the adoption (Romans 8:23).

Here we are like Israel in the wilderness, with only a sampling of the grapes of Canaan. *There* we will be in the vineyard. *Here* we see the manna falling in small bits, but *there* we will eat of the bread of heaven. We are only beginners in our spiritual education. We have learned the first letters of the alphabet, but we can't put sentences together yet—we can't even read words. But after five minutes in heaven, we will know more than all the philosophers of earth. At present, we have many ungratified desires, but soon all our wishes will be satisfied.

Anticipate heaven, my friend. Within a short time you will be rid of your troubles. Your teary eyes will weep no more. You will be gazing in love and wonder upon the splendor of the one who sits on the throne. In fact, you will be sitting on his throne yourself. You will share in the triumph of his glory. His crown, his joy, his Paradise—it will all be yours. You will be coheir with the One who is the heir of all things.

July 21

The daughter of Jerusalem tosses her head as you flee.
(Isaiah 37:22)

Reassured by the word of the Lord, the poor trembling citizens of Jerusalem grew bold, shaking their heads at Sennacherib's boastful threats. Strong faith enables the servants of God to look with calm contempt on their most haughty foes.

We know that our enemies are trying something impossible. They seek to destroy our eternal life, which cannot die while Jesus lives. They are trying to overthrow the fortress against which "the gates of hell shall not prevail" (Matthew 16:18 KJV).

We know their weakness. They are only human. They roar and swell like waves of the sea, foaming out their own shame. But when the Lord arises against them, they will fly like chaff before the wind and be thoroughly consumed. They are utterly powerless to do any damage to the cause of God. So even the weakest soldier of Jerusalem can laugh them to scorn.

Above all, *we know that the Most High God is with us.* When he puts on his armor, where are his enemies? When he steps into battle, the potsherds of earth will not survive for very long. His rod of iron will "dash them to pieces like pottery" (Psalm 2:9).

So put away your fears. The kingdom is safe in the King's hands. Let us shout for joy, for our God reigns. His enemies cannot win.

July 22

I am your husband. (Jeremiah 3:14)

Christ Jesus is joined to his people in a holy marriage. He married his church when she was a chaste virgin, long before she fell under the yoke of slavery. Full of burning affection, he worked hard, as Jacob did for Rachel, until he had paid the full price for her. Wooing her by his Spirit, he has brought her to know and love him. Now he awaits the consummation of their bliss, at the marriage supper of the Lamb.

The glorious bridegroom has not yet presented his fiancée, perfected and complete, before the Majesty of heaven. She has not yet begun to enjoy her exalted position as wife and queen. She is still a wanderer in a world of woe, but she is also the bride of Jesus, dear to his heart, precious in his sight, united with him.

On earth, he lovingly performs all the duties of a husband. He provides for her needs, pays her debts, allows her to assume his name and to share his wealth. He will always act this way. He will never even mention the word *divorce*—he hates it. Even death, which ends most mortal marriages, will not separate the partners in this immortal marriage. Jesus said that in heaven "people will neither marry nor be given in marriage" (Matthew 22:30), but here is a marvelous exception: In heaven Christ and his church will celebrate their joyous nuptials.

The love of even the best husband on earth is but a faint picture of the flame that burns in Jesus' heart. His mystical union with the church surpasses any human marriage, for he has left his Father, cleaves to his church, and has become one flesh with her.

July 23

You were like one of them. (Obadiah 1:11)

Edom, the nation descended from Esau, owed Israel some brotherly kindness in times of need. But instead, Edom allied herself with Israel's enemies.

In today's text, the word "you" deserves special stress, as in Caesar's cry, "And *you*, Brutus?" A bad action may be made worse because of the person committing it.

When *we* sin, there is a similar emphasis. We are the chosen favorites of heaven, so our offense is especially hurtful. If an angel were to catch us doing wrong, he would only have to say, "You? What are *you* doing here?" We have been forgiven, saved, taught, blessed, and enriched by our Lord. Do we dare set out to do evil? God forbid!

This morning might be a good time for a few minutes of confession. Have *you* been "like one of them"? At a party, someone starts telling offensive jokes, and everybody laughs, including you—you are like one of them. A co-worker begins to put down Christianity and faith in God, and no one says a word, even you—you are like one of them. People complain about money, fret about their bills, haggle for bargains, dream about their next major purchase—and you join in. You are like one of them, just as greedy for gain. Could anyone tell the difference?

This may be getting uncomfortable for you. Be honest with your own soul. Make sure you are a new creature in Christ Jesus. Once this is sure, live in such a way that no one can say, "You are like one of them." Side with the afflicted people of God and not with the world.

July 24

Stand firm and you will see the deliverance the Lord will bring you today. (Exodus 14:13)

These words contain God's command to the believer in trouble. What do you do when you face terrible trials? You can't go forward, you can't go back. You are stopped on the right and left. What do you do?

The Master says, "Stand firm." Don't listen to other advisers with their suggestions.

Despair whispers, "Lie down and die. Give it all up." But God wants us to maintain a cheerful courage, even in our worst times, rejoicing in his love and faithfulness.

Cowardice says, "Retreat! Go back to the ways of the world. It's too hard to be a Christian. Forget about your principles." But no matter how strongly Satan urges this upon you, you cannot follow it if you are a child of God. His divine fiat has ordered you to remain strong, and so you will. Neither death nor hell will turn you from your course. If the Lord wants you to stand still now, it is only to prepare for some future advance.

Restlessness cries, "Do something! Get moving! It's silly to just stand and do nothing!" But we are not "doing nothing." We are trusting in the Lord who will do everything.

Presumption boasts, "If the sea is in front of you, march into it and expect a miracle!" But true faith does not listen to presumption, or despair, or cowardice, or restlessness. It only hears God say, "Stand firm," and so it stands, immovable as a rock.

Stand firm. Keep an upright posture, ready for action, expecting further orders, cheerfully and patiently awaiting God's directing voice.

July 25

But he left his cloak in her hand and ran out of the house.
(Genesis 39:12)

With certain sins, there is no way to win except by running away. Ancient writers wrote about the basilisk, an evil monster whose eyes fascinated its victims and made them easy prey. In the same way, gazing upon wickedness puts us in serious danger. If you want to be safe from evil acts, hurry away from any opportunity to do them. Make an agreement with your eyes not even to look at a tempting sight. Some sins need only a spark to begin the blaze.

Would anyone carelessly enter a leper colony and sleep there? Only if he wanted to contract leprosy. If a captain of a ship knows how to avoid a storm, he does what he can to avoid it. A sensible captain would have no desire to see how close to quicksand the ship could go or how often it could brush against rocks without springing a leak. His aim is to stay in the middle of a safe channel.

Today I may be exposed to great danger, so let me have the serpent's wisdom to stay out of it. The wings of a dove may be more helpful than the jaws of a lion. Yes, it may seem that I am losing out by avoiding evil company, but it is better to lose my cloak then to lose my character. I don't need to be rich, but I must be pure. No ties of friendship, no chains of beauty, no flashes of talent, no arrows of ridicule should distract me from my wise decision to flee from sin. When I resist the devil, he will flee from me, but when I encounter the lusts of the flesh, *I* have to flee, or else they will win over me.

O God of holiness, preserve your Josephs.

July 26

Make every effort to add to your faith goodness; and to goodness, knowledge. (2 Peter 1:5)

If you want to enjoy your faith to the fullest, with the Spirit's help, do what Scripture says: "Make every effort." Make sure that your *faith* is the right kind—not a mere belief in doctrine, but a simple faith, depending on Christ, and Christ alone.

Make sure you have *goodness*. Live boldly, with an awareness of what's right. Study the Scriptures and get *knowledge*. Good knowledge of doctrine can confirm your faith. Try to understand God's Word. Let it dwell in your heart richly.

When you have done all this, add to your knowledge *self-control*. Take care both outside and inside—have control over both body and soul. Gain power over lip, life, heart, and thought. Add to this, by God's Holy Spirit, *perseverance*. Ask God to give you the perseverance that endures hard times and, once it is tried, turns to gold. Arm yourself with perseverance, and you won't complain so much about your afflictions.

Then pay attention to *godliness*. This is more than religion. Make God's glory the object of your life. Live in God's sight, close to him, in fellowship with him. Add to that *brotherly kindness*. Show love to all fellow believers. Then add *love*, which opens its arms to everyone and cares for their souls.

When you are adorned with all these jewels, you will be confident of your calling as a Christian. Make every effort to do so.

July 27

Very great and precious promises.
(2 Peter 1:4)

If you want to know how precious God's promises are and to enjoy them in your own heart, meditate often upon them. Many promises are like grapes in a winepress—when you tread them, the juice flows. Thinking over these sacred words is often the prelude to their fulfillment. While you are musing on them, the promised blessing comes to you. Many Christians have found this true.

But besides meditating on the promises, try to receive them as the very words of God. If you were dealing with the promise of some man or woman, you would carefully consider the ability and character of the person who had made the promise. So with the promise of God. You don't need to concentrate on how great the promise is—that may stagger you—but on how great the *promiser* is. That will encourage you. Remember it is God—God, who cannot lie—who speaks to you. His words are as true as his own existence. He is unchangeable. He has never had to alter one saying or call back a single sentence.

He certainly does not lack power. It is the God who made heaven and earth who made this promise. You can't even doubt his wisdom in choosing *when* to bestow his blessings. He knows when it is best to give and when it is better to hold back.

Therefore, seeing that this is the word of a God so true, so unchanging, so powerful, so wise—what is to keep you from believing the promise? If we meditate on the promises and consider the Promiser, we will ultimately experience their sweetness.

July 28

I was senseless and ignorant; I was a brute beast before you. (Psalm 73:22)

Remember that this is the confession of a man after God's own heart. In talking about his spiritual life, he calls himself "senseless and ignorant." He has just been describing how he has envied the "arrogant" and begrudged the "prosperity of the wicked." Their problem is that they ignore God. They act as if God is not there. But David finds himself doing the same thing. By envying their success, he has forgotten that God is ultimately in control of everyone's destiny.

Are we any better than David? Do we have a right to call ourselves wise? Is it possible that we have attained perfection? Has God's chastening taken away all our willfulness?

Of course not. If David was so "ignorant," we are, too. If we could see ourselves clearly, it would be apparent. Look back in your own life. Think back to the times you have doubted God, when he has proved himself faithful. You have said no to short-term affliction when God wanted to give you long-term blessings. You have mistaken his blessings for hindrances. You have cried out, "Everything's going against me!" when God is really working out all things for your good. You have often chosen sin because it seemed pleasing, when actually that pleasure turned out to be harmful.

If we knew our own hearts, we would have to plead guilty to this indictment. We, too, are senseless and ignorant. But we may also join the psalmist in saying, "You guide me with your counsel" (v. 24).

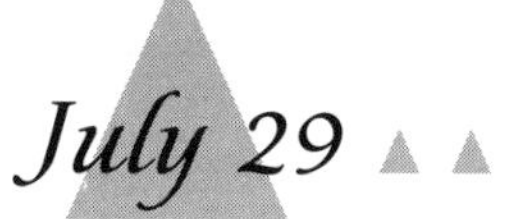

July 29

Yet I am always with you.
(Psalm 73:23)

"*Yet*," he says. In spite of all the senselessness and ignorance the psalmist had just been confessing, that did not decrease by one atom the fact that he was saved and accepted, enjoying the blessing of being constantly in God's presence. Fully aware of his own lost condition and how deceitful and vile he is, yet in a glorious outburst of faith, he sings, "Yet I am always with you."

Believer, you may enter into this confession and assurance. Try to say, in the same spirit as the psalmist, "Yet since I belong to Christ, I am always with God."

By this, we mean that we are always *on his mind*. He is always thinking about us. We are *before his eyes*. The Lord's eye never sleeps, but is always watching out for our welfare. We are always *in his hands*, so that no one can pluck us out. We are continually *on his heart*, worn there as a memorial, just as the high priest bore the names of the twelve tribes on his breastplate.

You are always thinking of me, O God. You are always providing what is best for me. Your love is as strong as death; many waters cannot quench it; rivers cannot wash it away (Song of Songs 8:6–7).

Surprising grace! You see me in Christ. Though I myself am hateful, you see me wearing Christ's garments, washed in his blood, so I stand accepted in your presence. So I am always in your favor.

This is a comforting thought for the afflicted soul. Troubled by the storm raging within you, look at the calm around you. "*Yet*"—say this in your heart and accept its peace—"yet I am always with you."

July 30

Then Peter remembered . . . and he broke down and wept.
(Mark 14:72)

Some have suggested that as long as Peter lived, whenever he remembered his denial of Christ, the fountain of his tears began to flow. This is not unlikely, because his sin was very great—even though he was completely forgiven, by God's grace.

Many of us who have been redeemed share a similar experience, now that the Spirit has removed our natural hearts of stone. Like Peter, we remember *our boastful promise*: "Even if all others forsake you, I will not." We eat our own words with the bitter herbs of repentance. When we think of what we promised to be and how different from that we were, we have good reason to weep.

Peter also thought of *his denial*: the place in which he did it, the small taunts that led him to do so, the curses he uttered to confirm his lies, and the dreadful hardness of heart that made him deny Christ again and again. Can we remain stoic when we remember our sins?

Peter also thought about *his Master's look of love*. After the rooster had crowed his warning, the Lord followed with an admonishing look of sorrow, pity, and love. That glance was never out of Peter's mind as long as he lived. It was far more effective than ten thousand sermons without the prompting of the Spirit could ever be.

The penitent apostle was sure to weep as he recalled *the Savior's full forgiveness*. To think that we have offended such a kind and gracious Lord—that is enough to make our tears flow.

July 31

I in them.
(John 17:23)

Consider how deep this union is between our souls and the person of Christ. This is no narrow pipe through which a threadlike stream may wind its way. No, this is a channel of amazing depth and breadth, along which a great volume of living water may flow.

Look, he has set before us an open door. We must not be slow to enter. The city of Communion with Christ has many pearly gates, and each gate is thrown open for us. We are assured of welcome. Even if there were only a small loophole through which we could talk to Jesus, that would be a wonderful privilege. But consider the blessing of having such a huge entrance.

If the Lord Jesus were far away, separated from us by many stormy seas, we would long to send a messenger to him, to express our love for him and bring back tidings from his Father's house. But he has built a house next door to ours. No, even more, he has moved in with us. He pitches his tent in our humble hearts, so that he may communicate with us constantly. It would be foolish for us not to take advantage of this close communion.

When friends are separated by great distance, it's understandable if they don't meet. But can they forget each other when they live nearby? A wife may go many days without conversing with her husband, if he is away on some trip—but not if he is right there in the house.

Seek the Lord, for he is near. Embrace him; he is your brother. Hold him close to your heart, for he is your own flesh and blood.

August 1

Let me go to the fields and pick up the leftover grain.
(Ruth 2:2)

Troubled Christian, come and glean today in the field of promise. There is an abundant supply of precious promises here that will meet your needs. Take this one: "'A bruised reed he will not break, and a smoldering wick he will not snuff out'" (Isaiah 42:3). Doesn't that fit your situation? A reed, helpless, insignificant, and weak. A bruised reed, which can produce no music. He will not break you. On the contrary, he will restore and strengthen you. You are like the smoldering wick. No light, no warmth can come from you. But he will not snuff you out. He will blow with his sweet breath of mercy, until he fans you to flame.

Do you want to pick up some more "leftover grain" from the field of Scripture? "Come to me, all you who are weary and burdened, and I will give you rest" (Matthew 11:28). What soft words! Your heart is tender, and the Master knows it. That is why he speaks so gently to you. Why not obey him, and come to him right now?

Glean some more grain: "'Do not be afraid, O worm Jacob, O little Israel, for I myself will help you,' declares the Lord, your Redeemer, the Holy One of Israel" (Isaiah 41:14). How can you be afraid with a wonderful assurance like this?

There is much more to glean:

"I have swept away your offenses like a cloud, your sins like the morning mist" (Isaiah 44:22).

"Though your sins are like scarlet, they shall be as white as snow" (Isaiah 1:18).

"The Spirit and the Bride say, 'Come!'" (Revelation 22:17).

Our Master's field is very rich. Look at all the promises. Gather them up, thresh them out by meditation, and feed on them with joy.

August 2

Who works out everything in conformity with the purpose of his will. (Ephesians 1:11)

Since we believe God is all-wise, we must believe he has a plan in his work of salvation. What would creation have been without his design? Is there a fish in the sea, a bird in the air, that was formed by chance? No, every bone, joint, muscle, sinew, gland, and blood vessel demonstrates the presence of God working everything according to his wise design.

Since God's hand is apparent in creation, it is also seen in his grace. If God's will prevailed in the old creation, he will certainly not leave the new creation to the fickle genius of human whims.

Look at his providence! He knows when a sparrow falls, and he numbers the hairs on your head. God weighs the mountains of our griefs on his scales. And if his providence is so ordered by his wisdom, shouldn't that be true of his grace, too?

He knows the end from the beginning. He sees where each of us belongs. He has not only laid the cornerstone, by the blood of his dear Son, but he takes each of us, as stones, out of the quarry of nature and polishes us by his grace. He sees the whole structure, from corner to cornice, from foundation to pinnacle. He has in his mind a clear idea of where each stone will be placed, how large the building will be, and when the last stone will be placed on top.

In the end, it will be clearly seen that God accomplished every part of this great work of grace, according to his purpose, to the glory of his Name.

August 3

The Lamb is its lamp.
(Revelation 21:23)

Quietly contemplate the Lamb as the light of heaven. Light in Scripture is a symbol of joy. And this is the joy of heaven: *Jesus* chose us, loved us, bought us, cleansed us, robed us, kept us, glorified us. We will be in heaven entirely because of Jesus.

Light is also a source of *beauty*. When light is gone, there is no beauty to be seen. Similarly, all the beauty of the saints comes from Jesus. They are like planets, reflecting the light of the Sun of Righteousness. Their lives are beams emanating from the central orb.

Light also symbolizes *knowledge*. In heaven, our knowledge will be perfect, and the Lord Jesus will be the source of it. Dark mysteries, never understood before, will then be clearly seen, and everything that puzzles us now will become plain to us in the light of the Lamb.

Light also *reveals*. In this world, "what we will be has not yet been made known" (1 John 3:2). But when Christ receives his people into heaven, he will touch them with the wand of his love and change them into the image of his revealed glory. What a transformation! Once stained with sin, with one touch of his finger they become bright as the sun, clear as crystal! All of this proceeds from the glorified Lamb. Whatever light there is, Jesus will be at the center and soul of it—our King of Kings and Lord of Lords.

August 4

The people who know their God will firmly resist him.
(Daniel 11:32)

Every believer understands that knowing God is the best form of knowledge we can have. This spiritual knowledge strengthens us. It strengthens our *faith*. The Scriptures often speak of believers as those who have been enlightened and taught by the Lord. It is the Spirit's unique task to "lead us into all truth," and all of this is for the advancement of our faith.

Knowledge of God also strengthens our *love*. Knowledge opens the door, and through that door we see our Savior. Or to use another image, knowledge paints a portrait of Jesus, and when we see that portrait, we love him. We cannot love a Christ we do not know, at least to some degree. But the more we know him, the more we love him.

Knowledge also strengthens *hope*. How can we hope for something if we don't even know it exists? Hope may be a telescope, but until we know something, our ignorance covers the lens, and we see nothing. Knowledge removes the obstacle. Then, when we gaze through the telescope of hope, we see the glory that will be revealed, and we anticipate it with joyous confidence.

Knowledge also gives us reasons for *patience*. How can we be patient unless we know something of the sympathy of Christ and understand the good that will result from our present trials?

There is no Christian virtue that is not advanced by the knowledge of God. That makes it crucial that we grow not only in grace, but also in the "knowledge of our Lord and Savior Jesus Christ" (2 Peter 3:18).

August 5

And we know that in all things God works for the good of those who love him. (Romans 8:28)

There are some things a believer can be absolutely sure about. We know, for instance, that God is in control. Even when the seas are rough, we know an invisible hand is steering our ship. That confidence prepares us for everything. We can look over the raging waters and see Jesus walking on the waves. We hear his voice: "It is I. Don't be afraid" (Matthew 14:27).

We also know that God is always wise. Knowing this, we are confident that there can be no accidents, no mistakes. Nothing can occur that should not occur. Even if we lose all we own, we can see that as a good thing—if God has willed it.

"And we know that in all things God works for the good of those who love him" (Romans 8:28). The Christian does not merely hold this as a theory, but as a matter of fact. Everything *has* worked for good so far. Even toxic drugs, mixed in the right proportions, can cure an ailment. The sharp cut of a lancet is often required to cleanse a wound and facilitate healing. And every event up to now has brought results that God has blessed—even the painful events.

So believing that God is in control, that he governs wisely, and that he brings good out of evil, we can rest assured, able to meet each trial calmly as it comes. The believer can, in the spirit of true submission, pray, "Send me whatever you wish, Lord—as long as it comes from you."

August 6

Watchman, what of the night?
(Isaiah 21:11 KJV)

What enemies are out there? False teachings are a numerous horde, and new ones appear every hour. What heresies do I need to guard against? Sins creep from their lurking places when it is dark. I must climb the watchtower and watch and pray. Our heavenly Protector foresees the attacks that are about to come against us. He prays that our faith will not fail, when Satan sifts us like wheat (Luke 22:31). O gracious Watchman, continue to warn us about our enemies.

What weather is coming for the church? Are the clouds rolling in, or is all clear overhead? We need to be concerned about the situation of the church. We need to read the signs of the times.

What stars are visible? What precious promises apply to our present situation? O Watchman, you who sound the alarm, give us comfort, too. Christ, our polestar, is always fixed in place, and all the stars are secure in their Lord's right hand.

And watchman, *when will the morning come*? The Bridegroom has not come yet. Are there any signs of the rising of the Sun of Righteousness? Has the morning star come up yet? When will the day dawn and the shadows flee away? O Jesus, even if you do not come in person to your waiting church today, please come in Spirit to my sighing heart and make it sing for joy.

August 7

The upright love thee.
(Song of Songs 1:4 KJV)

Believers love Jesus with a deeper affection than they would dare to give any other being. They would rather lose their fathers and mothers than to part with Christ. All their earthly possessions they hold loosely, but they carry Christ close to their hearts. They will gladly deny themselves for his sake, but you can't get them to deny him.

People have tried to separate the faithful from their Master, but in every age these attempts have been fruitless. Neither crowns of honor nor frowns of anger have untied this more-than-Gordian knot.

This is no everyday attachment that the world's power will eventually dissolve. Neither man nor devil has found the key that opens this lock. It is written, and nothing can blot out this sentence: "The upright love thee."

Yet we constantly lament the fact that we cannot love *more*. We wish our hearts could hold more and reach farther. We want a love for Christ that goes around the world and over heaven, but all our affection goes only so far. It is a drop in a bucket compared to what he deserves. Measure our love by our intentions, and it is very great. We hope the Lord measures it this way. Wouldn't it be wonderful if we could put together all our love, from all believers, in one great collection, and offer it to our great Lord, who is "altogether lovely"?

August 8

They . . . spin a spider's web.
(Isaiah 59:5)

The spider's web is a picture of the hypocrite's religion. How? *It is meant to catch his prey.* The spider fattens himself on flies; the Pharisee has a different catch. Foolish people are easily entrapped by the loud professions of pretenders—and sometimes even the wiser ones cannot escape. Philip, for instance, baptized Simon Magus; it took Peter's stern rebuke to burst Simon's greedy pretensions (Acts 8:9–25). Reputation, praise, and advancement—these are the flies that hypocrites catch in their webs.

A spider's web is *a marvel of skill*. But isn't the hypocrite's religion just as amazing? How can he make such barefaced lies appear to be truths? How can he make his tinsel seem like gold?

A spider's web also *comes from within the creature itself.* In the same way, hypocrites find their trust and hope within themselves. They forge their own anchor and twist their own ropes. They lay their own foundation and carve the pillars of their own house. They would hate to owe anything to the grace of God.

But the spider's web is *very frail*. A whisk of a broom destroys it. Similarly, the hypocrite's religion will be whisked away when the Lord begins his purifying work.

One final thought: Cobwebs *are not to be tolerated in God's house*. Be sure you're resting on something sturdier.

August 9

The city does not need the sun or the moon to shine on it.
(Revelation 21:23)

The inhabitants of that better world have no need of creature comforts. Their white robes never wear out, nor are they ever stained. They need no medicine to cure their diseases, for "no one living in Zion will say, 'I am ill'" (Isaiah 33:24). They need no sleep to refresh their bodies, but they tirelessly praise God day and night in his temple.

They don't need teachers there. Of course, they talk with each other about the things of God, but it is the Lord himself who teaches them. We on earth are like beggars receiving alms at the king's gate, but in heaven they feast at his table. Here we lean on the friendly arms of God's people, but there they rest on the bosom of their beloved Jesus. Here we strive for food that perishes and clothes that wear out, but there they find everything in God.

We use a bucket to fetch water from the well. But there they drink directly from the fountain, putting their lips to the living water. Here, angels bring us blessings, but there we will need no middlemen. They need no Gabriels to bring love notes from God, for they see *him* face-to-face.

What a blessed time that will be, when we will finally surpass every secondary blessing and rest on the bare arm of God! What a glorious day, when we will find our joy each day in God and not in his creatures, in the Lord and not in his works. Our souls will have attained perfect bliss.

August 10

Christ, who is your life.
(Colossians 3:4)

Paul's marvelously rich expression indicates that Christ is the *source* of our life. God "made us alive in Christ even when we were dead in transgressions" (Ephesians 2:5). The same voice that brought Lazarus out of the tomb raised us to newness of life.

He is also the *substance* of our spiritual life. It is by his life that we live. He is in us, the hope of glory, the spring of our actions, the central thought that moves every other thought.

Christ is also the *sustenance* of our life. What else can we feed on, other than Jesus' flesh and blood? "But here is the bread that comes down from heaven, which a man may eat and not die" (John 6:50).

Christ is the *solace* of our life. All our true joys come from him. In times of trouble, he is our consolation. There is nothing worth living for, apart from him. His loving-kindness is better than life (Psalm 63:3).

Christ is the *object* of our life. As a ship speeds toward its port, so the believer hurries toward the haven of his Savior. As the soldier fights for his captain, so the believer contends for Christ and finds triumph in the triumphs of his Master. As Paul said, "For to me, to live is Christ" (Philippians 1:21).

Christ is the *model* for our life. If we live in close fellowship with Jesus, we will grow to be like him. We will walk in his footsteps, until he becomes the *crown* of our life, in heaven.

August 11

How I long for the months gone by.
(Job 29:2)

Many Christians view the past with pleasure, but are dissatisfied with the present. They look back on the past days of their Christian life as the sweetest and best they have ever known. But the present seems shrouded in gloom and dreariness. Once they lived close to Jesus, but now they feel that they have wandered from him. So they moan, "How I long for the months gone by!" They complain that they have no peace of mind; or they're not enjoying their faith anymore; their consciences are seared; or they lack zeal.

There are many possible causes for such a state. It may arise through a *neglect of prayer*. This is the beginning of all spiritual decline. Or it may be the result of *idolatry*. Their hearts may be preoccupied with something else, more than with God. They may have set their affections on the things of earth and not on those of heaven. A jealous God will not be content with a divided heart. He must be loved first and best.

The present malaise may also result from *self-confidence and self-righteousness*. Pride stays busy in our hearts, puffing up our sense of self rather than laying it down at the foot of the cross.

Christian, if you are longing for the "months gone by," don't just *wish* for a return to the way it was—go to your Master and tell him about your sorry state. Ask for his grace and strength to help you walk more closely with him. Humble yourself, and he will lift you up. Don't just sit down and sigh. As long as our beloved Physician lives, there is hope. Even the worst cases have been known to recover.

August 12

The Lord reigns, let the earth be glad.
(Psalm 97:1)

There is no reason to be sad as long as this wonderful sentence is true. *On earth*, the Lord's power controls the rage of the wicked just as easily as it controls the rage of the sea. His love refreshes the poor with his mercy just as easily as it refreshes the soil with rain. Majesty gleams in the flashes of lightning in the middle of the storm. The Lord's glory is seen even as empires fall and kingdoms come crashing down. In all our conflicts and trials, we may see the hand of our divine King.

In hell the tormented spirits acknowledge God's supremacy. They are chained by the heel. Behemoth is bridled; Leviathan is on the hook. Death's darts are kept under the Lord's lock and key, and the grave's prisons answer to the Lord as their warden. The terrible vengeance of the Judge of all the earth makes fiends cower and tremble, like dogs in a kennel.

In heaven no one doubts the sovereignty of the Eternal King. All fall on their faces to do him homage. Angels serve him, the redeemed love him, all delight to honor him day and night.

May we arrive soon in that city of the great King!

August 13

The cedars of Lebanon that he planted.
(Psalm 104:16)

Lebanon's cedars are symbolic of the Christian. *They owe their planting entirely to the Lord*. This is true of every child of God. We are not man planted or self-planted but God planted. The mysterious hand of God's Spirit dropped the living seed into a heart that he himself had prepared.

Also the cedars of Lebanon *do not rely on man for their watering*. They stand on their mountain, far away from human irrigation, yet our heavenly Father cares for them. So it is with the Christian who has learned to live by faith. He is independent of other humans, looking to God alone for support.

Similarly, the cedars of Lebanon *are not protected by human effort*. They face the winds and storms quite apart from human protection. They are God's trees, kept and preserved by him. It is exactly the same with the Christian. The believer is not some houseplant, sheltered from temptation. He is quite exposed to the elements. He has no shelter, except for the broad wings of the eternal God.

Like cedars, Christians *are full of sap*. That is, there is a life force flowing through us, even in the dead of winter—the life of Christ.

Finally, the majesty of the cedars is *for the glory of God alone*. The Lord has done everything for these trees, which is why even the psalmist calls "fruit trees and all cedars" into his symphony of praise (Psalm 148:9). In the believer, there is nothing that can magnify man. The Lord has done it all. To him be all the glory.

August 14

For you make me glad by your deeds, O Lord.
(Psalm 92:4)

Do you believe that your sins are forgiven, that Christ has fully atoned for them? Then you should be very happy. With that assurance, you can live above the common trials and troubles of the world. Since sin is forgiven, does it matter what else happens to you? You can honestly say, "Come what may—sickness, poverty, losses, crosses, or persecution—as long as God has forgiven me, my soul is glad!"

Along with your gladness, then, be *grateful and loving*. Cling to the cross that took your sin away. Serve the one who served you. As Paul put it, "I urge you, brothers, in view of God's mercy, to offer your bodies as living sacrifices, holy and pleasing to God—this is your spiritual act of worship" (Romans 12:1).

Don't let your love for God evaporate in a few simple choruses of praise. Express your love in strong ways. Love the brothers and sisters of the One who loved you. If there is a Mephibosheth somewhere, someone disabled and needy, help him for Jonathan's sake. If there is some poor, struggling believer, weep with him and bear his cross, just as Jesus wept for you and carried your sins.

Since you have been forgiven freely in Christ, go and tell others the joyful news of God's mercy. Don't keep it to yourself. Holy gladness and holy boldness will make you a good preacher, and the whole world will be your pulpit. Cheerful holiness makes a most powerful sermon. It is the Lord's work we rejoice in. We don't need to worry about being too glad.

August 15

He went out to the field one evening to meditate.
(Genesis 24:63)

Isaac chose a good thing to do. Imagine all the time wasted in idle chatter, light reading, and useless pastimes. If we were wise, we would spend that time meditating on God's Word—and we would find it more interesting. We would all know more, live closer to God, and grow in grace. Meditation chews the cud and extracts the real nutrition from whatever mental food we're considering. When Jesus is our theme, meditation is very sweet. And Isaac found Rebecca while involved in private musings; many others have found someone to love there, too.

Isaac chose a good place to do it. The field presented Isaac with a great deal of food for thought. From the cedar to the hyssop, from the soaring eagle down to the chirping grasshopper, from the blue sky to a drop of dew—all of it was full of teaching. When God opens our eyes, that teaching flashes through our minds more vividly than the material from any written book. We tend to coop ourselves up in little rooms to do our studying. But these are often uninspiring and unhealthy, compared to the outdoors. All of creation points to its Maker, so even the fields can be a holy environment.

Isaac chose a good time to do it. As it draws the veil over the daytime, sunset is appropriate to the kind of meditation that carries us from earthly cares to heavenly communion. The glory of the setting sun delights us, and the oncoming night brings awe.

If you can arrange it, it would be good for you to spend an hour in the fields in the evening. But if not, the Lord is in the city, too. He will meet you in a crowded street or alone in your room. Go to meet him.

August 16

Ascribe to the Lord the glory due his name.
(Psalm 29:2)

God's glory is the result of his nature and his actions. He is glorious in his character, for he holds within him everything that is holy, good, and lovely. Glorious actions flow from his character. He loves to reveal his goodness, mercy, and justice to his creatures, but he is also concerned that the glory associated with these actions should be given back to him and to him only.

We have nothing in ourselves to boast of, for all that we have we received from God. So we should take care to *walk humbly before the Lord*. There is room for only one glory receiver in the universe. So the moment we glorify ourselves, we set ourselves up as rivals to the Most High God.

Should the piece of pottery exalt itself above the man who fashioned it on the wheel? Should the dust of the desert fight against the whirlwind? "Ascribe to the Lord, O mighty ones, ascribe to the Lord glory and strength. Ascribe to the Lord the glory due his name" (Psalm 29:1–2). Yet perhaps the hardest struggle of the Christian life is to learn this sentence: "Not to us, O Lord, not to us, but to your name be the glory" (Psalm 115:1). This is a lesson God is always teaching us, sometimes by very painful discipline.

If a Christian begins to boast, "I can do everything," without adding, "through him who gives me strength" (Philippians 4:13), before long he will be groaning, "I can't do anything." When we do anything for our Lord, and he is pleased to accept our service, let us lay our crowns at his feet and shout, "Not I, but the grace of God that was with me!" (1 Corinthians 15:10).

August 17

Remember, O Lord, your great mercy.
(Psalm 25:6)

Meditate a little on the mercy of the Lord. It is *tender mercy*. With a gentle, loving touch, he heals the heartbroken and binds up their wounds. It is *great mercy*. There is nothing little in God. His mercy is like himself—it is infinite. You cannot measure it. His mercy is so great that it forgives great sinners for their great sins and then bestows great blessings and great privileges and raises us up to great delights in the great heaven of the great God.

It is *underserved mercy*, as all mercy is. Deserved mercy is just another name for justice. The sinner has no right to the kindness of the Most High God. We all deserve to be condemned immediately to eternal fire. Our salvation has nothing to do with our merit; God's mercy is the only reason for it.

It is *rich mercy*. There are some things that may be great and impressive, but they don't work. Not so with God's mercy. It lifts our spirits, soothes our wounds, bandages our broken bones, and provides a chariot for our weary feet.

It is *abounding mercy*. Millions have received it, but the supply is not exhausted. In fact, it is just as fresh and full and free as ever.

It is *unfailing mercy*. It will never leave you. It will stay with you, to keep you from yielding to temptation, to keep you from sinking in times of trouble. It will be your delight as long as you live; and as you die, it will still be the joy of your soul.

August 18

Foreigners have entered the holy places of the Lord's house. (Jeremiah 51:51)

This was a shameful thing for the Lord's people. The Holy Place of the temple was reserved for priests alone. It was a terrible desecration for strangers to intrude there.

But we see similar causes for grief nowadays. How many ungodly people are now being educated for the ministry? How many people in our land consider themselves Christians merely because they live here? In how many churches do people take communion without any realization of what it means? And how many of our more enlightened churches are woefully lax in their discipline?

To corrupt the church is to pollute a well, to pour water on a fire, to scatter stones on a fertile field. May we all have the grace to maintain the purity of the church as an assembly of believers and not merely a collection of unconverted citizens.

Our zeal, however, must begin at home. We should examine *ourselves* to see if we belong at the Lord's Table. We should make sure that we ourselves are not intruders in the holy place. Many are called, but few are chosen. The way is narrow.

The One who struck down the well-meaning Uzzah for touching the ark (2 Samuel 5:6–7) is very protective of his ordinances of baptism and communion. As a true believer, I may approach them freely. As a stranger, I must stay away. Those who approach these ordinances must search their own hearts. "Search me, O God, and know my heart" (Psalm 139:23).

August 19

He will stand and shepherd his flock in the strength of the Lord. (Micah 5:4)

Christ reigns in his church *as a shepherd-king*. He has supremacy, but it is the superiority of a wise and tender shepherd over his needy and loving flock. He commands and receives obedience, but it is the willing obedience of well-cared-for-sheep, offered joyfully to their beloved Shepherd, whose voice they know so well. He rules by the force of love and the energy of goodness.

His reign is *practical*. He is actively engaged in providing for his people. He does not hold a scepter without wielding it. No, he stands and shepherds his flock. The Hebrew word for *shepherding* means "to feed, to guide, to watch, to protect, to restore, to tend"—to do everything expected of a shepherd.

His reign is *continual*. The text does not say, "He will shepherd his flock from time to time, when he feels like it." It does not say, "He will inspire a revival one day and then abandon his church to its barrenness." His eyes never sleep. His hands never rest. His heart never stops beating with love. His shoulders never weary of carrying his people's burdens.

His reign is *powerful*. It is in Yahweh's strength that he shepherds us. Wherever Christ is, there is God. Think about that. The One who stands and cares for the interests of his people is very God of very God, to whom every knee shall bow. We are fortunate to belong to such a shepherd, whose humanity interacts with us and whose divinity protects us. "Come let us bow down in worship . . . for he is our God and we are the people of his pasture" (Psalm 95:6–7).

August 20

The sweet psalmist of Israel.
(2 Samuel 23:1 KJV)

Of all the saints whose lives are recorded in Scripture, David has the most striking, varied, and instructive experiences. In his history, we find trials and temptations we don't come across elsewhere. This makes him an even more appropriate precursor of our Lord.

David knew the trials of all levels of humanity. Kings have their troubles, and David knew them. Peasants have their cares, and David knew these, too. The wanderer goes through many hardships, and David certainly had his share in the caves of En Gedi.

The psalmist also had difficulty with his friends. His counselor Ahithophel turned against him. His worst enemies came from his own family: His children caused him many problems. The temptations of poverty and wealth, of honor and reproach, of health and sickness, all worked their power upon him. Temptations from without disturbed his peace, and temptations from within marred his joy. He no sooner escaped from one trial than he fell into another.

All of this may explain why David's psalms are so universally loved by Christians. Whatever our frame of mind, whether ecstasy or depression, David has described our emotions perfectly. He is able to instruct our hearts, because he himself was tutored in the best of all schools—the school of heartfelt personal experience. As we are taught in that same school, we appreciate David's psalms more and more.

August 21

He who refreshes others will himself be refreshed.
(Proverbs 11:25)

This teaches us a great lesson: To get, we must give. To accumulate, we must scatter. To make ourselves happy, we must make others happy. To become spiritually vigorous, we must seek the spiritual good of others.

How does this work? First, our efforts to be useful bring out our own powers of usefulness. We have latent talents that become apparent only when they are used. We never know how strong we are until we test that strength in some challenging situation. We don't know what tender sympathy we have until we try to dry the widow's tears or soothe the orphan's grief.

Also, we often find that, in trying to teach others, we learn a great deal ourselves. As we converse with needy saints, we often get a deeper insight into divine truth.

Refreshing others also humbles us. We see how God's grace overshadows our efforts. He grants blessings beyond our expectations, and the people we're trying to help often help us.

We can also gain comfort ourselves from the comfort we share with others. It's like the two men trapped in a snowdrift. One rubbed the other's limbs to keep him from dying and in so doing kept his own blood circulating and saved his own life. The widow of Zarephath gave from her scarce supply to meet Elijah's needs—and she never lacked supplies again (1 Kings 17). So "give, and it will be given to you. A good measure, pressed down, shaken together and running over, will be poured into your lap" (Luke 6:38).

August 22

O daughters of Jerusalem, I charge you—if you find my lover, what will you tell him? Tell him I am faint with love. (Song of Songs 5:8)

This is the language of the believer who longs for fellowship with Jesus. He is faint with love. Believing souls are never perfectly at ease unless they are close to Christ. When they are away from him, they lose their peace.

But when they are close to him, they enjoy the perfect calm of heaven. The closer they are, the fuller their hearts are—full of life, energy, and joy, all coming from Jesus.

What the sun is to the day, what the moon is to night, what the dew is to the flower—that's what Jesus Christ is to us. What bread is to the hungry, a coat to the shivering, a place of shade to a desert traveler—that is Jesus to us.

So if we are not consciously united with him, it is no wonder that our spirits cry out, "If you find him, tell him I am faint with love!"

Behind this desperation, there is a blessing. Jesus said, "Blessed are those who hunger and thirst for righteousness" (Matthew 5:6). So those who thirst for the Righteous One are even more blessed. That hunger comes from God. If I can't have the full blessing of being utterly filled with Christ, at least let me have the blessing of desiring him. There is a holiness to that hunger—it sparkles among our Lord's beatitudes.

But the blessing involves a promise. Such hungry ones *will be filled* with what they desire. If Christ makes us long for him, he will certainly satisfy those longings. When he comes to us, how sweet it will be!

August 23

The sound of weeping and of crying will be heard in it no more. (Isaiah 65:19)

Why will there be no weeping in heaven? *All external causes of grief will be gone*. There will be no broken friendships, no disappointments. Poverty, famine, peril, persecution, and slander will be unknown in heaven. There will be no pain to distress us, no thought of death or bereavement to sadden us.

We will be perfectly sanctified. No longer will temptations lure us away from the living God. We will stand without fault before his throne, fully conformed to his image.

All fear of change will be past. We will know that we are eternally secure. Sin will be shut out, and we will be shut in. We will dwell in a city that will never be stormed, basking in a sun that will never set, drinking from a river that will never run dry, eating fruit from a tree that will never wither and die. The cycles of seasons may continue to revolve, but eternity will never be exhausted, and our blessedness will go on and on. We will be forever with the Lord.

Every desire will be fulfilled. Eye and ear, heart and hand, judgment, imagination, hope, will, and desire—all our faculties will be completely satisfied. Our present ideas of what heaven will be like are imperfect. But we know, by the revelation of God's Spirit, that the saints above are supremely blessed. They revel in the joy of Christ, the fullness of delight. They bathe in a bottomless sea of blessing. That same joyful rest awaits us. It may not be too far away. "Therefore encourage each other with these words" (1 Thessalonians 4:18).

August 24

One who breaks open the way will go up before them. (Micah 2:13)

Because Jesus has gone before us, everything is different. He has conquered every enemy that stood in our way. So cheer up! Not only has Christ traveled the road before you, but he has also defeated your enemies. Do you dread sin? He has nailed it to the cross. Do you fear death? He has been the death of death. Are you afraid of hell? He has closed it off to all of his children; they will never set foot there.

Whatever foes might come up against the Christian, they have all been overcome. There are lions, but their teeth are broken. There are serpents, but their fangs have been removed. There are rivers, but they are now bridged. There are flames, but we now wear fireproof garments. The sword that strikes at us has already been blunted. Through Christ, God has taken away all the power that is wielded against us.

Well, then, the army can march safely on. You may go on your journey joyously. Your enemies are vanquished, beaten. All you have to do is divide the spoil. It is true, you will sometimes have to engage in combat—but you will be fighting an already-beaten foe. He may try to injure you, but he will not have the strength to do so. Your victory will be easy, and your reward will be huge.

Proclaim aloud the Savior's fame,
Who bears the Breaker's wondrous name;
Sweet name, and it becomes him well,
Who breaks down earth, sin, death, and hell.

August 25

His fruit is sweet to my taste.
(Song of Songs 2:3)

Faith, in Scripture, is spoken of in terms of all the senses. It is *sight*: "Look unto me, and be ye saved" (Isaiah 45:22 KJV). It is *hearing*: "Hear me, that your soul may live" (Isaiah 55:3). Faith is also *smell*: "All your robes are fragrant with myrrh and aloes and cassia" (Psalm 45:8). Faith is spiritual *touch*: "That which was from the beginning, which . . . our hands have touched" (1 John 1:1)—and remember the woman who came up behind Jesus and touched the hem of his robe (Matthew 9:20–22). In one of its higher stages, faith is also *taste*: "How sweet are your words to my taste, sweeter than honey to my mouth!" (Psalm 119:103).

Faith begins with *hearing*. We hear God's voice, not only with our physical ears, but with our spirits as well. We hear it as God's Word, and we believe that it is from God. Then our minds *look* at the truth as it has been presented to us. That is, we understand it, we perceive its meaning. Then we discover how precious it is; we admire it; we sense its fragrance. That is faith in its "smell."

When we appropriate the mercies of Christ, claiming them for our own, that is *touch*. Then comes the enjoyment—peace, delight, communion. This is the *tasting* of faith.

Any one of these acts is saving. To hear Christ's voice as the true voice of God will save us, but the full enjoyment comes when we "taste" Christ, and he becomes food for our souls.

August 26

He ordained his covenant forever.
(Psalm 111:9)

The Lord's people delight in the covenant itself. It is a constant source of comfort as the Holy Spirit leads us to the banquet table, waving a banner of love.

We love to contemplate how *old* the covenant is. Before the daystar knew its place or the planets began to make their rounds, the covenant was already looking out for our interests. We also think about how *sure* the covenant is. It is signed, sealed, and secured for us—the "sure mercies of David" (Isaiah 55:3 KJV).

Our hearts thrill with joy as we consider how *unchanging* the covenant is. Neither time nor eternity, life nor death, will ever be able to violate it. This agreement is as everlasting as the Rock of Ages.

We rejoice also in the *fullness* of the covenant. All things are provided for us. God is our portion, Christ our companion, the Spirit our comforter. The earth is our temporary lodging, and heaven is our home. The inheritance is reserved for us—and for every soul that has an interest in this ancient deed. To read about these promises in the Bible is exciting enough, but to realize that they are all bequeathed to *us*—that gladdens our souls immeasurably.

It is also our pleasure to meditate on how *gracious* the covenant is. The law depended on us to keep it, and therefore that covenant was voided. But this covenant is based on grace through and through. This covenant is a rich treasure chest, a warehouse overflowing with good food, a fountain of life-giving water, a treaty of lasting peace, and a haven of joy.

August 27

How long will they refuse to believe in me?
(Numbers 14:11)

Work as hard as you can to keep the monster of unbelief away. It dishonors Christ to such an extent that he will withdraw his presence if we insult him by indulging in unbelief. It is a weed—we can never quite extract its seeds from the soil, but we must keep trying to get at its roots. It is abhorrent.

In your case, Christian, it is all the worse. You have received so many mercies from the Lord in the past, how can you doubt him now? When you distrust the Lord Jesus, you crown his head with even more thorns.

It is a cruel thing when a wife mistrusts her kind and faithful husband. It is foolish and entirely unnecessary. Yet that is what is happening here. Jesus has never given us the slightest grounds for suspicion. He has been consistently affectionate and true to us. He has shared his great wealth with us. How can we doubt the all-powerful, all-sufficient Lord?

He has more than enough to meet our needs. The "cattle on a thousand hills" are plenty for us, and we will not even come close to emptying the granaries of heaven. If Christ were just a reservoir of some kind, we might eventually exhaust his resources. But he is a fountain! We will never drain it. Countless souls have drawn nourishment from him, and no one has gone away hungry.

So away with this lying traitor, unbelief! He is only trying to cut the ties between us and Christ.

August 28

Oil for the light.
(Exodus 25:6)

We all need this oil. Our lamps will not burn long without it. There is no "oil well" within our own natures, so we need to go out and get some—or else we will have to cry, with the foolish virgins, "Our lamps are going out!" (Matthew 25:8).

Even these sacred lamps in the tabernacle required oil. They needed to be fueled and trimmed—just like us. Even under the best circumstances, we can hardly last an hour without a fresh supply of God's grace.

It was not just any oil that was to be used for the tabernacle lamps. Oil might be extracted from the earth, from fish, even from nuts, but only the finest olive oil was to be used in the Lord's service. Similarly, the true believer cannot be satisfied with the fake grace of those who say we are naturally good or the manufactured grace of religious rituals. Even rivers of this kind of oil will not please the Lord. No, the Christian goes to the olive press of Gethsemane and draws his supply from the one who was crushed there.

The oil of God's true grace is pure and free from dregs. So our light is clear and bright. Our churches are the Savior's candelabra, and they require plenty of his grace to shine in this dark world.

We should be praying for ourselves, our ministers, and our churches, that we might always have a full supply of the oil of God's grace.

August 29

Have mercy on me, O God.
(Psalm 51:1)

When William Carey, the great missionary, was suffering from a serious illness, he was asked, "If this sickness should prove fatal, what passage would you select for your funeral sermon?"

He replied, "Oh, I feel that such a poor sinful creature is unworthy to have anything said about him. But if a funeral sermon must be preached, let it be from the words, 'Have mercy upon me, O God, according to thy lovingkindness; according unto the multitude of Thy tender mercies blot out my transgressions'" (Psalm 51:1 KJV).

In the same spirit of humility, he directed in his will that his tombstone should read:

WILLIAM CAREY, BORN AUGUST 17TH, 1761
DIED—
"A wretched, poor, and helpless worm
On Thy kind arms I fall"

Even the most experienced and most honored of Christians can only approach God by his free gift of grace. The best men and women seem to be most aware that they are just men and women. Empty boats float high, but heavily laden vessels are low in the water. Those who merely profess their faith may boast of their spirituality, but the true children of God cry for mercy.

We need the Lord to have mercy on our good works, our prayers, our preachings, our offerings, all our holiest things. The Passover blood was sprinkled not only on the houses of Israel, but also on the sanctuary. If we need mercy for our *good* works, what can we say about our sins? It is a great comfort to remember that God's inexhaustible mercy is waiting for us, to restore us when we backslide and to bind our broken bones.

August 30

Wait for the Lord.
(Psalm 27:14)

Waiting may seem easy, but it takes years to learn. Most of God's soldiers find it easier to march, even double-time, than to stand still. There are times of confusion when the most zealous soul, eagerly wanting to serve the Lord, just does not know what to do.

What *do* you do in cases like that? Worry? Rush backward in cowardice or forward in presumption? No. Just wait.

Wait in prayer. Call on God and spread the case before him. Tell him your difficulty and remind him that he has promised to help.

Wait with a simple heart. Be humble as a child. When we realize our own inability to choose wisely, we are more willing to be guided by God.

Wait in faith. Express your unstaggering confidence in the Lord. To wait in a doubting manner is an insult to him. Keep believing that he will answer you at the right time, whenever that may be.

Wait in quiet patience. Don't complain about your situation, but thank God for it. Accept it as it is and put it all into God's hands, as simply and wholeheartedly as you can. Say, "Not my will, but your will be done. I don't know what to do. I am at my wit's end. But I will wait for you to provide relief. I will wait for days and days, if need be, because my heart is fixed on you alone. My spirit waits for you in the full conviction that you will come through, for you are my joy and salvation, 'my refuge, a strong tower against the foe'" (Psalm 61:3).

August 31

And wait in hope for my arm.
(Isaiah 51:5)

In times of severe trial, the Christian has nothing on earth he can trust in, so he is compelled to cast himself on the Lord. When the storm is raging and wrecks his ship, he must simply and entirely trust himself to the providence and care of God. We can actually thank God for these hurricanes that blow our souls toward him.

Sometimes, however, we find it hard to get to God because we have too many friends. But the poor, friendless man has nowhere else to turn. He flies to his Father's arms and is happily embraced. When he is burdened by problems that he can't talk to anyone else about, he can be glad for them—because they drive him to his God, and he will learn much about the Lord in those times of crisis.

Since we have only God to trust in, let us put our full confidence in him. Do not dishonor your Lord by entertaining doubts and fears. Be strong in your faith, giving glory to God. Show the world that your God is worth ten thousand worlds to you. Show the wealthy how wealthy you are, even in your poverty, when the Lord is your helper. Show the strong how strong you are, even in your weakness, when you are supported by the "everlasting arms." Now is the time for feats of faith and valiant exploits. Be strong and very courageous. The Lord your God will certainly glorify himself in your weakness and magnify his might in the midst of your distress.

Imagine how it would ruin the scenery if the sky had to be held up by a visible column. In the same way, your faith would lose its beauty if it relied on anything visible to the natural eye.

September 1

You guide me with your counsel, and afterward you will take me into glory. (Psalm 73:24)

The psalmist felt his need for divine guidance. He had just been discovering the foolishness of his own heart, and to keep himself from being led astray, he decided to let God's wisdom guide him. A sense of our own ignorance is a good first step toward becoming wise, if it leads us to rely on God's wisdom. A blind man leans on a friend's arm and reaches home safely. In the same way, we should lean on God's direction: Though we cannot see, it is always safe to trust the all-seeing God.

"*You guide me*," the psalmist says, and there's no qualification. He was sure the Lord would not refuse this task. We, too, can be sure that God is our counselor and friend. He will guide us.

Scripture itself fulfills this promise in part. He guides us through his written Word. Where would a sailor be without a compass? Where would the Christian be without the Bible? This is the map that marks out every shoal, every pit of quicksand, and shows the way clearly toward the haven of salvation.

We praise you, O Lord, that we can trust you to guide us now—and that you will steer us all the way to glory!

What a great thought this is! God himself will take us into glory. We have wandered, strayed, sinned—but he will welcome us home. Live with this assurance in your heart today. If you find yourself surrounded by problems, take this verse and march right up to God's throne.

September 2

Simon's mother-in-law was in bed with a fever, and they told Jesus about her. (Mark 1:30)

This glimpse into Peter's home is quite interesting. We see that household matters are not necessarily a hindrance to one's ministry. In fact, since they give us opportunity to see the Lord's grace at work with our own flesh and blood, concerns of the home may even be our most valuable education in the faith.

Peter's house was probably a poor fisherman's hut, but the Lord of Glory entered it, lodged there, and worked a miracle. If you find yourself in a humble house, this fact should encourage you. We find God more often in simple huts than in gaudy palaces. Jesus is looking around your room right now, waiting to show his grace to you.

Sickness had entered Peter's home. A deadly fever had stricken his mother-in-law. As soon as Jesus heard of this, he hurried to her bedside. Is there sickness in your house this morning? You will find that Jesus is by far the best physician. Go to him right now and tell him about your problem. Lay the case before him. He will not consider it trivial, since it concerns one of his people.

We can't be sure that the Lord will immediately remove all disease from those we love, yet prayer is more likely to bring about healing than anything else. Where this does not happen, we must meekly bow to the Lord's will. He is the one who determines life and death.

The tender heart of Jesus waits to hear our griefs.

September 3

You whom I love.
(Song of Songs 1:7)

Can you truly say this about Jesus—"you whom I love"? Many can only say that they *hope* they love him, or they *think* they love him. But only the shallowest spirituality will stay at this level. We should not rest until we are quite sure about this, since it is a matter of vital importance. A superficial "hope" will not do. The saints of old did not usually speak with "ifs" and "buts" or "I hope" or "I think." No, they spoke positively and plainly. "I know whom I have believed," said Paul (2 Timothy 1:12). "I know that my Redeemer lives," said Job (Job 19:25). Make sure of your love for Jesus, and don't be satisfied until you can speak of your affection for him as a reality, sealed by the witness of God's Spirit.

True love for Christ always comes from the Holy Spirit. He may bring it about, but the logical reason for loving Jesus lies in Jesus himself. *Why* do we love Jesus? *Because he first loved us* (1 John 4:19). *Why* do we love Jesus? Because he "gave himself up for us" (Ephesians 5:2). We have life through his death. We have peace through his blood. Though he was rich, yet for our sakes he became poor (2 Corinthians 8:9). *Why* do we love Jesus? Because of his excellence. We are filled with a sense of beauty, an awareness of his infinite perfection. His greatness, goodness, and loveliness combine to enchant our souls, until we cry, "He is altogether lovely" (Song of Songs 5:16).

September 4

"I am willing," he said. "Be clean!"
(Mark 1:41)

The primeval darkness heard the divine command—"Light be!"—and immediately light was. The word of the Lord Jesus has authority equal to that ancient word of creation. Jesus speaks, and it is done. Leprosy yielded to no human remedies, but it went running the moment it heard the Lord's "Be clean!" There was nothing natural about this healing; it was only the word of Christ that worked this wonder.

The sinner is in a plight worse than the leper. Sinners should follow the leper's example, coming to Christ and begging on their knees, summoning whatever faith they have, to say, "If you are willing, you can make me clean." Is there any doubt what would happen? Jesus heals all who come. He turns no one away.

Notice that Jesus touched the leper. This unclean person had broken the health regulations and approached Jesus, but Jesus did not scold the man. He broke the regulations himself in touching the leper. In a way, he traded places with the man. By touching the leper, Jesus cleansed him, but made himself legally defiled. In the same way, Jesus was made "to be sin for us," though he had not sinned, "so that in him we might become the righteousness of God" (2 Corinthians 5:21). The hand that multiplied the loaves, that saved sinking Peter, that lifts up troubled saints and crowns believers—that same hand will touch every sinner who seeks Christ and in an instant make him clean.

September 5

Woe to me that I dwell in Meshech, that I live among the tents of Kedar! (Psalm 120:5)

As a Christian, you have to live in the midst of an ungodly world. It does little good to cry, "Woe is me!" In Jesus' priestly prayer, he pointedly did *not* ask his Father to take believers out of this troublesome world (John 17:15), and since he didn't pray for it, we should not desire it. It is far better to meet the problem head on, in the Lord's strength, and to glorify him in it.

The enemy is always on the watch to detect some inconsistency in your behavior. So be very holy. Remember that people are watching you. Because you are a Christian, they expect more from you than from others. So try to avoid giving anyone an opportunity to find fault with you. Let your goodness be the only thing "wrong" with you. Like Daniel, make them say of you, "We will never find any basis for charges against this man Daniel unless it has something to do with the law of his God" (Daniel 6:5).

Try to be useful as well as consistent. You may be thinking, *If I lived in better surroundings, I could serve the Lord, but I can't do any good where I am*. But the worse the people around you are, the more they need your help. If they are evil, they need you to turn their proud hearts to the truth.

Where's the best place for a doctor? Where there are sick people. Where will a soldier win the most honor? In the heat of the battle. And when you grow weary of the sin that confronts you at every turn, remember that the saints of old went through the same trials. They had to risk their lives in difficult surroundings to win their crowns. So "stand firm in the faith . . . be strong" (1 Corinthians 16:13).

September 6

In a crooked and depraved generation, in which you shine like stars in the universe. (Philippians 2:15)

We use lights *to make things clear*. A Christian's life should shine to such an extent that a person could not live with him for a week without knowing the gospel. His conversation should be such that everyone around him can see clearly whose he is and whom he serves. They should see the image of Jesus reflected in his daily actions.

Lights are also intended for *guidance*. We should be helping those around us who are in the dark. We should be holding out to them the Word of life. We should be pointing sinners to the Savior. Sometimes people read their Bibles and don't understand them. We should be ready, like Philip (Acts 8:26–40), to explain the meaning of God's Word, the way of salvation, and the Christian life.

Lights are also used for *warning*. People desperately need a lighthouse to point out the rocks and shoals of this world. But there are many false lights around. We need to put up a true light on every dangerous rock, pointing out sin and what it leads to.

Lights also have a very *cheering* influence. So do Christians. A Christian ought to be a comforter, with kind words on his lips and sympathy in his heart. He should carry sunshine wherever he goes and spread happiness all around.

September 7

Since they could not get him to Jesus because of the crowd, they made an opening in the roof above Jesus and, after digging through it, lowered the mat the paralyzed man was lying on. (Mark 2:4)

Faith is full of inventions. The house was full. A crowd blocked the door. But faith found a way of getting to Jesus and bringing the sick man to him. If we cannot get sinners to Jesus by ordinary methods, we must use extraordinary ones. It seems, according to Luke's account (5:19), that these friends had to remove some tiling. That would create dust and cause some danger to those below. But when the situation is urgent, we shouldn't mind running some risks and shocking some people's sense of propriety. Jesus was there to heal, so these faithful friends risked everything to get their friend to the Savior. I wish we had more daring faith among us! Why not try today to perform some gallant act for the love of souls and the glory of God?

The world is constantly inventing. Genius serves all the whims of human desire. So why shouldn't faith be just as inventive in reaching the outcasts around us? It was the presence of Jesus that excited courage in the friends of the paralytic. Isn't Jesus present with us now? If so, then let us break through all barriers—door, window, roof—let us work to bring needy souls to Jesus. When in faith and love we are truly seeking to bring people to Christ, all methods are good and proper.

O Lord, make us quick to invent new ways of reaching those lost in sin, and give us the courage to carry these out, whatever the hazards.

September 8

Your fruitfulness comes from me. (Hosea 14:8)

How does this happen? Through our *union* with Christ. The fruit on the branch of a tree is connected to the roots of that tree. Sever that connection, and the branch dies—no fruit is produced. Similarly, we bring forth fruit from our union with Christ. Every bunch of grapes has started its life in the roots, passed through the stem, and grown into the external fruit. So every good work we may do begins in Christ and only comes out in us. Treasure your union with Christ. It is the source of all your fruitfulness. If you weren't joined to Jesus, you would be very barren.

We also owe our fruitfulness to God's *spiritual providence*. The fruit on a tree is not only dependent on the roots, but also on the dewdrops, the rainclouds, the bright sun. All of these external influences bring forth that fruit. For us, it is God's gracious providence that influences us to be fruitful. He is always inspiring, teaching, comforting, strengthening, or whatever. Without his provision, we would be useless.

But our fruit also results from God's *wise gardening*. The gardener takes his sharp knife to a fruit tree, cuts off the unnecessary branches, thinning the clusters. In so doing, he enhances the fruitfulness of the tree. It is the same way with the pruning God does to us. "My Father is the gardener," Jesus said. "He cuts off every branch in me that bears no fruit, while every branch that does bear fruit he prunes so that it will be even more fruitful" (John 15:1, 2).

In all these ways, God is responsible for our fruitfulness. So let us give him all the glory.

September 9

I will answer you and tell you great and unsearchable things you do not know. (Jeremiah 33:3)

Some parts of the Christian experience are reserved and special. Not all the developments of spiritual life are easy to attain. There are the common feelings of repentance, along with faith, joy, and hope, that are enjoyed by the entire family. But there is an upper realm of communion with Christ which goes beyond where most believers are. We do not all have the privilege John had, of leaning on Jesus' bosom. Nor have we been caught up, like Paul, into the "third heaven" (2 Corinthians 12:2). There are heights in experimental knowledge of the things of God that you cannot reach by philosophy or personal brilliance—only God can take us there. But the chariot in which he takes us is made of prayer.

Prayer can take the Christian to Mount Carmel, where he can summon clouds of blessing to rain down mercy on the earth (1 Kings 18). Prayer lifts the Christian to Mount Pisgah, and shows him the Promised Land (Deuteronomy 34). It elevates us to Mount Tabor and transfigures us into the image of our Lord Jesus (Matthew 17).

If you want to reach for something higher than everyday experience, look to the Rock that is higher than you (Psalm 61:2), and gaze with the eye of faith through the window of prayer. When you open that window on your side, it will not be bolted on the other.

September 10

Jesus went up on a mountainside and called to him those he wanted, and they came to him. (Mark 3:13)

Here was sovereignty. Impatient souls may fret and fume when they are not called to the highest places of ministry. But Jesus calls the ones he wants, to go where he wants, and we should rejoice in that. If he wants me to be a doorkeeper in his house (Psalm 84:10), I will cheerfully thank him for letting me serve him at all.

The call of Christ's servants comes from above. Jesus stands on the mountain, always above the world in terms of holiness, zeal, love, and power. The people he calls must go up the mountain to him. They must seek to rise to his level by living in constant communion with him. Jesus went off by himself when he wanted close fellowship with his Father, and if we want to be of any service to our fellowmen, we must have that same divine companionship. No wonder the apostles were clothed in power when they came down from the mountain where Jesus was! (Mark 3:15).

This morning, let us climb the mount of communion. There we may be set apart and empowered for our lifework. It is best not to see anyone today until we have seen Jesus. Time spent with him is precious. We, too, will cast out devils and work wonders if we go back down to the world equipped with divine energy from Christ. It makes no sense to enter the Lord's battle until we are armed with heavenly weapons. We *must* see Jesus. This is essential.

September 11

Be separate.
(2 Corinthians 6:17)

The Christian is *in* the world but should not be *of* the world. He should be distinct from the world in terms of *his life's goal*. To him, "to live is Christ" (Philippians 1:21), or should be. Whether he eats or drinks, or whatever he does, he should do all for God's glory (1 Corinthians 10:31). You may store up treasure—but store it in heaven, away from the ravages of moths, rust, and thieves (Matthew 6:19–20). You may strive to be rich—but make it your ambition to be rich in faith and good works (James 2:5; 1 Timothy 6:18). You may seek pleasure—but when you are happy, sing psalms and make music in your hearts to the Lord (Ephesians 5:19).

You should also differ from the world in your *spirit*. Waiting humbly before God, always aware of his presence, enjoying close fellowship with him, seeking to know his will—in all these ways you will prove you belong to him.

Your *actions* should also set you apart. You must do the right thing, even if you lose out. You must avoid wrong for Christ's sake, even if you would benefit from it. Remember that you are a child of the King of kings. Walk worthy of your heritage. Keep yourself from being polluted by the world (James 1:27). Do not soil the fingers that will soon be sweeping heavenly harpstrings. Your eyes will soon be seeing the King in all his beauty; don't let them become windows of lust. And do not fill your heart with pride or bitterness; before long it will be filled with heavenly joy.

September 12

The Lord is a jealous . . . God.
(Nahum 1:2)

Your Lord is very jealous of your love. Didn't he choose you? He cannot bear it when you choose someone else. Didn't he buy you with his own blood? He hates it when you insist that you are your own person or that you belong to the world. He loved you with such a great love that he couldn't stay in heaven without you. He would sooner die than to see you die. He can't stand anything that comes between your love and himself.

He is very jealous of your trust. How can you trust in your own flesh? How can you rely on broken cisterns when an overflowing fountain is always available to you? God is glad when we lean on him, and he gets upset when we depend on others or on our own wisdom.

He is also very jealous of our company. We should be talking with Jesus more than anyone else. But when we prefer to converse with others—even with other Christians—it saddens him. He wants us to abide in him, to stay close to him. Many of the trials he sends our way are merely to wean our hearts away from the world and toward him. But his jealousy can also comfort us. For if he loves us this much, he will certainly allow nothing to harm us. He will protect us from our enemies.

May we have the grace today to keep our hearts in sacred chastity for our beloved Lord, with his sacred jealousy shutting our eyes to the fascinations of the world.

September 13

As they pass through the Valley of Baca, they make it a place of springs; the autumn rains also cover it with pools. (Psalm 84:6)

What is the lesson here? When someone finds comfort for himself, the benefits often overflow to others. The wells dug by previous inhabitants are still there when we move in. It is the same way with Scripture. We read some book full of comforting words, and we say, "Aha! Someone has been here before us and has dug a well that we can use."

This is especially true of the Psalms. The psalmist writes, "Why are you downcast, O my soul? Why so disturbed within me?" (Psalm 42:5, 11). Later travelers have been delighted to see this footprint on an otherwise barren shore. Someone has been in this foul mood before us!

Interestingly, in today's text, the pools are filled not by the newly discovered springs, but by the rains. Blessing comes from above rather than below. The well may be dug by the previous pilgrims, but heaven fills it with rain. The effort helps to create the environment for blessing, but it does not cause the blessing itself. The pools are useful reservoirs—the pilgrims' labor is not wasted—but it does not supersede God's provision.

Grace can be compared to rain—in its purity, its refreshment, its source (in the heavens), and the will of God that sends it. I pray that you may have showers of blessing, that the pools dug by others may overflow for you. For what are all our efforts worth unless heaven smiles on us?

O God of love, open the windows of heaven and pour us a blessing!

September 14

There were also other boats with him.
(Mark 4:36)

Jesus was the Admiral of the sea that night. His presence preserved the whole fleet. It is good to sail with Jesus, even if you are in a little ship. When we sail in Christ's company, we can't be assured of fair weather. Furious storms rage even around our Lord's vessel, so we shouldn't expect the sea not to toss our little boat. When we go with Jesus, we face the same obstacles he does, but we know we will eventually reach land again.

When the storm swept over Galilee's dark lake, everyone grew worried, expecting shipwreck. When all human efforts proved useless, the slumbering Savior rose up and, with a word, transformed the riot of the tempest into the quiet of a calm. All the little boats could rest again.

Jesus is the star of the sea. There may be sorrow on the sea, but when Jesus is there, there is joy, too. May our hearts make Jesus their anchor, their rudder, their lighthouse, their lifeboat, and their harbor. The church is the Admiral's flagship, leading the way. We should follow in his wake, look for his signals, steer by his chart—and we have no reason to fear when he is close by. Not a single boat in this convoy will suffer wreck. The Commodore will lead us all safely to port. Winds and waves will not yield to us, but they obey him. So whatever squalls may occur, by faith we will be calm. He is always in the center of our little fleet. We can rejoice in him.

September 15

He will have no fear of bad news.
(Psalm 112:7)

Christian, you should not dread the arrival of bad news. If you did not have your God to run to, that would be different. No wonder unbelievers cower in fear—they don't know how strong and faithful our God is. But we do, or at least we say we do. We have been given new birth into a living hope (1 Peter 1:3). Our hearts are not bound by earthly things. So if you are just as fearful as others, what good is the grace you have received? Where is the dignity of your new nature?

Fear of bad news may lead you into sin. The ungodly, when they worry about bad news, rebel against God. They complain against God, blaming him for treating them harshly. Will you do the same?

In addition, unbelievers often run toward wrong solutions, in their efforts to escape their difficulties. If you begin to be afraid, you may do the same thing. Trust in the Lord. Wait patiently for him. Do what Moses did at the Red Sea: "Stand firm and you will see the deliverance the Lord will bring you today" (Exodus 14:13).

If you give way to fear when you hear bad news, then you won't be able to meet the crisis with the composure you need. How can you glorify God if you play the coward? If you are doubting and despairing, as if there were no hope, how does that magnify the Lord? Take courage. Rely on the faithfulness of God. "Do not let your heart be troubled" (John 14:1).

September 16

You may participate in the divine nature.
(2 Peter 1:4)

What does this mean? To participate in the divine nature is not to become God. That cannot be. The *essence* of deity is not participated in. There will always be a gulf—in terms of essence—between the creature and the Creator. Yet Adam and Eve were made "in the image of God," and we, by the renewal of the Holy Spirit, are *re*made in his image—so even more than the first couple, we participate in God's nature.

"God is love," and we become love: "Everyone who loves has been born of God" (1 John 4:16, 7). God is truth, and we become true—we love what is true. God is good; and he makes us good by his grace: We become the "pure in heart" who will "see God" (Matthew 5:8).

We participate in the divine nature in an even higher sense than this. Don't we become members of the body of Christ? Yes, the same blood that flows in the head flows in the hand. The same life that energized Christ now energizes his people.

More than that, we are married to Christ. He has taken us to himself in righteousness and faithfulness, and "he who unites himself with the Lord is one with him in spirit" (1 Corinthians 6:17).

What a marvelous mystery! We can study it and study it, but who can understand it? We are one with Jesus! Remember that those who participate in the divine nature will demonstrate their holy character in their involvement with others, in their daily life.

September 17

Bring the boy to me.
(Mark 9:19)

In despair, the boy's disappointed father turned from the disciples to Jesus. His son was in the worst possible condition. All attempts to help him had failed. But the child was delivered from the evil one when his father obeyed Jesus' simple command: "Bring the boy to me."

Children are a precious gift from God, but a lot of anxiety comes with them. They can bring great joy and great agony to their parents. They may be filled with the Spirit of God or possessed by a spirit of evil. In each case, the Word of God gives the simple answer for curing their ills: "Bring them to me."

We should begin when they are babies, praying earnestly for them. Sin is present even then, so we should begin to attack it with our prayers. In fact, our cries of prayer should even come before the cries with which these babies enter our world. As they grow, we may see the sad symptoms of a deaf and dumb spirit—when they neither pray properly nor hear the voice of God in their souls. But Jesus still commands: "Bring them to me." In young adulthood, they may wallow in sin, even proclaiming their defiance toward God. Even with our hearts breaking, we should remember the Great Physician's words: "Bring them to me." We must never stop praying until they stop breathing. No case is hopeless as long as Jesus lives.

Sometimes the Lord allows us to be driven into a corner so that we may learn how much we need to trust him. Ungodly children, by showing us how powerless we are, can make us turn to God for strength, and there is blessing here. Whatever this morning's need may be, let it carry you like a swift current to the ocean of God's love.

September 18

Since we live by the Spirit, let us keep in step with the Spirit.
(Galatians 5:25)

The two most important things in our religion are *the life of faith* and *the walk of faith*. If you understand these properly, you are not far from being a master of practical theology. These are vital points for the Christian.

You will never find true faith unaccompanied by true godliness. On the other hand, you will never find a truly holy life that is not rooted in a living faith in Jesus. It is pointless to try to cultivate one without the other.

Some try to develop faith and forget about holiness. They may get high marks for orthodoxy, but they remain under condemnation because they "hold the truth in unrighteousness" (Romans 1:18 KJV). Others struggle to be holy, but deny the faith. Like the Pharisees of old, they are "whitewashed tombs." We must have faith, for this is the foundation. We must have holy lives, for this is what is built on top. What good is a mere foundation to a person who seeks shelter from a storm? Can he hide himself in it? In the same way, we need the superstructure of holiness to protect us from the ravages of doubt.

But it doesn't help to build a house without a foundation, either. Faith and life must go together. Like the two abutments of an arch, they will make our piety strong and enduring. Like light and heat emanating from the same sun, they both are full of blessing. They are two streams from the fountain of grace, two lamps lit with holy fire.

O Lord, give us faith within, which comes out in holy lives, glorifying you.

September 19

It is for freedom that Christ has set us free.
(Galatians 5:1)

We are free. We have free access to the Bible. We are free to enjoy the promises of God. "When you pass through the waters," he says, "I will be with you" (Isaiah 43:2). "Though the mountains be shaken and the hills be removed," he adds, "yet my unfailing love for you will not be shaken" (Isaiah 54:10). You are a welcome guest at the banquet of promises. Scripture is a treasury always well stocked with grace. It is the bank of heaven. Withdraw as much as you like; there are no limits.

Come in faith, and you are welcome to all the blessings of the covenant. Not a single promise in God's Word will be held back. In serious trials, this freedom can comfort and cheer you. When sorrow surrounds you, this liberty will soothe you. It is your Father's token of love.

You also have free access to the throne of grace. Whatever your desires, difficulties, or wants, you may spread it all before him. It doesn't matter how much you have sinned, you may always ask for pardon and expect to receive it. No matter how poor you are, you may refer to God's own promise that he will provide all you need. We have permission to approach his throne at any time—at the heat of noon or the dark of night. So exercise your rights as a believer; use your privileges. You are free to enjoy everything that is stored up for you in Christ—wisdom, righteousness, sanctification, and redemption. What a great freedom this is!

September 20

The sword of the Lord, and of Gideon.
(Judges 7:20 KJV)

Gideon ordered his men to do two things. They carried torches, but hid them in earthen pitchers. Their first task was to break the pitchers, at the proper signal, and let the light shine. But they also had trumpets. The second task was to blow the trumpets and shout, "The sword of the Lord, and of Gideon!"

This is precisely what all Christians must do. First, *we must shine*. Break the pitcher that hides your light. Throw aside the bowl that covers your candle (Matthew 5:15), and let your light shine! Let your good works be such that, when people watch you, they will know that you have been with Jesus.

Second, *there must be a sound*, the blowing of a trumpet. We must boldly proclaim Christ crucified for sinners. Take the gospel to those who need it. Carry it to their door. Put it in their way. Don't let them ignore it. Blow the trumpet right in their ears.

Remember that battle cry: "The sword of the Lord" God must win the battle. But that doesn't leave us with nothing to do: "and of Gideon!" We are the instruments he uses.

We must blend these two truths. We can do nothing by ourselves, but we can do everything with God's help. So let us determine, in his power, to go out and serve him, with our blazing torches of holy living and our trumpet tones of bold testimony. God will be with us. Our enemies will be routed. And the Lord of hosts will reign forever.

September 21

I will rejoice in doing them good.
(Jeremiah 32:41)

Why should God take such pleasure in us? We can't delight very much in ourselves, because we often feel burdened. We are sadly aware of our own sin and unfaithfulness. And the rest of God's people can't find much joy in us either, for they must see all our foibles and imperfections. They probably mourn our weaknesses rather than admiring our virtues.

But this one truth, this glorious mystery, cheers us up: As the bridegroom rejoices in his bride, so the Lord rejoices in us. He does not find this much delight in the cloud-capped mountains or the sparkling stars. He does not even find so much joy in his angels. To which of his angels did he ever say, "You will be called Hephzibah . . . ; for the Lord will take delight in you" (Isaiah 62:4)? Yet that is exactly what he says to poor, fallen creatures like ourselves, corrupted by sin, but saved, exalted, and glorified by his grace. What strong language he uses to express his happiness! Who would guess that the eternal One would burst forth into song? Yet Scripture says, "He will take great delight in you . . . he will rejoice over you with singing" (Zephaniah 3:17).

As he looked over the world he had made, he said, "It is very good" (see Genesis 1:31). When he saw those he purchased through Christ's blood, it seemed as if his great heart could not restrain itself, but he overflowed in exclamations of joy. We should certainly join his song, singing, "I will rejoice in the Lord, I will be joyful in God my Savior" (Habakkuk 3:18).

September 22

Let Israel rejoice in their Maker.

(Psalm 149:2)

You have every reason to be glad, my friend, but make sure your gladness has its source *in the Lord*. You can be glad that the Lord reigns. Rejoice that he sits on the throne. You can sing with the psalmist, "God, my joy and my delight" (Psalm 43:4).

Every attribute of God becomes a fresh ray in the sunlight of our gladness. His wisdom makes us glad, because we are very aware of our own foolishness. His strength makes us rejoice, because we tremble at our own weakness. We exult in the fact that he is eternal, because we know that we wither like grass. His unchanging nature inspires us to sing, because we seem to change every hour. Above all, his grace—the overflowing grace of his covenant, the grace that keeps us, makes us holy, perfects us, and brings us to glory—this grace makes us very glad in him.

Gladness in God is like a deep river. We have just touched its surface, so we know only a little of its sweet streams, but we know it gets deeper farther on and the current surges with joy.

The Christian can find delight not only in what God *is*, but also in what he *has done*. As we see in the Psalms, God's people in olden days thought a great deal of God's actions—so much that they seem to have a song for each of them. So why can't we rehearse the deeds of the Lord? We should never stop singing, for his new mercies each day should inspire new songs of thanksgiving.

September 23

Accepted in the beloved.

(Ephesians 1:6 KJV)

What a privilege! Our acceptance involves our *justification* before God, but it means much more than that. It indicates that we are objects of divine delight. How can we—worms, mortals, sinners—be objects of God's love? Only "in the beloved," that is, in Christ.

Some Christians seem to think that they are only accepted on the basis of their day-to-day experience with the Lord. Some days their spirits are lively, full of bright hopes, and they feel sure that God accepts them because they feel so high, so heavenly minded. But on other days, their souls are hugging the dust. They fear that they are no longer accepted. If they could only see that the Father's acceptance does not depend at all on their highs and lows, but that they stand accepted on the basis of the One who never changes, the One who is always perfect, without stain or wrinkle, the Beloved One of God—how much happier they would be, and how much more they would honor their Savior!

You may look at yourself and say, "There is nothing acceptable *here*!" But look at Christ—there is everything acceptable *there*. Your sins bother you. But God has put your sins behind his back and accepted you in the Righteous One. You regularly fight with temptation, but you are accepted in the One who has overcome the powers of evil. Rest assured of your glorious standing in Christ, the beloved.

September 24

I was ashamed to ask the king for soldiers and horsemen to protect us from enemies on the road, because we had told the king, "The gracious hand of our God is on everyone who looks to him, but his great anger is against all who forsake him." (Ezra 8:22)

For many reasons, Ezra's pilgrim band could have used an armed escort, but Ezra was embarrassed to ask for one. He was afraid that the pagan king would think that his profession of faith in God was just hypocrisy, or perhaps the king would think that the God of Israel lacked the strength to protect his own worshipers. Since Ezra could not bring himself to trust in such human protection, the caravan set out guarded only by God, the sword and shield of his people.

Unfortunately, few believers today feel this same kind of holy jealousy for God. Even those who generally walk by faith will occasionally mar the brilliant shine of their lives by asking for human aid where God's is sufficient. It is a wonderful thing to stand upright on the Rock of Ages, upheld by God alone. Would we run so hastily to friends and relatives for assistance if we realized how much our Lord is glorified when we rely on him alone?

"But wait," you say. "Doesn't God use others to help us?" Yes, at times. But we often begin to trust in them rather than in God. Few of us are in danger of neglecting human help, but many of us learn to count on it. We must learn to honor God by counting on him first of all.

September 25

Just and the one who justifies those who have faith in Jesus. (Romans 3:26)

Since we have been justified by faith, we have peace with God. Conscience no longer accuses us. Judgment is now in our favor. Memory looks back on the sins of the past and mourns for them, but has no fear of future punishment. Christ has paid our debt, to the last iota. Only an unjust God would demand double payment.

One of the basic principles of any reasonable person is that God is just. When we really think about it, this can be a terrifying thought—unless we also realize that he is a *justifier*. If God is just, as a sinner I must be punished. But Jesus stands in my place. He takes the punishment for me. Now, if God is truly just, he can never punish me, since my punishment has already been taken. God would have to change his nature radically in order to lash out against even a single soul who was covered by Jesus.

So since Jesus has taken our place, bearing the full brunt of divine wrath on our account, we can shout with glorious triumph, "Who will bring any charge against those whom God has chosen?" (Romans 8:33). Not God, for he has justified us. Not Christ, for he has died and risen again for us. No one can condemn us.

My hope, then, rests not in the fact that I am a sinner, but that I am a sinner for whom Christ died. I do not trust in my own holiness, but Christ has become my righteousness. My faith does not depend on what I am or will be or will feel or will know, but in what Christ is, in what he has done, and in what he is now doing for me.

September 26

Among the myrtle trees in a ravine.
(Zechariah 1:8)

The vision in this chapter describes the condition of Israel in Zechariah's day. But as we look at it, it can describe the church as it exists today in the world. The church is compared to a grove of myrtle trees flourishing in a small valley. It is *hidden*, unobserved, secret. It attracts no attention from the casual onlooker. The church, like its Lord, has glory, but it is concealed from carnal eyes—until the time comes to burst forth in radiant splendor.

We also find a hint of *tranquil security*. The myrtle grove in the valley is still and calm, while a storm sweeps over the mountaintops. In the same way, the church enjoys a great inner tranquility. Even when opposed and persecuted, the church has a peace that the world cannot give—and cannot take away. The peace of God "which transcends all understanding" (Philippians 4:7) guards the hearts and minds of God's people.

The image of myrtle trees also suggests a picture of *constant growth* for believers. The myrtle doesn't drop its leaves, but remains green. And the church, even in its worst crisis, still has the color of grace. In fact, the color seems brighter in the fiercest winters. The church prospers most when adversities are most severe.

So our text also hints at *victory*. The myrtle is a symbol of peace and triumph. Conquerors of old would have their brows crowned with myrtle and laurel. Aren't we "more than conquerors through him who loved us" (Romans 8:37)?

September 27

Blessed are you, O Israel! Who is like you, a people saved by the Lord? (Deuteronomy 33:29)

Anyone who says Christianity makes people miserable knows nothing about it. That would make no sense. When we become Christians, we enter God's family. And why would God give all the happiness to his enemies and make his own children mourn? Should the sinner, who has no interest in Christ, be rich in joy, while we go moping like beggars? No, you can rejoice in the Lord always, and glory in your inheritance, "For you did not receive a spirit that makes you a slave again to fear, but you received the Spirit of sonship. And by him we cry, 'Abba, Father'" (Romans 8:15).

At times, like any child, we must be disciplined. But this just helps us to grow in righteousness. With the help of the divine Comforter, we still rejoice in the God of our salvation.

We are married to Christ. Would the Bridegroom allow his wife to languish in constant grief? No! Our hearts are kin to his. We are his members—and even though we must suffer sometimes as he suffered, we also receive tremendous blessings in him. The Spirit is in our hearts, as God's down payment, and he provides substantial benefits even now. But we still look forward to our full inheritance in heaven. Our riches lie beyond the sea. Gleams of glory from that spiritual world cheer us on each day.

September 28

From heaven the Lord looks down and sees all mankind.
(Psalm 33:13)

There's probably no image that shows God in a better light than when he is depicted stooping from his throne, coming down from heaven to see firsthand the wants and needs of his people. When Sodom and Gomorrah reeked with sin, he would not destroy them until he had made a personal visit. He regularly bends his ear to hear the prayers of dying sinners who long for reconciliation. He pays special attention to us: He counts the hairs of our heads; he marks out our paths; he directs our ways.

We love him for this. How can we help but pour out our hearts in affection? He becomes all the more precious when we realize how deeply he cares for our spiritual needs. A huge distance lies between creature and Creator, yet he regularly spans it. When you are in tears, don't think that God isn't watching. "As a father has compassion on his children, so the Lord has compassion on those who fear him" (Psalm 103:13). Your simple sigh can move Yahweh's heart. Your whisper bends his ear. Your prayer of faith can move his arm.

No, don't ever think that God sits high and mighty and doesn't care about you. However poor and needy you may be, he is thinking about you. "For the eyes of the Lord range throughout the earth to strengthen those whose hearts are fully committed to him" (2 Chronicles 16:9).

September 29

If the disease has covered his whole body, he shall pronounce that person clean. (Leviticus 13:13)

This rule seems strange at first, but there is wisdom in it. If the leper had been completely infected by the disease and still survived, that proved his constitution was basically sound.

It might do us good to look for an application of this unusual regulation in our lives. We, too, are lepers. When someone sees that he is completely lost, ravaged by sin, when he gives up on all righteous efforts of his own and pleads guilty before the Lord—then he is clean through the blood of Jesus and the grace of God. Hidden, unfelt, unconfessed sin is the true leprosy. But when sin is detected and confessed, it has received its death blow.

Nothing is more deadly than self-righteousness, and nothing heals better than repentance. We must come to God, confessing that we are thoroughly sinful—any confession short of that is not the whole truth. (The Holy Spirit will help us realize how sinful we are, prompting a heartfelt confession.) But once we confess, there is great comfort. However foul our sin has been, it will not shut us out from Jesus. "Whoever comes to me," he said, "I will never drive away" (John 6:37).

You may be as dishonest as the thief on the cross, as promiscuous as the "sinful woman" with the perfume, as violent as Saul of Tarsus, as cruel as Manasseh, as rebellious as the Prodigal Son—but God will look lovingly on the person who realizes he has no merit of his own. When he trusts in Jesus, God will pronounce him clean.

September 30

Sing the glory of his name; make his praise glorious!
(Psalm 66:2)

It is not up to us whether or not we praise God. Praise is due to God, and every Christian, as a recipient of his grace, owes him thanks daily. True, we have no stipulated pattern for our praise. We have no rules prescribing certain hours for singing and giving thanks. But there is a law written on our hearts, and this teaches us that it is right to praise God.

Yes, it is the Christian's *duty* to praise God. It is not only a pleasurable exercise, but an absolute obligation. If you find yourself complaining and despairing, don't think that you are exempt. You are bound by the bonds of his love to bless his name as long as you live. His praise should always be on your lips (Psalm 34:1).

Why do you think he has blessed you? So that you may bless him back. "The people I formed for myself, that they may proclaim my praise" (Isaiah 43:21). If you do not praise God, you are not bringing forth the fruit that he, the Divine Gardener, has a right to expect from you. So don't let your harp hang on the willows. Take it down! Play your music as loud as you can. Chant his praise. With the dawning of each day, raise a song of thanks, and close each sunset with hymn. Surround the earth with your praises, create an atmosphere of melody. God himself will appreciate your music.

October 1

At our door is every delicacy, both new and old, that I have stored up for you, my lover. (Song of Songs 7:13)

The beloved bride wants to give Jesus all she can. Our hearts are filled with "every delicacy, both new and old," stored up for Jesus, the lover of our souls. At this harvest season, let's see what fruits we have available to give him.

We have *new* delicacies. We brim with new life, new joy, and new gratitude. We want to make new resolutions and carry them out in new surges of effort.

But we have *old* delicacies, too. There is our "first love." That is one of our choicest fruits, and Jesus delights in it. There is our first faith—the simple faith that lifted us from a state of utter poverty and allowed us to share in God's great riches. There is that joy we had when we first came to know the Lord—can we revive this?

We also have all the old promises. God has been faithful, delivering us time after time. Yes, we have many of these old delicacies, for his mercy has been great. We regret our old sins, but he has even led us to repentance. We have wept our way to the cross and learned how valuable his blood really is.

So we have these delicacies, new and old, but here's the point—*they are all stored up for Jesus*. Whatever blessings or talents or virtues we have, let's give them all to our Beloved. That is when they shine brightest—when Jesus' glory is the solitary aim of our soul. We must not let the lure of human acclaim sneak in and steal from our storehouse. These delicacies are for you, Jesus, and for you only.

October 2

The hope that is stored up for you in heaven.
(Colossians 1:5)

Our hope in Christ and the heavenly future he prepares for us keeps us going. It cheers us up to think of heaven, because all that we desire awaits us.

Here we are weary. But that is a land of *rest*, where the sweat of labor will no longer drip from the worker's brow. Fatigue will be banished.

Here we feel embattled—attacked by internal temptations and external opponents. We have little or no peace. But in heaven, we will enjoy the *victory*. The banner will be hoisted high, the sword put into its sheath, and the Captain will say, "Well done, good and faithful servant."

Here we have suffered much bereavement. But we are headed for a place of *immortality*. Graves are unknown there.

Here sin constantly besieges us. But there we will be perfectly *holy*. Nothing will creep in to defile that perfect kingdom.

It is sheer joy to realize that we will not be wandering in this wilderness forever, that we will soon inherit the Promised Land. But let's not dream so much about the future that we forget the present. The future can sanctify the present. Through God's Spirit, the hope of heaven can produce great righteousness within us. It is the basis for a cheerful holiness. The person who has this hope inside has a new vigor in his work—for the joy of the Lord is his strength (Nehemiah 8:10). He fights against temptation with renewed power, for the hope of the next world repels the devil's darts. He can labor without an immediate reward, because he knows he will be rewarded in the world to come.

October 3

Are not all angels ministering spirits sent to serve those who will inherit salvation? (Hebrews 1:14)

Angels are the invisible bodyguards of the saints of God. "They will lift you up in their hands, so that you will not strike your foot against a stone" (Psalm 91:12). Loyalty to their Lord leads them to take a deep interest in the children he loves. They rejoice over the return of the runaway son (Luke 15), and they welcome the entry of the believer into the King's heavenly palace.

In biblical times, God's people were sometimes visited by angels. This still happens, though we don't see them. The angels of God still ascend and descend to visit the heirs of salvation (Genesis 28:12), only now their ladder is Jesus himself. Seraphim still fly with burning coals from the altar to touch the lips of the people God chooses (Isaiah 6:6–7). If our eyes were opened, we would see horses and chariots of fire around us and an army of angels protecting us (2 Kings 6:17).

Consider the dignity that goes along with this. We are served by the brilliant courtiers of heaven! We are defended by the greatest army ever known! To whom do we owe all this? To Jesus Christ, of course. God has "seated us with him in the heavenly realms" (Ephesians 2:6). It is his camp that the angel of the Lord sets up around those who fear him (Psalm 34:7).

All praise to you, Jesus! We glorify you today!

October 4

When evening comes, there will be light.
(Zechariah 14:7)

We often dread the onslaught of old age. We forget that, "when evening comes, there will be light." For many believers, old age is the best time of their lives. As the sailor approaches the shore, a balmier breeze fans his cheek, fewer waves ruffle the sea, and a deep quiet reigns. So it is with those who near the shore of immortality.

Fire no longer flashes from the altar of youth, but the deep glow of earnest feeling remains. It is as if these pilgrims have reached a beautiful land—not quite heaven, but nearly so. Angels visit; heavenly breezes blow over it; the flowers of paradise grow; and the air is filled with glorious music. Some live here for years, and others only reach it a few hours before they depart, but it is Eden on earth.

We don't need to dread this time; we can look forward to it. The sun seems larger when it is setting, and it lends a special glory to all the clouds around it. Even pain does not break the calm of this twilight time, for strength is made perfect in weakness (2 Corinthians 12:9).

The Lord's people can also see light in the hour of death. Doubters may mourn the coming of night. But the faithful ones say, "No, the night is quickly passed. The day is already near. The light of immortality is dawning, and the Father's sweet face is brightening. See the angels carrying our beloved one to the kingdom of light. The pearly gates are wide open. We can see those golden streets gleaming. Good-bye, dear friend. You are enjoying great light, even in the evening. Someday we will, too."

October 5

So he got up and ate and drank. Strengthened by that food, he traveled forty days and forty nights. (1 Kings 19:8)

God supplies us with great strength when we need it, but he wants us to use that strength in his service, not in wanton pleasure seeking or boasting. When the prophet Elijah woke up and found a cake of bread baked on the coals and a jar of water, it was not just so he could lie back and take it easy. Far from it! He was commissioned to travel forty days and nights, heading for Horeb, the mountain of God.

When the Master invited his disciples to "Come and have breakfast" (John 21:12), he followed the meal with a challenge to Peter: "Feed my sheep." Later he added, "Follow me" (vv. 17, 19).

So it is with us. We eat the bread of heaven so that we may be strengthened to serve our Master. We come to the Passover meal and eat the sacrificial lamb as the Israelites did, "with your cloak tucked into your belt, your sandals on your feet and your staff in your hand" (Exodus 12:11), because we must move on after we have satisfied our hunger.

Many Christians are all in favor of living *on* Christ, but they're not so anxious to live *for* Christ. Earth should be a preparation for heaven. Heaven is a place where the saints feast and work. They sit down at the Lord's table and serve day and night in his temple. They eat of the heavenly food and offer him perfect service.

Believer, use the strength Christ gives you to work for him. We have much more to learn about his grace. Why do you think he sends rain and sunshine on the earth? To help the crops grow. Why does he feed and refresh our souls? So that we may glorify him.

October 6

Whoever drinks the water I give him will never thirst.
(John 4:14)

The one who believes in Jesus finds enough to satisfy him now and forever. The believer is not one to walk around depressed and glum. No, his relationship with Christ is a spring of joy, a fountain of comfort. Put him in a dungeon, and he will find a companion there. Drop him in the desert, and he will eat the bread of heaven. Isolate him from his friends, and he will spend time with the "friend who sticks closer than a brother" (Proverbs 18:24). Take away his shade, and he will rest under the Rock of Ages. Shake the foundation of his earthly hopes, but his heart will still be secure, trusting in the Lord.

The heart is as insatiable as the grave until Jesus enters it. Then it is a cup that overflows. The true saint is so completely satisfied with Jesus that he is no longer thirsty—except for another drink from the living fountain.

That is the only kind of thirst you should feel, my friend, not a thirst of pain but of love. It is a sweet thing to be panting after a fuller enjoyment of Jesus' love. Is this the way you feel today? Do you feel that all your desires are satisfied in Jesus, and that you only want to know more of him? Then keep on coming to the fountain and drink freely of the water of life. Jesus will never scold you for drinking too much. On the contrary, he will say, "Drink on, my friend! Drink as much as you want!"

October 7

Why have you brought this trouble on your servant?
(Numbers 11:11)

Why does our heavenly Father bring troubles on his servants? *To try our faith*. If our faith is worth anything, it will stand the test. The phoney gem can't stand to be touched by the diamond, but the true jewel does not fear that test. If you can only trust God when your friends are faithful, your body healthy, and your business profitable, then your faith is poor. True faith relies on the Lord's faithfulness when friends are gone, when the body is sick, when spirits are depressed, and when it seems that even God is hiding his face. A heaven-born faith will be able to say with Job, "Though he slay me, yet will I hope in him" (Job 13:15).

The Lord also troubles his servants *to glorify himself*. He derives glory as our character grows. As "suffering produces perseverance; perseverance, character; and character, hope" (Romans 5:3–4), the Lord is honored, because he is the one creating these changes in us. We would never know the beauty of harp music if the strings were left untouched. Nor would we enjoy the juice of the grape if it were not trodden in the winepress. Nor would we enjoy the warmth of a fire unless coals were consumed. Similarly, the wisdom and power of the Potter is seen in the trials that his workmanship can bear.

Our present troubles also tend *to heighten our future joy*. In a painting, there must be shadows in order to bring out the beauty of the light. Isn't peace sweeter after conflict and rest more welcome after a hard day's work? So the memory of our past troubles will enhance our heavenly bliss.

October 8

Put out into deep water, and let down the nets for a catch.
(Luke 5:4)

This story teaches us, first, *the necessity of human effort*. The catch of fishes was miraculous, but it still required the use of the fisherman, his boat, and his net. In the saving of souls, the same principle applies. God uses human means. It is certainly his grace alone that saves people, but he still chooses to use the foolishness of preaching.

By themselves, the instruments are ineffective. "Master," Peter complained, "we've worked hard all night and haven't caught anything" (v. 5). Why not? Weren't they experienced as fishermen? Yes! Did they lack skill? No! Did they lack effort? No, they had *worked hard*. Did they lack perseverance? No, they had worked hard *all night*. Was there a lack of fish in the sea? Certainly not. Once the Master arrived, the fish swarmed into the net. So how do we explain this? Is it because there is no power in the instruments themselves, apart from the presence of Jesus? As Jesus put it, "Apart from me, you can do nothing" (John 15:5). But with Christ, we can do all things (Philippians 4:13).

Christ's presence brings success. Jesus sat in Peter's boat, and in some mysterious way, his will drew the fish into the net. When Jesus is "lifted up" in his church, his presence is the church's power. "But I, when I am lifted up from the earth," he said, "will draw all men to myself" (John 12:32).

So let us go about our soul fishing today, looking upward in faith and outward in compassion. Let's work hard and trust that the one who goes with us will fill our nets.

October 9

Able to keep you from falling.
(Jude 24)

In a way, the path to heaven is very safe. But in another sense, it is the most dangerous road you could travel. It is beset with difficulties. One false step (and how easy that is to take, if grace is not with us) and down we go. We often find ourselves exclaiming, along with the psalmist, "My feet had almost slipped; I had nearly lost my foothold" (Psalm 73:2).

If we were strong, surefooted mountaineers, this might not matter much. But in ourselves we are very weak. Even on the best roads we often falter. These feeble knees of ours can hardly support our tottering weight. A pebble can wound us; a mere straw can trip us up. We are children taking our first steps in the walk of faith. If our heavenly Father were not holding us up by the arms, we would soon stumble.

All this makes us appreciate our patient Lord all the more. When we consider how prone we are to sin, how easily we choose the dangerous ways, how strong our tendency is to trip over our own feet—these reflections make us sing Jude's song even more sweetly: "Glory to him who is able to keep us from falling!"

We also have many enemies trying to push us down. They lurk in ambush, rushing upon us when we least expect them. They try to trip us or to throw us over the cliff. Only an Almighty arm can save us from these invisible foes, who seek to destroy us. We have such an arm enlisted in our defense. He has promised to be faithful. He is more than able to keep us from falling.

October 10

Before his glorious presence without fault. (Jude 24)

Turn around that wonderful phrase in your mind: "without fault." We are far from that now. But our Lord never stops short of perfection in his work of love—and we will reach it someday. Ultimately, the Savior will present us to himself as "a radiant church, without stain or wrinkle or any other blemish, but holy and blameless" (Ephesians 5:27).

All the jewels in the Savior's crown are of the finest quality, without a single flaw. How will Jesus make *us* flawless? He will wash us clean from our sins in his own blood, until we are as fair as God's purest angel. We will be clothed in his righteousness, a robe that makes us faultless in God's eyes. Not only will his perfect law have no charge against us, but it will be perfectly modeled in us.

In addition, the work of the Holy Spirit will be completed within us. He will make us so thoroughly holy that we will have no lingering tendency to sin. Our judgment, memory, and will—every power and passion we have will be set free from our captivity to evil. We will be holy as God is holy, and we will live in his presence forever.

Christians will not be out of place in heaven. Our beauty will match the place prepared for us. What a great day that will be! Sin gone, Satan shut out, and temptation out of the way—and we are presented "without fault" before God!

October 11

Let us lift up our hearts and our hands to God in heaven.
(Lamentations 3:41)

The act of prayer teaches us our own unworthiness. This is a very important lesson for proud beings like us. If God gave us favors without asking us to pray for them, we would never know how poor we were. A true prayer is an inventory of wants, a catalog of necessities, that reveals to us our hidden poverty. Through prayer, we stake our claim on divine wealth, but we also confess our human emptiness.

The healthiest state for a Christian is to be always empty of self and constantly dependent on the Lord for supplies—poor in self and rich in Jesus. That is why we pray. We adore God, and at the same time we recognize our own position—in the dust.

So prayer in itself, apart from the answer it brings, is a great benefit to the Christian. As a runner gains strength for a race with daily exercise, so we get the energy we need for the race of life through the exercise of prayer. Prayer arms God's warriors and sends them out to combat. The diligent prayer warrior comes out of his closet as the sun itself emerges "from his pavilion, like a champion rejoicing to run his course" (Psalm 19:5). Prayer is the uplifted hand of Moses that routs the enemy, even more effectively than the sword of Joshua (Exodus 17:10–13). Prayer turns human folly into heavenly wisdom and gives to troubled mortals the peace of God. In fact, we don't know anything that prayer cannot do!

We thank you, great God, for your mercy seat. You prove your marvelous loving-kindness every time you hear our prayers.

October 12

I meditate on your precepts.
(Psalm 119:15)

Sometimes solitude is better than company, and silence is wiser than speech. We would be better Christians if we spent more time alone, waiting on God, meditating on his Word, gathering spiritual strength to serve him.

Why should we muse upon the things of God? Because they nourish us. Truth is something like a cluster of grapes. If we want its juice, we must crush it. We must press it and squeeze it and stomp on it. If we don't, the juice will not flow, the precious liquid will be wasted. By meditation, we tread the clusters of truth to get the wine of divine comfort.

Our bodies do not derive nourishment merely by taking food into the mouth. The process that builds us up is *digestion*. That's how the external food begins to make a difference inside of us. Similarly, our souls do not get fed merely by listening to this or that expression of God's truth. Hearing, reading, studying, and learning—all of these require digestion in order to be truly useful, and digesting truth involves meditation.

Why is it that some Christians, though they have heard hundreds of sermons, are progressing very slowly in their Christian lives? Because they do not thoughtfully meditate on God's Word. They love the wheat, but they don't grind it. They want the corn, but they won't harvest it. The fruit hangs there on the tree, but they won't pluck it. The water is flowing at their feet, but they won't stoop to drink.

Deliver us, Lord, from this foolishness. Let this be our honest statement: "I meditate on your precepts."

October 13

Godly sorrow brings repentance.
(2 Corinthians 7:10)

Genuine spiritual mourning for sin is *the work of God's Holy Spirit*. Repentance is too precious a flower to grow naturally. Pearls may grow naturally in oysters, but repentance is always the result of God's supernatural grace. If you have even one particle of hatred for sin, God gave it to you. The thorns of human nature do not produce figs. "Flesh gives birth to flesh, but the Spirit gives birth to spirit" (John 3:6).

True repentance *always involves Jesus*. We must have one eye on our sin and another on the cross. Better still, we should fix both eyes on Christ and see our sins only in the light of his love.

True sorrow for sin is also *very practical*. No one can truly say he hates sin as long as he is living in it. Repentance makes us see the evil of sin—not theoretically, but through experience, as a burned child dreads fire. We will be as afraid of sin as the man who has recently been robbed is afraid of thieves. We will seek to avoid it at all costs. We will stay away from small sins as well as great sins. True repentance will make us careful what we say, and what we do each day. We will take care not to offend or hurt others. Each night we will close the day by confessing our shortcomings, and each morning we will start by asking God to keep us from sinning against him.

Sincere repentance is also *continual*. Believers keep repenting until their dying day. Every other sorrow we experience fades with time, but this one grows as we grow. But it is such a sweet sorrow that we can thank God that he has allowed us to feel it.

October 14

I consider everything a loss compared to the surpassing greatness of knowing Christ Jesus my Lord.
(Philippians 3:8)

Our knowledge of Christ is *personal*. I cannot rely on anyone else's relationship with Jesus. I must know him *myself*.

It is an *intelligent* knowledge. I know him not as some visionary might dream of him, but as Scripture shows him to be. I must know his human nature as well as his divine nature. I must know the positions he holds, the attributes he possesses, the works he has done, the shame he bore on my account, his heavenly glory. I must meditate on him until I "grasp how wide and long and high and deep is the love of Christ" (Ephesians 3:18).

It is an *affectionate* knowledge. If I know him at all, I have to love him. An ounce of heart knowledge is worth a ton of head learning.

Our knowledge of Christ is also *satisfying*. When I know my Savior, my mind is full to the brim. I have what my soul has been panting after.

At the same time, this knowledge is also *exciting*. The more I know of my Beloved, the more I want to know. The higher I climb, the higher I want to go. It is like the miser's treasure: I want more as I get more.

In conclusion, the knowledge of Jesus Christ is a *happy* one. It sometimes lifts me up above all my trials, doubts, and sorrows. Not only does it cheer me up in the present moment—it also grants me the Savior's eternal joy.

So sit down for a few moments. Sit at Jesus' feet and get to know him.

October 15

But who can endure the day of his coming?
(Malachi 3:2)

Jesus' first coming was quiet, without a great deal of fanfare or powerful display. But even then there were few who passed the test. Herod and all Jerusalem were stirred by the news of this remarkable birth. But those who claimed to be waiting for their Savior showed how shallow their convictions were. They rejected him when he arrived.

Jesus' life on earth was a winnowing fork, tossing the great heap of religious profession into the air and letting the wind blow the chaff away. Few could endure this process.

But what will his second advent be like? Can any sinner even stand to think of it? "He will strike the earth with the rod of his mouth; with the breath of his lips he will slay the wicked" (Isaiah 11:4). In the garden, Jesus merely said, "I am he," and the soldiers fell backward (John 18:6). How will his enemies react when he fully reveals himself as the great "I Am"? His death shook earth and darkened heaven—what will the day be like when the living Savior summons the living and dead before him?

Why don't these future terrors persuade people to forsake their sins and "kiss the Son, lest he be angry" (Psalm 2:12)? He is the sacrificial Lamb, but he is also the Lion of Judah, tearing his prey in pieces (Revelation 5:5). None of his enemies will be able to withstand the storm of his wrath.

Yet his beloved, blood-washed people look forward with joy to his appearing. Let us examine ourselves this morning and reassure ourselves of our place among his people, so that his coming will not worry us in the least.

October 16

Jesus said to them, "Come and have breakfast."
(John 21:12)

With these words this morning, you are invited into a holy *nearness to Jesus*. Jesus invites you to his table, to share his food, perhaps to sit by his side, or to lay your head on his chest. These words welcome you into his banquet hall, under the banner of his redeeming love (Song of Songs 2:4).

This invitation also speaks of an even closer *union with Jesus*, because the only food we can feast on when we're with Jesus is Jesus himself. This goes beyond our understanding, but he has said, "Whoever eats my flesh and drinks my blood remains in me, and I in him" (John 6:56).

This also welcomes us into *fellowship with the saints*. Christians may differ on various points, but they share the same appetite. Even if we cannot all *feel* the same way, we can all *feed* the same way, on the bread of life. Get closer to Jesus, and you will find yourself linked more and more to other believers.

We also see in these words a *source of strength* for the Christian. To look at Christ is to live, but for strength to serve him, we must eat. Do you wonder why you are wearing yourself out in the Master's service? Maybe you're forgetting to eat properly. None of us needs to go on a diet, as far as Christ is concerned. On the contrary, we must fatten ourselves up, feasting on the gospel, in order to have maximum strength.

So do you want nearness to Christ, union with him, love for his people, and strength for his service? Then start today with a healthy breakfast—with Jesus himself.

October 17

But David thought to himself, "One of these days I will be destroyed by the hand of Saul." (1 Samuel 27:1)

This thought that David had was false. He certainly had no good reason to think that his own anointing by Samuel was intended as an empty promise. The Lord had never deserted him. He had often been placed in perilous positions, but in every instance God had delivered him. His trials had been varied—they came in many forms—yet the Lord always provided a way of escape. David could not put his finger on any entry in his diary and say, "Here is proof that the Lord will forsake me." His whole life had proven just the opposite!

David should have concluded, on the basis of what God had already done for him, that God would continue to defend him. That's easy for us to say, but don't we doubt God in the same way? Have we ever had the slightest reason to doubt our Father's goodness? Hasn't his mercy been consistently marvelous? Has he ever failed to justify our trust in him? No! Our God has never left us! We have had dark nights, but the star of his love shines through the darkness. We have gone through many trials, but they have always resulted in our benefit. We can safely conclude that if God has been with us in six troubles, he'll be with us in the seventh. All the evidence indicates that he will be with us to the end. How can we doubt this?

Lord, throw down the Jezebel of our unbelief, and let the dogs devour it.

October 18

Your carts overflow with abundance.
(Psalm 65:11)

What are these "carts" that overflow with good things for us? One special one is certainly the cart of prayer. If a believer frequents the prayer closet, he or she will never lack spiritual nourishment. Starving souls are the ones who live at a distance from God's mercy seat. They become like parched fields during a drought. But when you wrestle with God in prayer, you grow strong—even if the wrestling is sometimes difficult.

If you spend a great deal of time alone with Jesus in prayer, you will have a great deal of assurance. If you are seldom alone with Jesus, your faith will be shallow, polluted with doubts and fears, not sparkling with the joy of the Lord.

This overflowing cart of prayer can be driven by even the weakest saint. You don't need any advanced degree. All believers are invited for the ride. Take advantage of this opportunity. Make a habit of being on your knees. This is how Elijah drew the rain for Israel's famished fields (James 5:17–18).

But there's another cart that overflows with nourishment for the Christian—the cart of communion. How delightful it is to have fellowship with Jesus! Earth has no words to describe this holy sense of calm. There are even few Christians who understand it. They spend all their time in the valleys and seldom climb the mountain. They live in the outer court and never enter the holy place. Don't make that mistake, dear reader. Sit under the shadow of Jesus. Enjoy his presence, and you will be greatly satisfied.

October 19

Mere infants in Christ.
(1 Corinthians 3:1)

Do you feel that your spiritual life is weak? Does it bother you that your faith is small, your love feeble? Cheer up. You still have reason to be thankful. Remember that in some things you are equal to the most experienced, most full-grown Christian.

You are bought with the blood of Christ, just as much as the greatest saint is. You are just as much an adopted child of God. Think about it—a baby is just as truly a child of its parents as an adult is. You are just as completely justified, because justification doesn't happen in degrees. Even your small faith has made you thoroughly clean. You have just as much right to the promises in the covenant as the most advanced believer has. These promises depend not on your growth, but on the covenant itself. You are as rich as the richest Christian, even if you feel frustrated at the moment.

The smallest star that gleams in the night still has a place in the heavens. Its faint ray of light is one with the brilliance of the sun. In the family register of heaven, both small and great are written with the same pen. You are as dear to your Father's heart as anyone else in the family. Jesus feels very tender toward you. You may be a "bruised reed" (Isaiah 42:3) that anyone else would snap in two and throw away, but Jesus will never break you. Instead of feeling depressed about what you are, you should triumph in Christ. You may be poor in faith, but in Jesus you are the heir of all things.

October 20

In all things grow up into him.
(Ephesians 4:15)

Many Christians have stunted their growth in spiritual things. Every year, they're the same. There's no advance, no upspringing. They *exist*, but they do not *grow*. Jesus talked about how grain grows: "first the stalk, then the head, then the full kernel in the head" (Mark 4:28). Should we be content with being merely stalks when we could ripen and produce kernels for his glory? Should we be satisfied just believing in Christ—at least we are "safe"—and not longing to move more and more into his fullness? No! As good traders in heaven's market, we should keep trying to gain more of the knowledge of our Lord.

Why should it always be wintertime in our hearts? Granted, we must have time for planting, but we must move on into spring and a summer that gives the hint of an early harvest. To ripen in grace, we must live close to Jesus, in his presence, ripened by the sunshine of his smiles. We must hold sweet communion with him. We must never be satisfied with a distant view of his face. No, we must come close, as John did, and pillow our heads on his breast. Then we will find ourselves advancing in holiness, in love, in faith, in hope—in every precious gift.

The sun rises first on the mountaintops and spatters them with light, presenting the traveler with a very charming scene. But there is a similar beauty when we see the glow of the Spirit's light on the head of some saint who has grown and grown until he stands, spiritually, head and shoulders above his companions. Such a person reflects the beams of the Sun of Righteousness and glorifies the Father of lights.

October 21

For Christ's love compels us.
(2 Corinthians 5:14)

How much do you owe the Lord? Has he ever done anything for you? Has he forgiven your sins? Has he covered you with a robe of righteousness? Has he "set your feet on a rock" and given you "a firm place to stand" (Psalm 40:2)? Has he prepared heaven for you? Has he prepared you for heaven? Has he written your name in his book of life? Has he given you countless blessings? Has he prepared for you a supply of mercies that "no eye has seen, no ear has heard, no mind has conceived" (1 Corinthians 2:9)?

Then do something for Jesus that is worthy of his love. Don't just give some wordy offering to your dying Redeemer. How will you feel when your Master shows up and you have to confess that you did nothing for him, that you kept your love dammed up, like a stagnant pool?

Even human beings do not think much of a love that never shows itself. As the saying goes, "Open rebuke is better than secret love." Who wants to accept a love that does not motivate you to a single act of self-denial, generosity, or heroism?

Think of how *he* has loved you and given himself for you. Do you know the power of that love? Then let it be like a powerful wind sweeping through your soul, blowing away the clouds of worldliness and the mists of sin. "For Christ's sake"—let that be the "tongue of fire" that lights upon your head. "For Christ's sake"—let that be the force that lifts you from earth, making you bold as a lion and swift as an eagle in your Lord's service. Love should give wings to feet that serve him. Fix your heart on God with a steadfast confidence, and honor him with acts of heartfelt devotion.

October 22

I will . . . love them freely.
(Hosea 14:4)

This simple sentence is a powerful theology lesson. The one who understands it fully is a true master of divinity. It capsulizes the glorious message of salvation that was given to us by Jesus Christ our Redeemer.

The sense of this verse hinges on the word "freely." This is the glorious way that love streams from heaven to earth, a spontaneous love flowing forth to those who don't deserve it, can't afford it, and don't seek it. It is, in fact, the only way God can love us, considering how sinful we are.

This text deals a deathblow to any idea that we can earn God's favor. "I will love them *freely*," he says. Now if there were any way that we earned his love, that would diminish the freeness of it. But it stands: "I will love you freely."

"But Lord," we protest, "my heart is so hard."

"*I will love you freely*."

"But I don't even feel that I need Christ as much as I should."

"*I will love you, not on the basis of what you feel, but freely.*"

"But I don't feel that my spirit is softened and made sensitive to you."

"*I will love you freely*."

Remember, there are no conditions to the covenant of grace. We can set foot on the promise of God and stand secure. Isn't it great to know that God's grace is utterly free to us—without preparation, without our merit, without money, and without price?

The text is urging backsliders to return. "I will heal their waywardness," he says, "and love them freely."

October 23

You do not want to leave too, do you?
(John 6:67)

Many have forsaken Christ and have stopped walking with him. But what reason could *you* have to make such a change?

Has there been any reason from the *past* that would make you do this? Hasn't Jesus always proved himself sufficient for your needs? When you have simply trusted Jesus, have you ever been let down? Haven't you always found Jesus to be a compassionate and generous friend? Hasn't he given you peace? Can you dream of anyone who would be a better friend? Then why exchange the tried and true for a new and false?

Is there anything in the *present* that would make you leave Christ? When this world is especially troubling, we find it very relaxing to rest upon our Savior. We have the joy of salvation—why give that up? Who trades gold for mud? We will never give up the sun until we find a better light, and we'll never leave our Lord until a brighter lover appears. And that will never happen.

As for the *future*, can you imagine anything that might arise that would make it necessary to mutiny?

I don't think so. If we are poor, Christ enriches us. If we are sick, Jesus makes our bed. Who could want anything more? And even when we die, "neither death nor life, . . . neither the present nor the future, . . . will be able to separate us from the love of God that is in Christ Jesus our Lord" (Romans 8:38–39). We say with Peter, "Lord, to whom shall we go?" (John 6:68).

October 24

The trees of the Lord are well watered.
(Psalm 104:16)

Without water, the tree cannot flourish—or even exist. In the same way, *vitality* is essential to a Christian.

There must be *life*—the vital force infused into us by God's Holy Spirit. It is not enough to bear the name *Christian*: We must be filled with the spirit of divine life.

This life is *mysterious*. We cannot see how the tree's roots take in the water and circulate it, generating sap that rises through the trunk and out to the branches. In the same way, the spiritual life within us is a sacred mystery. Regeneration is a miracle of the Holy Spirit, entering into a person and becoming his life. This divine life feeds on the flesh and blood of Jesus and thrives on a daily interaction with him, but where this life force comes from and where it's going, we don't know (John 3:8). The roots of the tree suck up the water underground, shrouded in darkness. Our root is Christ Jesus, and our life is hidden in him.

But consider how *constantly active* the moisture is within the tree. Similarly, the Christian life is full of energy, not always bearing fruit, but often in inner growth. The believer's character is always developing, becoming more like Christ.

With the tree, the water *eventually produces fruit*. So it is with a truly healthy Christian. The work of the Spirit can be seen in how he walks and talks. He can't help but tell you about Jesus. If you observe his actions, you will note that he has been with Jesus (Acts 4:13). There is so much of the life-giving Spirit within, that his whole being vibrates with divine power.

October 25

Because of the truth, which lives in us and will be with us forever. (2 John 2)

Once the truth of God enters the human heart and gets control of a person, nothing can dislodge it. We entertain it not as a guest, but as the master of our house. This is an essential part of the gospel. Those who know the power of the Holy Spirit—opening the Word, applying it to our lives and sealing it there—would rather be torn in pieces than to be torn away from the gospel. A thousand mercies are wrapped up in this assurance: The truth will be with us forever. It will be our support as long as we live and our comfort as we die. It will be a song in our hearts and our glory through all eternity.

This is one of the great blessings of being a Christian. Without God's truth, our faith is worth little. Some truths we grow out of—they are merely basics for beginners. But God's truth is not like that. Yes, it is sweet food for babies, but it is also nourishing food for the strongest adults. It is painful to acknowledge the truth that we are sinners, but it is exciting to realize the truth that whoever believes on Jesus will be saved.

Our experience hasn't loosened our grip on the doctrines of grace. On the contrary! It has knit us even tighter to these truths. We now have even more reason to believe than ever before, and we expect that we will keep learning more reasons until the Savior himself holds us in his heavenly arms.

As our love for God's truth grows, we grow in love as well. Our compassion goes beyond boundaries. The truth we receive is sometimes mixed with error—we must oppose the error, but we still strive to love the brother who is erring. There is still a measure of truth in him that we can affirm.

October 26

"You expected much, but see, it turned out to be little. What you brought home, I blew away. Why?" declares the Lord Almighty. "Because of my house, which remains a ruin, while each of you is busy with his own house." (Haggai 1:9)

Stingy people cut back their contributions to church ministry and missionary support, and they call such saving "good economy." Little do they know that they are impoverishing themselves. Their excuse is that they *must* care for their own families, but they forget that neglecting the house of God is a sure way to bring ruin on their own houses. God is able to make our efforts succeed beyond our expectations or fail dismally. By a turn of his hand, he can steer us toward profit or bankruptcy.

Scripture teaches that the Lord enriches the one who gives freely and allows the miser to discover the sad result of his penny-pinching. I have noticed that the most generous Christians I have met have always been the happiest—and almost always the most prosperous. I have also seen stingy souls fall into poverty from the very "economy" they thought would help them.

If a broker invests your money well, you will give him more money to invest. God treats us the same way. If we give out bushels, he gives us cartfuls. Even when he does not give us material wealth, he fills us with contentment.

Selfishness looks first to its own house, but godliness seeks first the kingdom of God and his righteousness (Matthew 6:33). In the long run, selfishness is loss, and godliness is great gain (1 Timothy 6:6). It takes faith to be so generous, but surely the Lord deserves it.

October 27

Here is a trustworthy saying.
(2 Timothy 2:11)

Paul has four of these "trustworthy sayings." The first occurs in 1 Timothy 1:15—"Here is a trustworthy saying that deserves full acceptance: Christ Jesus came into the world to save sinners."

The next is in 1 Timothy 4:8—"godliness has value for all things, holding promise for both the present life and the life to come. This is a trustworthy saying that deserves full acceptance."

The third comes in 2 Timothy 2:12—"if we endure, we will also reign with him."

And the fourth is in Titus 3:7–8—"having been justified by his grace, we might become heirs having the hope of eternal life. This is a trustworthy saying. And I want you to stress these things, so that those who have trusted in God may be careful to devote themselves to doing what is good."

We may trace a connection between these sayings. The first lays the foundation of our eternal salvation in the free grace of God, as shown to us in Jesus' mission. The next affirms the double blessing we get through this salvation—present and in the life to come. The third shows us our duties as God's chosen people. Among them is the call to suffer for Christ's sake. The last one sends us off into Christian service, making sure we do "what is good."

Treasure these trustworthy sayings. Let them guide your life, comfort you, and teach you. The apostle found them trustworthy and they are trustworthy still. They deserve full acceptance. Let them be written on the four corners of your house.

October 28

I have chosen you out of the world.
(John 15:19)

Some of us are the special objects of divine affection. Don't be afraid to dwell on this doctrine of election. When you get depressed, this is a refreshing thing to think about. Those who doubt the doctrines of grace or prefer not to consider them are missing the choicest clusters of God's vineyard. Nothing compares to them. If the honey Jonathan found in the woods brightened his eyes (1 Samuel 14:27), this is honey that brightens the heart—to love and learn the mysteries of God's kingdom. Eat up, and don't worry about eating too much. Feast on this delicate morsel and don't think that it won't be enough for you. The food from the King's table is very filling.

Seek to enlarge your mind, so that you can comprehend more and more of the eternal love of God. When you have climbed the mountain of the doctrine of election, vault over to that other mountain, the covenant of grace. God's covenant is our protection, our assurance, our place of rest. When everything else on earth fails us, we can still rest on his unchanging grace.

Consider this: If Jesus himself promises to bring you to glory, and if the Father himself promised to give you to the Son as part of his infinite reward, what can happen to you? Unless God himself is unfaithful, or unless Jesus goes back on his promise, you are utterly safe.

When David danced before the ark of God, he explained to his complaining queen that election made him do it (2 Samuel 6:21). God had chosen him, and he rejoiced. So come, exult before the God of grace and leap with joy—because he has chosen you.

October 29

This, then, is how you should pray: "Our Father in heaven."
(Matthew 6:9)

This prayer begins where all true prayer starts, with the spirit of *adoption*: "Our Father." No prayer is acceptable unless it is in the spirit of "I will set out and go back to my father" (Luke 15:18).

But then the childlike soul begins to understand the grandeur of the Father "in heaven" and ascends into *heartfelt adoration*: "hallowed be your name." The child who lisps, "Abba, Father," grows into the cherub who sings, "Holy, holy, holy."

There is only a small step from adoring worship to a *glowing missionary spirit*: "your kingdom come, your will be done on earth as it is in heaven."

Next follows an *expression of dependence* on God: "Give us today our daily bread."

As you are illuminated by the Spirit, you realize that you are not only dependent but also sinful, so you *beg for mercy*: "Forgive us our debts as we also have forgiven our debtors."

Then once you are forgiven, with the righteousness of Christ credited to your account, knowing that you are accepted by God, you *ask for strength*: "Lead us not into temptation." The person who is truly forgiven is anxious not to sin again. Awareness of justification leads to a desire for sanctification. "Forgive us our debts"—that is justification. "Lead us not into temptation, but deliver us from the evil one"—that is sanctification in both positive and negative forms.

Finally, as a result of all this, there is *triumphant praise*: "for yours is the kingdom and the power and the glory forever." We rejoice that our King reigns and will continue to reign in grace.

October 30

I will praise you, O Lord.
(Psalm 9:1)

Praise should always follow answered prayer—just as the mist rises with earth's gratitude when the sun warms the ground. Has the Lord been gracious to you? Has he heard your prayer? Then praise him as long as you live. Let the ripe fruit drop onto the fertile soil that gave it life to begin with.

To be silent over God's mercies is to be guilty of ingratitude. In that case, you are like the nine lepers, cured of their leprosy, who did not return to thank the healing Lord. To forget to praise God is to neglect a great benefit for ourselves. Praise, like prayer, is one great way to develop our own spiritual life. It removes our burdens, excites our hope, increases our faith. It is an invigorating exercise that quickens our pulse and prepares us for new ways of serving God.

Blessing God for the mercies we have received can also benefit those around us. Others who have been in similar situations can be comforted if we say, "Glorify the Lord with me; let us exalt his name together. . . . This poor man called, and the Lord heard him" (Psalm 34:3, 6). Weak hearts will be strengthened. Dreary saints will be revived when they hear our songs of deliverance. Their doubts and fears will be challenged, as we "speak to one another with psalms, hymns and spiritual songs" (Ephesians 5:19). They will join our song.

Praise is the most heavenly of Christian duties. The angels do not pray, but they never stop praising, night and day. And the redeemed, clothed in white robes, waving palm branches, never grow weary of singing their anthem of praise: "Worthy is the Lamb."

October 31

Renew a steadfast spirit within me.
(Psalm 51:10)

When a backslider is restored, the experience is similar to the original conversion. Repentance is required. We needed God's grace to come to Christ at first, and we need it to come back to him. We longed for a word from God Almighty, a simple invitation of love to calm our fears. Now we need a new word of forgiveness to restore us.

No one can experience this renewal without the same burst of the Holy Spirit's energy that he felt at his conversion. The effort is just as great. Flesh and blood are once again in the way.

If you feel weak, my friend, let your weakness lead you to pray for help. Look at what David did when he felt powerless. He did not fold his arms or close his mouth, but he rushed to God's mercy seat and begged, "Renew a steadfast spirit within me." It is true that, by yourself, you can do nothing. But don't let that fact lull you to sleep. Let it push you toward the Helper of Israel. Plead with God for a new spirit.

If you sincerely pray to God about this, you are already proving your sincerity by relying on prayer. Prayer is the method God uses to achieve his results. So pray often. Dwell on God's Word. Kill the lusts that have driven the Lord out of your life. Guard against future uprisings of sin. The Lord will act in his way, at his time. Be ready. Sit by the roadside and wait for him to come by. Keep doing the things that nourish your spiritual life and keep praying David's prayer: "Renew a steadfast spirit within me."

November 1

The church that meets in your home.
(Philemon 2)

Is there a "church" in your home? Are parents, children, grandparents, boarders, visitors all part of it? Or are some of these still unconverted?

It would make a father's heart jump for joy and bring tears to a mother's eyes to know that all their children were saved. If this is not the case for your home, pray for God to grant this great mercy.

That was probably a great desire of Philemon, to have his entire household know the Lord, but it was not granted to him at first. His wicked servant, Onesimus, wronged him and ran away. But the master's prayers followed him, and ultimately, as God arranged the events, Onesimus happened to hear the preaching of Paul. The servant's heart was touched, and he returned to Philemon, not only as a now-faithful servant, but also as a brother in Christ. So another member was added to the church in Philemon's home.

Is there someone from your household or a friend of the family who needs to know Christ? Pray especially for that person this morning, that he or she would "return home," refreshing the hearts of all the saints (Philemon 7).

And if there is a "church" in your home, make sure it is well-ordered. We should all be moving through our activities with holiness, diligence, kindness, and integrity. You see, more is expected of a church than a mere household. Family worship must be more devout and exciting. Love within the home must be warm and unbroken. And our external conduct must be more Christlike. Let's trust Christ to give us grace to shine before others with his glory.

November 2

I the Lord do not change.
(Malachi 3:6)

Despite all the changes in the world around us, there is One who never changes. Life is variable in every aspect, it seems, but there is One whose heart is fixed. The sun itself grows dim with age. The world gets old. This is just the beginning of the "folding up" of the worn-out robe. The heavens and earth will soon pass away. But there is One who is immortal, whose years go on and on, and whose personality is constant.

Think of the delight a sailor feels when, after being tossed by the sea for days, he sets foot again on the solid shore. This is the delight a Christian feels when, amid all the changes of this trying life, he rests again on this truth: "I the Lord do not change."

This is the stability that an anchor gives a ship. It is the basis for Christian hope. God "does not change like shifting shadows" (James 1:17). Whatever his character has been in the past, it still is now. His power, his wisdom, his justice, and his truth—all are unchanged. He has always been a refuge for his people, their stronghold in the day of trouble, and he will continue to be their strong helper.

And his love never changes. He loves his people "with an everlasting love" (Jeremiah 31:3). He loves us now as much as he ever did. When all earthly things have melted in the final fire of judgment, his love will still be fresh and new. This gives us precious assurance. The wheel of providence may revolve, but its axle is eternal love.

November 3

For he is praying.
(Acts 9:11)

Prayers are instantly noticed in heaven. The moment Saul began to pray, the Lord heard him. Here is comfort for the distressed (but praying) soul. Often a brokenhearted person will get on his knees but can only utter his plea in the language of sighs and tears. Yet that groan makes all the harps of heaven vibrate with music. The tear is caught by God and treasured—the psalmist pictured God putting his tears in a bottle (Psalm 56:8). Tears are the diamonds of heaven. Sighs are part of the music of God's court. Even though the one who prays this way may find his words choked off by fear and grief, he is still understood by the Lord. Do not think that your prayer, even weak and trembling, will go unnoticed. Jacob's ladder is steep, but our prayers attach themselves to the angel of the covenant, who climbs swiftly.

Not only does God hear our prayers, but he *loves* to hear them. "He does not ignore the cry of the afflicted" (Psalm 9:12). He does not care for pompous looks and pretentious words. He does not go for the pageantry of kings. He does not listen for a marching band accompanying some victory parade. He does not pay attention to proud prayers.

But wherever there is a heart bursting with sorrow or a lip quivering with pain or a deep groan or a repentant sigh—then the heart of Yahweh is open. He puts our prayers, like rose petals, between the pages of his book of remembrance. When the book is finally opened, a precious fragrance will spring up from it.

November 4

My power is made perfect in weakness.
(2 Corinthians 12:9)

A primary qualification for success in serving God is a sense of our own weakness. When God's warrior marches out to battle, strong in his own power, defeat is not far away. God does not go along with anyone who marches in his own strength. The one who figures he will win on his own figures wrongly, for it is "'not by might nor by power, but by my Spirit,' says the Lord Almighty" (Zechariah 4:6). Those who go out to fight boasting in their own ability will return with their flags trailing in the dust and their armor stained with disgrace.

Those who serve God must serve him in God's way, in God's strength, or he will not accept their service. Whatever man does without God's help, God can never claim as his own. He throws away the fruit of the earth—he wants only the grain that grows from the seed sown from heaven, watered by grace and ripened by the sun of divine love.

God will empty out everything that's in you before he fills you with himself. He must clean out the silo before he fills it with his fine grain. The river of God is full of water, but not one drop of it flows from earthly springs.

Are you bothered by your own weakness? Take courage, because there must be an awareness of weakness before the Lord gives you victory. Your emptiness is just the preparation for being filled.

November 5

No weapon forged against you will prevail.
(Isaiah 54:17)

The history of the church is full of examples of weapons forged against God's people. At first, the early Christians in Judea had to withstand opposition from their fellow Jews. King Herod, possibly intending to gain favor among his subjects, "had James, the brother of John, put to death with the sword" (Acts 12:2). But soon it was Rome that took up the sword against believers. For about 250 years, the Roman Empire had Christians arrested, tortured, and killed in savage ways.

But even these horrendous methods did not prevail against Christ's church. "Take heart!" Jesus said. "I have overcome the world" (John 16:33). That promise has often been claimed by persecuted saints. Christianity emerged as the official religion of the empire, outlasting its attackers.

In the following years, new weapons were forged, weapons of false teaching. The apostles had warned that many would attempt to pervert Christ's teaching, and that has continued to happen throughout history. But those weapons have not prevailed either. God's truth goes on.

At some times, Christians who have tried to reform the church have been viciously opposed by the church itself. Weapons of tradition and authority can be especially potent. But these weapons, in their various degrees, failed to put down the Protestant movement or the Methodist movement or the Baptist movement, and the church has been greatly enriched by all of these.

"We have heard without ears, O God; our fathers have told us what you did in their days, in days long ago" (Psalm 44:1). Let us praise the Lord today that he has delivered his people from the many weapons forged against them.

November 6

For I will pour water on the thirsty land.
(Isaiah 44:3)

When a believer falls into a depressed state, he sometimes tries to lift himself out of it by scolding himself. This is not the way to rise from the dust—it just keeps you down there. You might as well chain the eagle's wings and expect it to fly.

It is not the law that saves us, but the good news of the gospel. That's what restores us when we sink into sadness. It is not fear that brings the backslider back to God, but the sweet wooings of love.

Are you thirsting this morning for the living God? Are you depressed because the delight of God is missing from your heart? Have you lost the "joy of your salvation" (Psalm 51:12)? Are you becoming aware that you are barren, like the dry ground, that you are not bringing forth the fruit that God expects of you? Do you find that you are not as useful in the church or in the world as you would like to be?

Then here is exactly the promise you need: "I will pour water on the thirsty land." You *will* receive the grace you need; you will have plenty. As water refreshes the thirsty, so grace will gratify your desires. As water awakens the sleeping plants, so a fresh supply of grace will awaken you. As water swells the buds and makes fruit ripen, so will you become fruitful in the ways of God. Any good quality that there is in God's grace—you will enjoy it. All its riches will overflow to you. You will be drenched by grace. Have you ever seen fields flooded by bursting rivers? That is how you will be. The thirsty land will become springs of water.

November 7

See, I have engraved you on the palms of my hands.
(Isaiah 49:16)

There is an excitement in the word "see." It presents a way out of the doubting cry of verse 14: "But Zion said, 'The Lord has forsaken me, the Lord has forgotten me.'"

The Lord seems to be amazed at this unbelief. When you think about it, what can be more absurd than the doubts and fears of God's favored people? It should make us blush to hear the Lord's loving rebuke: "How can I forget you? I have engraved you on my hands! How can you doubt the fact that I am *always* thinking of you, since my very flesh is a constant reminder."

What a strange thing unbelief is! We don't know what to marvel at more—the faithfulness of God or the unbelief of his people. He keeps his promise a thousand times, but the very next trial makes us doubt him. He never fails. He is never a dry well. He is never a setting sun, a shooting star, or a dissipating vapor. But we are constantly vexed with anxieties, disturbed by fears, as if God were just a mirage in the desert.

See! Look for yourselves! Here is the truth! We are engraved on his hands! All creation may marvel that rebels like us are given such a precious place. And note: He doesn't say he has engraved our *names*, but *us*, on the palms of his hands. Think of it! He has engraved your image, your circumstances, your sins, your temptations, your weaknesses, your wants, and your works—everything about you is on his hands. How could you ever think he has forgotten you?

November 8

As you received Jesus Christ as Lord.
(Colossians 2:6)

The life of faith is a *receiving*. This implies the very opposite of any idea that we could earn our salvation. It is just the accepting of a gift. As the earth drinks in the rain, as the sea takes in the streams, as night accepts light from the stars, so we partake freely of the grace of God. Saints are not wells or streams, but cisterns, into which living water flows. We are empty vessels into which God pours his salvation.

The idea of receiving implies a sense of *realization*, that is, making the matter a reality. You can't receive a shadow. You receive something substantial. So it is with our faith—Christ becomes real to us. As long as we are without faith, Jesus is a mere name to us—a person who lived a long time ago, a piece of history. But by an act of faith Jesus becomes a real person in our consciousness.

But receiving, of course, also means *grasping* or *getting possession of*. The thing I receive becomes my own. When I receive Jesus, he becomes *my* Savior, so much mine that neither life nor death can rob me of him.

Salvation may be described as the blind receiving sight, the deaf receiving hearing, the dead receiving life. But we have not only received these blessings, we have received *Christ Jesus himself*. It is true that he has given us much—life, pardon, and righteousness. These are all precious, but we have even more—Christ himself! The Son of God has been poured into us, and we have received him.

November 9

Continue to live in him.
(Colossians 2:6)

If we have received Christ into our innermost hearts, our new life will demonstrate our intimate acquaintance with him. The word for "live" in this verse, as elsewhere in the New Testament, is the word for "walk." The apostles pictured us walking through life *in Jesus*.

Walking implies *action*. Our religion shouldn't stay in a closet. We must carry it out. If a person "walks" in Christ, he acts as Christ would act. Since Christ is in him, he bears the image of Jesus. People will say, "He is just like his Master; he lives like Jesus."

Walking also signifies *progress*. Keep moving forward until you reach the ultimate level of the knowledge of our beloved Lord.

Walking means *continuance*. The New Testament also speaks of "abiding" or "remaining" in Christ (John 15). But how many Christians spend time with Christ in the morning or evening and then give their hearts to the world all day long? This is no way to live.

Walking also has to do with *habit*. You walk a certain way. Similarly, Christ must fill us to the point that he affects our instincts and he changes our habits. We must keep clinging to him. We must live and move and have our being in him. Yes, we received Christ as Lord—he entered our lives through no merit of our own. But now we must "walk" *in him*.

November 10

The eternal God is your refuge.
(Deuteronomy 33:27)

The word "refuge" may also be translated "mansion" or "home," which yields a great new thought. *God is our home*. This is a sweet image for most of us. Home is precious, even if it's a humble cottage. Yet God is even more dear to us than that.

At home we *feel safe*. We shut out the rest of the world and rest in quiet security. In the same way, when we are with God, we "fear no evil" (Psalm 23:4). He is our shelter and retreat.

At home we *rest*. After the labor of the day, we go home and relax. So our hearts find rest with God after we get tired of life's conflicts.

At home, we *express ourselves freely*. We don't worry about being misunderstood or having our words misconstrued. Similarly, we can communicate freely with God, speaking of all our hidden desires. If "the Lord confides in those who fear him" (Psalm 25:14), they can certainly confide in him.

Home is also the place of our *greatest happiness*. And in God we find our deepest delight. Our joy in the Lord surpasses all other joys.

We also *work for* our home. The thought of home and family gives us the motivation we need to work hard all day. In the same way, our love for God strengthens us. We think of his dear Son, and the image of his suffering face makes us work harder in his cause. There are others who need to know him, and we long to make our Father's heart glad by bringing home other wandering children. That will fill our heavenly home with joy.

November 11

Underneath are the everlasting arms.
(Deuteronomy 33:27)

God—the eternal God—is *our support* at all times, especially when we are sinking in some deep trouble or concern.

Sometimes a Christian sinks low in shame and humility. He has such a deep sense of his own sinfulness that he hardly knows how to pray. In his own eyes, he seems worthless. If that is your situation, child of God, remember that, even at your lowest, *still* "underneath are the everlasting arms." Sin may drag you down, but Christ's atonement still supports you.

On some occasions, a Christian will be sinking from an external trial. Every earthly support has been cut away. What then? Underneath are *still* the "everlasting arms." You cannot fall so far that God's gracious arms cannot reach you. You may even be sinking under internal struggles, but the everlasting arms are still embracing you. While the Lord is holding on to you like that, Satan can do nothing to harm you.

This assurance of support is a great comfort to those who are working hard in God's service. It implies a promise of strength for each day, grace for each need, and power for each duty. Even when death comes, the promise still holds true. As we approach the grave, we will be able to say with David, "I will fear no evil, for you are with me" (Psalm 23:4). We may descend into the grave, but that's as far as we'll go, because God's eternal arms keep us from falling farther. At every point of life—and even at its close—the everlasting arms are strong to save us, for "he will not grow tired or weary" (Isaiah 40:28).

November 12

So that your faith . . . may be proved genuine.
(1 Peter 1:7)

If faith is not tested, it may be true faith, but it will certainly be *small* faith. It will probably remain undersized until it is tested. Faith prospers most when things go against it. Storms are its teachers, and lightning just reveals its truths.

When the sea is utterly calm, it doesn't matter how you spread the sails, the sailing ship will not advance toward its port. But let the winds howl and let the waters churn, and—although it may rock and its deck be washed with waves and its mast may even creak from the pressure of the swelling sail—the vessel will make headway toward the harbor.

The loveliest flowers grow at the foot of the frozen glacier. The brightest stars shine in the polar sky. The sweetest water comes from springs in the desert. And no faith is as precious as the faith that triumphs through adversity.

Tested faith brings experience. How else will you learn your own weakness and the power of God to help you, unless you have to rely on his support to pass through the raging rivers? The more it is exercised, the firmer faith becomes. It grows in strength and intensity through trials.

This should not, however, discourage those who are young in the faith. You don't have to seek trials; they will come to you. And you will have plenty of them soon enough. But even if you can't claim the benefits of a lengthy experience of tested faith, thank God for the grace he gives you now.

November 13

No branch can bear fruit by itself.
(John 15:4)

How did you begin to bear fruit? It was when you came to Jesus, threw yourself on his great atonement, and rested on his righteousness. Remember those early days? Remember all the fruit you had then? Your vine was flourishing, the tender grapes appeared, the pomegranates were budding, and the beds of spices emitted their luscious odors.

But have you declined since then? If so, then think back on that special, loving time, repent, and return to those early ways.

The strategy is simple: Discover those activities that have drawn you closest to Christ, and spend time doing them. If you want to bear fruit, you have to stay close to him. So any activity that gets you close to him will help you bear fruit. Consider the role of the sun in creating fruit on the trees in the orchard. Jesus plays that role for the trees in his garden of grace.

Consider your own life. When have you lacked fruit? Hasn't it been when you lived farthest from Jesus, when you got lazy about your prayer life, when you left the simplicity of your faith, when you became cocky about your own righteousness and forgot where your true strength comes from?

Some of us have to learn the hard way that all good things come from Christ. We reach a point of utter barrenness in our own lives before we realize how weak we really are. Then we simply depend again on the grace of God; we wait on the Holy Spirit; and the fruit returns.

November 14

I will cut off from this place . . . those who bow down and swear by the Lord and who also swear by Molech. (Zephaniah 1:4–5)

Those people thought they were safe because they belonged to both parties. They worshiped with the followers of Yahweh, and they also bowed to Molech. But God hates such duplicity. He can't stand hypocrisy. The idolater who gives himself totally to his false god actually has one less sin than the one who offers his polluted sacrifice in God's temple, while his heart still plays with the world and its sins.

In the affairs of everyday life, a double-minded man is not respected, but in religion he is detestable. The penalty that God pronounces in today's text is substantial but well-deserved. How could a just God spare the sinner who knows what is right, approves it, and even claims to follow it, when at the same time he loves evil and lets that rule his heart?

My friend, search your own soul this morning. See whether you are guilty of double-dealing. You profess to be a follower of Jesus—do you really love him? Is your heart right with God? To have one foot on the land of truth and another on the sea of falsehood will lead to a major fall and total ruin. Christ will be all or nothing. God fills the whole universe, so there is no room left for any other god.

If he reigns in your heart, there will be no space left for another master. If you do find yourself double-minded this morning, ask God to forgive you, and pray, "Give me an undivided heart, that I may fear your name" (Psalm 86:11).

November 15

For the Lord's portion is his people.
(Deuteronomy 32:9)

In what way are his people "his"? First, *by his own sovereign choice*. He chose them. He decided to show them his love. He did this without seeing any goodness that they possessed at the time or would possess in the future. He had mercy on the ones he wanted to have mercy on (Exodus 33:19).

But God's people are not only his by choice, but also *by purchase*. He has bought and paid for them, so there can be no disputing his claim. He bought them not with perishable things like silver and gold, but with the precious blood of Jesus (1 Peter 1:18–19). There is no mortgage he has yet to pay off. No suit can be filed by other claimants. The price was paid in open court, and the church belongs to the Lord forever. The blood mark is on all his chosen ones, invisible to the human eye, but seen clearly by Christ. "The Lord knows who are his" (2 Timothy 2:19). He doesn't forget anyone he has redeemed. He counts all the sheep for whom he laid down his life.

The church is also his *by conquest*. He fought a great battle in our hearts. He laid siege to our souls, offering us treaty after treaty, but we barred the gates against him. Yet wasn't it a glorious moment when he stormed our hearts, placing his cross against the wall and scaling our ramparts, firmly planting his blood-red flag of mercy? Yes, we are the conquered captives of his omnipotent love. We have been chosen, bought, and won, and the Lord's rights to us are incontestable. So let us live each day to do his will and to show forth his glory.

November 16

I say to myself, "The Lord is my portion."
(Lamentations 3:24)

It is not, "The Lord is *partly* my portion." No, he makes up the sum total of my soul's inheritance. Within the circumference of that circle lies everything we possess or desire. The *Lord* is my portion. Not only his grace or his love or his covenant, but Yahweh himself. He has chosen us as his portion, and we have chosen him as ours. It is true that his choosing comes first, but if we are truly chosen by him, then we choose him in return.

The Lord is our *all-sufficient* portion. God is complete in himself. If he is all-sufficient for himself, he must be all-sufficient for us. It is not easy to satisfy all of a person's desires. We may dream that we are satisfied, but then we wake up to the thought that there is something more that we need, something beyond, and our hearts cry out for it.

But when the Lord is our portion, our attitude is completely different. We say, "Whom have I in heaven but you? And earth has nothing I desire besides you" (Psalm 73:25). We delight in the Lord, who lets us drink freely from the river of his pleasures. Our faith stretches its wings and rises like an eagle to the heavenly nest of divine love. "The boundary lines have fallen for me in pleasant places," said the psalmist. "Surely I have a delightful inheritance" (Psalm 16:6). We can say the same thing about our "portion," the Lord himself. Let us rejoice in him, showing the world how much God has blessed us, so that they reply, "Let us go with you, because we have heard that God is with you" (Zechariah 8:23).

November 17

To him be the glory forever! Amen.
(Romans 11:36)

This should be the greatest desire of any Christian. All other wishes must give way to this one. The Christian may want prosperity in business, but only as long as it helps him promote God's glory. He may want to improve his character, but only for the purpose of giving God glory. You should not be driven by any other motivation. As a Christian, you are "from" God and "through" God—so live your life "to" God as well. Don't let anything make your heart beat as strongly as your love for God does. Let this be your ambition, the foundation of every enterprise you undertake. Make God your *only* object. Depend on this. Where self begins, sorrow begins. Let God be your sole delight.

Your desire for God's glory should be a *growing* desire. In your youth, you praised him. But don't be content with that. If God has allowed you to prosper in business, give him more (since he has given you more). If God has enriched you with experience, then praise him with a stronger faith than you had at first. Have you gained knowledge over the years? Then you can sing his praises even more sweetly. If you have enjoyed happy times, if you have been healed from sickness, if your sorrow has been turned to joy, then you can build your music; let it swell with glory for God. Put more coals and incense into the censer of your praise. And put the "Amen" on this doxology by serving him and living in holiness.

November 18

A spring enclosed, a sealed fountain.
(Song of Songs 4:12)

This metaphor can apply to the inner life of the believer. First, we find the idea of *secrecy*. It is a spring *enclosed*. In biblical times there were springs that had buildings constructed over them, so that no one could get to them except those who knew the secret entrance. So is the heart of the believer, when it has been renewed by God's grace. There is a mysterious life within that no other human can touch. It is a secret, so secret that you can't even talk about it with a friend.

Today's text speaks not only of secrecy, but also of *separation*. This is not the community spring, which everyone can drink from. It is set apart from the others. It bears a unique mark, a king's royal seal, so that everyone knows that it is special. So it is with the spiritual life. Those whom God has chosen have been set apart. They have a spiritual life that others lack. It is impossible for them to feel at home in the world or to delight in its pleasures.

We also find a sense of *sacredness*. The spring is preserved for the use of some special person, just like the Christian's heart. It is a spring kept for Jesus. Every Christian should feel that he has God's seal on him.

The enclosed spring also has *security* and so does the believer. Even if all the powers of earth and hell join forces against us, they cannot harm us. For God is our protector.

November 19

But avoid foolish controversies.
(Titus 3:9)

It is better to spend our time doing good than arguing about things that are, at best, of minor importance. Scholars have wasted a great deal of time with their endless discussions of subjects that have no practical value. Our churches have suffered greatly from petty battles over obscure points and trivial questions.

After everything has been said that can be said, neither party in the debate is any wiser, and the discussion does not promote knowledge. It certainly doesn't promote love. What good is it? It is foolish to sow seed in such a barren field. Wise believers avoid questions on points where Scripture is silent, on mysteries that belong to God alone, on prophecies of doubtful interpretation, and on methods of observing human rituals. It is not our business to ask or answer foolish questions. If we follow the apostle's advice and devote ourselves to doing what is good (Titus 3:8), we won't have time to take any interest in insignificant and contentious debates.

There are, however, some questions that are the opposite of foolish. We must not avoid these, but confront them fairly and honestly: Do I believe in the Lord Jesus Christ? Am I renewed in the spirit of my mind (Romans 12:2)? Am I keeping in step with the Spirit (Galatians 5:25)? Am I growing in grace? Do I conduct myself in a manner worthy of the gospel of Christ (Philippians 1:27)? Am I looking for Christ's coming? What more can I do for Jesus? Questions like these urgently demand our attention.

November 20

O Lord, you took up my case.
(Lamentations 3:58)

Notice how positively the prophet speaks. He does not say, "I *hope*, I *trust*, I *sometimes think*, that God has taken up my case." No, he speaks of it as something that cannot be disputed. In the same way, we must shake off our doubts and fears. Let us get rid of the harsh voice of suspicion and second-guessing and pray with the clear, musical voice of assurance: "Lord, you took up my case."

See how gratefully the prophet speaks, giving all the glory to God alone. He doesn't say a thing about the case, about its merits. He doesn't credit any human effort with his redemption. No, it's "*you* took up my case; *you* redeemed my life." We should always be cultivating a grateful spirit. Whenever God helps us, we should prepare a song of thanks. Earth should be a temple filled with grateful anthems from God's saints, and every day should be a censer smoking with the sweet incense of thanksgiving.

How *joyful* Jeremiah seems to be when he writes of the Lord's mercy! He has been in the miry pit—we think of him as the "weeping prophet"—yet in this book of Lamentations he sings a song of victory. It's as clear as the music of Miriam, shaking her tambourine, or the song of Deborah, celebrating her triumph.

Children of God, seek to have a vital experience of the Lord's mercy. When you have it, speak positively of it, sing gratefully, and shout triumphantly.

November 21

And do not grieve the Holy Spirit.
(Ephesians 4:30)

All the believer has must come from Christ, but it comes only through the channel of the Holy Spirit. Just as all blessings come *to* you through the Spirit, so all good things that come *from* you are a result of the Spirit's sanctifying work in your life. No holy thought, devout worship, or grace-filled act can happen apart from the Spirit in you.

Do you want to speak for Jesus? You can't unless the Holy Spirit empowers your tongue. Do you want to pray? It would be sheer drudgery without the Spirit making intercession for you. Do you want to conquer sin in your life? Do you want to be holy? Do you want to live as Jesus did? Do you want to rise to greater levels of spirituality? Do you want to be filled, like the angels, with a passion for Christ's cause? You cannot do any of these things without the Spirit.

Child of God, you have no life in you apart from the life God gives through his Spirit. So do not grieve the Spirit or make him angry by sinning against him. Do not quench the Spirit by ignoring his whispers in your soul. Be ready to obey every suggestion he offers.

Since the Holy Spirit is so powerful, it doesn't make sense to try anything without him. Don't begin a project, carry on an enterprise, or conduct a transaction without seeking the Spirit's blessing. We must realize how weak we are without him and then depend entirely on his strength. This should be our prayer: "Open my heart and my whole being to let you come in. Support me with your powerful Spirit."

November 22

Israel served to get a wife, and to pay for her he tended sheep. (Hosea 12:12)

Jacob, arguing with Laban, described how hard he had worked: "I have been with you for twenty years now. . . . I did not bring you animals torn by wild beasts; I bore the loss myself. And you demanded payment from me for whatever was stolen by day or night. This was my situation: The heat consumed me in the daytime and the cold at night, and sleep fled from my eyes" (Genesis 31:38–40).

Our Savior's life on earth was even more difficult. He watched over all his sheep: "I have not lost one of those you gave me," he prayed (John 18:9). And sleep "fled" from his eyes as he wrestled in prayer all night for his people. One night Peter needed prayer; soon it would be someone else. If Jesus had chosen to complain, he could have moaned louder than any underappreciated shepherd. His service was more exacting than anyone's. Like Jacob, he did it in order to win his bride.

We can go further with this spiritual parallel of Laban and Jacob. Laban required Jacob to account for all the sheep. If any were killed by beasts, Jacob had to make up for it. If any died, Jacob had to pay. Wasn't Jesus in a similar position? He was under obligation to bring every believer safely into the Father's hand—even if it meant his death.

Take a good look at Jacob, and you'll see a picture of the Lord Jesus. "He tends his flock like a shepherd" (Isaiah 40:11).

November 23

Fellowship with him.
(1 John 1:6)

When we were united to Christ by faith, we were brought into fellowship with him. His interests and ours became mutual. Let's look more closely at these interests.

We have fellowship with Christ in his *love*. What he loves, we love. He loves his church—so do we. He loves sinners—so do we. He loves the poor, perishing human race, and he longs to see earth's deserts transformed into the garden of the Lord—and so do we.

We have fellowship with him in his *desires*. He desires God's glory—and we work toward the same goal. He wants believers to be with him, where he is—and we want to be there, too. He desires to drive out sin—and we are fighting under his banner. He wants his Father's name to be loved and adored by all his creatures—and we pray, "Your kingdom come, your will be done on earth as it is in heaven" (Matthew 6:10).

We also have fellowship with Christ in his *suffering*. We are not nailed to a cross, but we share the burden of prejudice that people have against him. This is actually a privilege for us, to be blamed for his sake.

We also share Christ's *work*, ministering to people with words of truth and deeds of love. We share Christ's *joys*. We are happy when he is happy. Have you ever experienced that joy? There is no purer delight on earth than to have Christ's joy fulfilled in us.

Finally, his *glory* will complete our fellowship. We, the church, will sit with him, upon his throne.

November 24

There the Lord will be our Mighty One. It will be like a place of broad rivers and streams. (Isaiah 33:21)

Broad rivers and streams produce fertile ground and abundant crops. That is what God does for his church. With God, the church has *abundance*. Is there anything the church could ask for that the Lord would not give her? He promises to supply all our needs. "On this mountain the Lord Almighty will prepare a feast of rich food for all peoples" (Isaiah 25:6).

Do you crave the bread of life? It drops like manna from the sky. Do you thirst for refreshing streams? The rock that brings forth water is right in front of you—that Rock is Christ. If you are in need, it is your own fault.

Broad rivers and streams also bring about *commerce*. Our glorious Lord opens a place of heavenly merchandising for us. Through our Redeemer, we have commerce with the past—the wealth of Calvary, the treasures of the covenant, the riches of our election, the stores of eternity—all these come down the broad stream of our gracious Lord. We also do business with the future. Barges from the millennium float down the river, bearing visions of glorious days to come. Through our Lord we have commerce with angels; we commune with the bright spirits, washed in blood, who sing before the throne; and better yet, we have fellowship with the Infinite One.

Broad rivers and streams especially denote *security*. In ancient days, rivers were a defense. What a defense the Lord is for his church! Satan may try to invade, but he cannot cross this broad river of God.

November 25

To proclaim freedom for the prisoners.
(Luke 4:18)

No one but Jesus can offer freedom to prisoners. True freedom comes only from him.

It is a freedom *righteously granted*. The Son, heir of all things, has the right to make people free. Our salvation occurs within the perfect justice of God.

Our freedom has been *expensive to purchase*. Christ proclaims freedom with his powerful word, but he bought it with his blood. He won our freedom with his chains. We go free because he took our punishment. We have liberty because he faced suffering in our place.

But although it has been costly, our freedom is *freely given*. Jesus asks nothing from us. He finds us sitting in sackcloth and ashes and invites us to put on the beautiful clothes of liberty. He saves us just as we are, without any merit on our part.

When Jesus sets us free, our freedom is *eternally secure*. No chains can bind us again. Once Jesus says, "Captive, I have released you!" it is done. Satan may plot to enslave us again, but the Lord is on our side! Who is there to fear?

The world may try to trap us with temptations, but our Lord is mightier than our opponents. The workings of our own deceitful hearts may harass and annoy us, but we are confident that he who began a good work in us will carry it on to completion (Philippians 1:6).

So since we are free from the law, free from sin, let our freedom be *practically demonstrated* as we serve God in our daily lives with gratitude and delight.

November 26

Whatever your hand finds to do, do it with all your might.
(Ecclesiastes 9:10)

"Whatever your hand finds to do"—this refers to actions that are *possible*. There are many things that our hearts want to do that will never come about. That is fine, but if we want to be truly effective, we should not be content with talking about the schemes of our hearts. No, we must practically carry out "whatever our hands find to do." One good deed is worth more than a thousand brilliant theories.

We should not be waiting for great opportunities or for a different kind of work, but we should just do the things we "find to do" each day. We have no other time in which to live. The past is gone; the future has not yet arrived; we will never have any time but the present. So don't wait until your Christian experience has ripened into maturity—serve God *now*.

Don't fritter your life away thinking about what you intend to do tomorrow. Tomorrow's plans don't make up for today's idleness. No one ever served God by doing things "tomorrow." We honor Christ by what we do *today*. Whatever you do for Christ, throw your whole soul into it. Do not give Christ a little bit of half-hearted effort, done only now and then. When you serve him, do it with heart, soul, and strength (Mark 12:30).

But where is our "might" as Christians? Not in ourselves; we are nothing but weakness. Our might lies in the Lord, so let us seek his help. We should proceed with prayer and faith and seek his blessing in whatever our hands find to do.

November 27

Joshua the high priest standing before the angel of the Lord. (Zechariah 3:1)

In Joshua the high priest, we see a picture of every child of God who has been brought to God by the blood of Christ and taught to serve the Lord in holiness. Jesus has made us priests and kings unto God, and even here on earth we exercise the priesthood of holy living and devoted service.

But this high priest is described as "*standing* before the angel of the Lord," that is, standing to minister. This should be the position of every true believer. Every place is God's temple, and we can serve him just as well in our daily lives as in his house. We should always be ministering, offering the spiritual sacrifice of prayer and praise, and presenting ourselves as "living sacrifices."

Notice where Joshua stands—*before the angel of the Lord*. It is only through a mediator that we sinners can ever become God's priests. Our mediator is Jesus, the messenger of the covenant. I present what I have to him; he wraps my prayers in *his* prayers, and thus they are accepted. My praises become sweet when they are bundled up with myrrh, aloes, and cassia from Christ's garden. Sometimes I can bring him only tears, but he has wept, too. I put my tears, along with his, in his bottle. Even if I can only bring him groans and sighs, he will accept these, too, because he once was heartbroken and sighed heavily in his spirit.

Standing in him, I am accepted. All my polluted works are received because of Jesus. In him, they smell sweet.

November 28

It gave me great joy to have some brothers come and tell about your faithfulness to the truth and how you continue to walk in the truth. (3 John 3)

The truth was in Gaius, and Gaius was in the truth. If that first statement were not the case, the second would not be true either. If the second statement could not be said about him, then the first would be merely a pretense.

Truth must enter a soul, penetrate it, and saturate it, or else it does no good. A doctrine held as a matter of creed is like bread in your hand. It does not nourish you until you take it inside yourself. But once your heart begins to digest the true doctrine, it can sustain you and build you up. Truth must be a living force within us, an active energy, an indwelling reality, a part of the warp and woof of our beings. If it is *in us*, then we cannot do without it. A person may lose a garment or even one of his limbs, but his inner organs are vital and cannot be torn away without loss of life.

A Christian can die, but he cannot deny the truth. Now it is a rule of nature that the inside affects the outside, just as light shines from the center of a lantern through the glass. When the truth is kindled within us, its brightness soon beams forth in our external life and conversation. They say that some caterpillars spin cocoons of different colors, depending on the food they eat. So it is with us. The spiritual nourishment we take into ourselves colors the words and deeds that proceed from us. Walking in the truth, as Gaius did, involves a life of integrity, holiness, faithfulness, and simplicity—the natural products of the gospel of truth.

November 29

Do not go about spreading slander among your people. . . . Do not hate your brother in your heart. Rebuke your neighbor frankly so you will not share in his guilt."(Leviticus 19:16–17)

Slander contains a triple-action poison. It harms the teller, the hearer, and the person who is slandered. Whether the report is true or false, God's Word tells us not to spread it. The reputations of the Lord's people should be very precious in our sight. We should consider it shameful to help the devil dishonor the church and bring down the Lord's name.

Many people take a special delight in tearing down their fellow Christians, as if they were raising themselves up in the process. The wise sons of Noah put a cloak over their naked father; the foolish son who removed it earned a terrible curse. One of these days *you* may need understanding and silence from others, so give it cheerfully to those who need it now. This should be our general rule: "to slander no one, to be peaceable and considerate, and to show true humility toward all men" (Titus 3:2).

The Holy Spirit does allow us to stand up against sin. But this must be done face-to-face, not behind someone's back. Do we find this difficult? It can be. But we should emphasize the importance of a clear conscience. We would not want to become partners in our friend's sin by letting him continue in it. Hundreds have been saved from downfall by the timely, wise, and loving warnings of faithful believers.

November 30

Amaziah asked the man of God, "But what about the hundred talents I paid for these Israelite troops?" The man of God replied, "The Lord can give you much more than that." (2 Chronicles 25:9)

This seemed to be a very important matter to King Amaziah. Maybe you can understand that. Losing money is never pleasant, and even when it is a matter of principle, we often find ourselves unwilling to make that sacrifice. "Why lose money that could be used for good purposes? What will we do without it? I have a family to support!" All these things and a thousand more would tempt the Christian to forget his principles and go after money. When it's a matter of survival, the need for money can outweigh other doctrines.

But "The Lord can give you much more than that." Our Father holds the purse strings. What we lose for his sake he can repay a thousand times over (Luke 18:29–30). We must merely obey his will, and we can be sure that he will provide for us. Faithful believers know that an ounce of obedience is worth more than a ton of gold. God's smile and a dungeon are enough for the true believer. His frown and a palace would be hell. Let worse come to worst, let your fortune go. We cannot lose our real treasure, because that is deposited above, where Christ sits at God's right side. In the meantime, the Lord has bequeathed this earth to the meek (Matthew 5:5), and he will not withhold any good thing from those who live according to his principles (Psalm 84:11).

December 1

You made both summer and winter. (Psalm 74:17)

Let's begin this wintry month with God. The cold snows and piercing winds remind us that he keeps his covenant day and night. If he is true to his Word in the revolving of the seasons, he will certainly prove faithful in his dealings with his own beloved Son.

The winter of the soul is not a comfortable season at all. If you are going through it now, you know how distressing it can be. But this may comfort you: The Lord has made it. He sends the sharp blasts of adversity to nip the buds of expectation. He scatters the frost like ashes over the once-green meadows of our joy. He sends ice to freeze the streams of our delight. He does it all. He is the great Winter King, ruling in the realms of frost, so you cannot complain. Losses, crosses, depression, sickness, poverty, and a thousand other ills are all sent by the Lord. They come to us by his wise design. Frost kills dangerous insects and limits the spread of disease. Frost breaks up the earth and enriches the soil. In the same way, good things can result from our winters of affliction.

How great it is, on these cold days, to sit before a warm fire! We should appreciate our Lord in the same way. He is a constant source of warmth and comfort in our times of trouble. We should snuggle close to him, finding joy and peace in his presence. Let's wrap ourselves in the warm sweaters of his promises and then go out into the cold and continue our service for him.

December 2

All beautiful you are, my darling.
(Song of Songs 4:7)

The Lord's admiration for his church is wonderful. He describes her beauty in glowing terms. She is not merely "beautiful," but "*all* beautiful." He sees her in himself, washed in his atoning blood and clothed in his righteousness. No wonder he considers her beautiful! He sees his own perfection reflected in her. Holiness, glory, excellence—these are *his* robes that his lovely bride is wearing.

Notice, she is not simply "clean," or "well-proportioned." She is absolutely lovely and fair. She has real merit! Her deformities of sin have been removed. Through her Lord, she has gained a position of righteousness—and that makes her beautiful to behold.

Not only is the church lovely, she is *superlatively* lovely. The Lord calls her "most beautiful of women" (Song of Songs 5:9). Her excellence and worth cannot be rivaled by all the nobility and royalty of the world. If Jesus could exchange his chosen bride for any queen or empress or any angel of heaven, he would not do it, for he considers her the best of them all. Like the moon, she far outshines the stars.

This is no secret opinion he holds. He invites everyone to hear it. He has written it in his Word and he sounds it forth even now. One day, from his glorious throne, he will confirm it. "Come, you who are blessed by my Father," he will say (Matthew 25:34). That will be his solemn affirmation of the loveliness of his chosen bride.

December 3

There is no flaw in you.
(Song of Songs 4:7)

The Lord has just announced how beautiful his church is. Now he adds a precious negative: "there is no flaw in you." It is as if this Bridegroom thought that the cynical world might think he was only mentioning her good features and had left out her shortcomings. He answers this by declaring her thoroughly beautiful and free from any defect.

It might have been amazing enough to say that she was free from hideous scars or horrible deformities or deadly ulcers. But he goes beyond this. There is no flaw at all in her. It would have been wonderful enough to say that he would eventually get around to removing her flaws and blemishes. But he speaks as if it has already been done! This should bring us intense joy and delight!

Christ Jesus has no quarrel with his spouse. She often wanders from him, grieving his Holy Spirit, but he does not allow her faults to affect his love. He sometimes corrects her, but it is always in the tenderest way, with the kindest intentions. Even then, he calls her "my love." He does not remember our foolish errors. He does not harbor grudges. He forgives us, and he loves us just as much after we sin as he does beforehand. This is a good thing, because if he nursed grudges as we do, he would never speak to us. The fact is we sometimes hold grudges against *him*, blaming him for some slight turn of events. But our precious Husband knows our silly hearts too well to take offense at our bad manners.

December 4

I have many people in this city.
(Acts 18:10)

This should be a great motivation for us to take God's message to those around us. Among the people in your city—among the sinful, the degraded, the drunken—God has people whom he has chosen to save. When you take his Word to them, it means that God has chosen you to be the messenger of life to them. They must receive it, because God has chosen them to do so.

They may be unlikely candidates for the church *now*, but they have just as much a claim on Christ's redemption as any of the saints before God's throne. They are Christ's property, even if they are momentarily allied with the enemy. If Jesus Christ purchased them, he will have them. God will not forget the price his Son has paid. Tens of thousands of redeemed souls have not been regenerated yet, but they will be. And this spurs us on to reach them with God's enlivening Word.

Even beyond this, these ungodly people are being prayed for, before God's throne, by Christ himself. "My prayer is not for them alone," Jesus said. "I pray also *for those who will believe* through their message" (John 17:20, *italics added*). These souls are presently poor and ignorant. They don't know enough to pray for themselves, but Jesus prays for them. Before long they will bend their stubborn knees and breathe their repentant sighs before the throne of grace.

The chosen moment has not yet come for them. But when it comes, they will obey. They must, because the Spirit cannot be withstood when he operates in his full power. They *must* become willing servants of God.

December 5

Ask and it will be given to you.
(Matthew 7:7)

There is a place in England where a portion of bread is offered to every passerby who asks for it. Whoever the traveler may be, he only has to knock at the door, and he will be fed.

Jesus has established such a place. Whenever a sinner is hungry, he only needs to knock, and his needs will be supplied. In fact, he has done even more. In this place of his, there is also a bath. Whenever a soul is grimy and filthy, it can go there to be washed. The water is always flowing, and it always cleanses. Sins that were scarlet and crimson have disappeared; sinners have been washed whiter than snow (Isaiah 1:18).

As if this weren't enough, Jesus has added a great deal of closet space and filled it with clothing. The sinner merely needs to ask, and he will be clothed. If he wants to be a soldier, he will have armor, a sword, and a shield. Nothing that he needs will be denied. He will have spending money as long as he lives and a huge inheritance awaiting him in heaven.

All these things are to be had by merely knocking at mercy's door. Knock there this morning and ask for large things from your generous Lord. Do not leave the throne of grace until all your desires have been spread before the Lord. You don't need to be bashful. Don't let unbelief hinder you. Jesus invites you. Jesus has promised to bless you. Don't hold back.

December 6

As is the man from heaven, so also are those who are of heaven. (1 Corinthians 15:48)

The body of Christ is all of one nature. He is not at all like that monstrous image that Nebuchadnezzar dreamed about—head of gold, belly of brass, legs of iron, feet of clay. No, Christ's mystical body is no absurd combination of opposites. Its members were mortal, so Jesus died. Its head is immortal, and so the body is now immortal, too. As it is written: "Because I live, you also will live" (John 14:19). As our loving Head is, so is the body—chosen, accepted, living. If the head is pure gold, the body is, too—and *every member* of the body.

Pause for a moment and think about this. Isn't it amazing how Christ could humble himself to unite with such wretched souls as ours? Yet he lifts us into a glorious union with himself. We are so corrupt that death and decay are part of our nature. But in Christ we are born with a new nature—God becomes our "Abba," our Father; Christ is our beloved brother. You have seen how members of royal families tend to think highly of themselves. Well, we can do them one better. Our family is the most royal of all. Each one of us should be aware of our heritage; we should trace our lineage; we should take advantage of its privileges. We are one with Christ! In comparison, all earthly honors are empty.

December 7

He chose the lowly things of this world.
(1 Corinthians 1:28)

Walk the streets by moonlight, if you dare, and you will see sinners then. Go to the jail, walk down the row of cells, and see the men with hardened faces, men you would not like to meet at night—there are sinners there. Go to the juvenile reformatories and look at those who have displayed a bent toward wickedness at a young age, and you will see sinners there. Go to the primitive peoples across the seas, where tribalism and cannibalism reign, and you will see sinners there. Go wherever you want—you don't need to ransack the earth—sinners can be found everywhere, in every street of every city, town, village, and hamlet.

Jesus died for these people. Find me the grossest specimen of humanity; as long as he is human, there is hope, because Jesus came to seek and save *sinners*. In God's supreme love, he has chosen to turn some of the worst into the best. Pebbles of the brook become jewels for the crown, through God's grace. His redeeming love has invited many of the worst sinners to sit at the table of mercy. So there is always hope.

If you are reading this and do not know the grace of Jesus, I ask you not to turn away. Think about Jesus' love. See his tearful eyes, his bloody wounds. This is love that streams out for you—strong, faithful, pure, and lasting love. This love doesn't care where you have been or what you have done. Just trust in him, and you will be saved. Entrust your soul to him, and he will bring you into a glorious relationship with his Father.

December 8

Yet you have a few people in Sardis who have not soiled their clothes. They will walk with me, dressed in white, for they are worthy. (Revelation 3:4)

We may see this as *justification*. "They will walk with me, *dressed in white*." That is, they will enjoy a constant sense of being right with God. They will understand that the righteousness of Christ has been put on their account and that they have been washed, made whiter than the new-fallen snow.

This also refers to *joy and gladness*. White robes were festive garments for the Jews. Those who have not soiled their clothes will have bright faces; they will understand what the Preacher meant when he said, "Go, eat your food with gladness, and drink your wine with a joyful heart, for . . . God favors what you do. Always be clothed in white" (Ecclesiastes 9:7–8). The one who is accepted by God wears white clothing of joy and gladness, and walks in sweet fellowship with Jesus.

But why is there so much doubting, so much sadness? Because many believers soil their clothes with sin and lose the joy of their salvation.

But this promise also refers to *walking in white before the throne of God* (Revelation 7:9–17). Those who have not soiled their clothing here will certainly walk in white in heaven, where the white-robed hosts sing eternal hallelujahs to the Most High God. They will have unspeakable joy and a happiness they couldn't even dream of. They will have all this, not through their own merit, but by God's grace. They will walk with Christ in white, because he has made them worthy.

December 9

Therefore will the Lord wait that he may be gracious unto you. (Isaiah 30:18 KJV)

God often delays in answering prayer. We have several instances of this in Scripture. Jacob did not get a blessing from the angel until almost dawn—he had to wrestle all night for it (Genesis 32:24–32). The poor woman of Syrian Phoenicia did not receive an answer immediately—Jesus tested her first (Mark 7:24–30). Paul asked the Lord three times to remove his "thorn in the flesh" (2 Corinthians 12:7–8). His only answer was that God's grace would be sufficient for him.

If you have been knocking at the gate of mercy and have received no answer, do you want to know why the mighty Maker has not opened the door? Our Father has his own reasons for keeping us waiting. Sometimes it is to show his power and sovereignty. More often, the delay is to our advantage. You may be kept waiting so that your desires will grow stronger. God knows that this will happen, and he may want you to see your need even more clearly, so you will appreciate his mercy, when it does come, all the more.

There may also be something wrong in you that has to be removed before the Lord grants his joy. Maybe your view of the gospel is confused, or maybe you are relying too much on yourself, instead of trusting simply on Jesus.

Your prayers are all filed in heaven, and even if they are not answered immediately, they will not be forgotten. In a while, they will be answered. So don't lose hope. Keep praying.

December 10

And so we will be with the Lord forever.
(1 Thessalonians 4:17)

We can have occasional visits with Christ now, but oh, how short they are! One moment our eyes see him, and we rejoice with unspeakable joy, but then he withdraws from us again. He is like a deer that you might see in the mountains. He is there for a moment, but then he leaps away, gone to the land of spices, and he browses no longer among the lilies.

We look forward eagerly to the time when we will see him not at a distance, but face-to-face. He will not be like a tourist, lodging with us for the night, but he will be family, holding us close in his embrace.

In heaven, our fellowship will not be interrupted by sin or by worries. No tears will dim our eyes. No earthly business will distract us. We will have nothing hindering us from gazing forever on the Sun of Righteousness.

It is so sweet to see him, as we do, now and then—imagine what it will be like to be with him forever! Just to look at his blessed face, without a cloud in between us, never having to turn our eyes away to deal with the weary, woeful world—that will be a blessed time. May that day come quickly. Rise, O sun that will never set! We need not worry about the pain of death, because this sweet fellowship will make up for it. If dying means entering into uninterrupted communion with Jesus, then death truly is gain. That single, somber moment is swallowed up in eternal victory.

December 11

The one who calls you is faithful and he will do it.
(1 Thessalonians 5:24)

Heaven is a place where we will never sin. We will finally be able to stop watching out for our untiring enemy, because the tempter will not be around anymore to trip us up. The wicked will not trouble us, and we will be able to rest.

Heaven is the land of perfect holiness and complete security. But don't we on earth sometimes taste a bit of this security? God's Word teaches us that all who are united to the Lamb are safe. Those who have committed their souls to Christ's keeping will find that he will preserve them faithfully. Sustained by such a doctrine, we can enjoy security even on earth. This is not the same perfect security that will keep us free from every error, but it does spring from Jesus' promise that believers will never perish. We should often reflect on this great truth—the "perseverance of the saints." It should fill us with joy and make us glorify our faithful God.

I pray that God will convince you of your security in Christ. I pray that he will remind you that your name is engraved on his hands. I pray that you will hear him whisper, "So do not fear, for I am with you" (Isaiah 41:10). See Jesus as the Executor of the covenant. He is bound by his perfect honor to present you—even the weakest of his family—before God's throne. This thought should be a glorious one to nibble on, a tasty appetizer leading to the ultimate main course of heavenly joys. You can be sure it will happen, because he is faithful, "and he will do it."

December 12

His ways are eternal.
(Habakkuk 3:6)

Human ways are variable. But God's ways are eternal. Things that he has done he will do again. There are many reasons for this great truth.

The Lord's ways are *the result of wise deliberation*. He makes all things happen according to his own plans. Human action is often the hasty result of passion or fear and is frequently followed by regret. But nothing can take the Almighty by surprise. He has foreseen it all.

God's ways are *the outgrowth of his unchangeable character*. His glorious attributes are clearly seen in his actions. He is just, gracious, faithful, wise, tender—and his actions are distinguished by the same traits. All beings act according to their nature. When their natures change, their conduct varies, too. But God is constant; he "does not change like shifting shadows" (James 1:17). His ways will always be the same.

There is nothing else that can reverse God's actions, since they are *the expression of his irresistible might*. When Yahweh marches out to accomplish the salvation of his people, the mountains tremble, the ocean throws up its hands, and the sun and moon stand still. Who can keep him from doing what he wants?

But it is not only his might that gives stability; his ways are *the manifestation of the eternal principles of right*. Wrong breeds decay and comes to ruin. But truth and goodness have a vitality that never dissipates.

So go to God this morning with confidence. He is gracious to his people, and that will never change.

December 13

Salt without limit.
(Ezra 7:22)

Salt was used in every burnt offering made to the Lord. Due to its preserving and purifying properties, it became a symbol of God's grace in the soul. In that light, it is interesting that, when Xerxes gave salt to Ezra the priest, he set no limit on the quantity. Similarly, we can be quite sure that when the King of kings dispenses grace to his royal priests he does not cut short the supply. *We* may cut it short, for some reason, but God won't. The one who goes out to gather manna will find that he can have as much as he likes. There is no rationing here. Now some things in God's economy *are* limited. Vinegar and gall are given out in precise portions—never one drop too much. But there is no limit on the salt of grace.

Parents may need to lock away sweets from their children, but there's no need to restrict the salt. A person may have too much money, or too much honor, but he cannot have too much grace. More wealth brings more worry, but more grace brings more joy. Increased wisdom, said the Preacher, is increased sorrow, but to have God's gracious Spirit in overflowing proportions is to have fullness of joy.

So go to God's throne and get a large supply of heavenly salt. It will season your afflictions, preserve your heart, and kill your sins. You need a lot of it. Ask for it, and you'll get it.

December 14

They go from strength to strength.
(Psalm 84:7)

These words convey the idea of progress. Those who rely on the Lord get stronger and stronger as they walk in the Lord's way. Usually, as we walk, we go from strength to weakness. We start fresh, well-prepared for our journey, but pretty soon the road becomes rough, and the sun grows hot, and we sit down by the roadside to rest before plodding on. But the Christian pilgrim obtains a fresh supply of grace along the way. He is as energetic after years of hard travel and struggle as he was when he started. He may not be quite as buoyant or bubbly; he may not burn with the same fiery zeal; but when it comes to real power, he is stronger than he ever was. He travels on, perhaps more slowly, but far more surely.

There are some gray-haired veterans who are just as zealous now as they were in younger days, but that is not common. For many, their love grows cold and their sin increases—but that is their own fault. It does not disprove the promise we have: "Even youths grow tired and weary, and young men stumble and fall; but those who hope in the Lord will renew their strength. They will soar on wings like eagles; they will run and not grow weary, they will walk and not be faint" (Isaiah 40:30–31). Fretful souls sit down and worry about the future. "Oh, no," they say. "We go from trouble to trouble!" That may seem true, but it may also indicate that you are going from strength to strength. You will never find a bundle of trouble that does not have a nugget of grace wrapped up in it. God gives strength to match the troubles.

December 15

Then Orpah kissed her mother-in-law good-bye, but Ruth clung to her. (Ruth 1:14)

Both of these young women had affection for Naomi. Both of them started out with her on the way back to Judah. But then the test came. Naomi unselfishly presented them both with the struggles that awaited them. She warned them that if they wanted lives of ease and comfort they should turn back to Moab. At first, both of them declared that they would cast their lot with God's people. But after further consideration, Orpah made the difficult decision to leave her mother-in-law and return to her idolatrous countrymen. But Ruth devoted herself fully to Naomi, as well as Naomi's people and Naomi's God.

It is one thing to love the ways of the Lord when things are easy and quite another to cling to them when it's difficult. The kiss of outward respect is cheap and easy, but *clinging* to the Lord, making that decision for truth and holiness, is no trifling matter.

Where do you stand? Is your heart clinging to Jesus? Have you counted the cost? Are you solemnly prepared to suffer loss in this world for the Master's sake?

The reward will be substantial. Orpah is heard of no more. In glorious ease and idolatrous pleasure, her life melts away. But Ruth lives on, in history and in heaven. She even became an ancestor of our Lord Jesus. Those who renounce everything else for Christ's sake will be blessed forever. But those who turn back, yielding to temptation, will be forgotten and worse than forgotten.

Do not be satisfied this morning with a casual devotion to Christ. That is as empty as Orpah's kiss. By God's Holy Spirit, cling to Jesus.

December 16

Come to me.
(Matthew 11:28)

This is the cry of the Christian religion: "Come." The Jewish law essentially said, "Go, walk in God's way. But be careful. Break the commandments, and you will die. Keep them, and you will live."

The law was an instrument of terror, driving people with fear. But the gospel draws people with love. Jesus is the Good Shepherd, going before his sheep, calling them to follow him, always leading them on with the sweet word, "Come." The law repels; the gospel attracts. The law shows the distance between God and humanity; the gospel bridges that chasm and brings the sinner safely across.

From the first moment of your spiritual life to the time you are ushered into glory, this is what Christ says to you: "Come, come to me." As a mother invites her child to walk toward her by beckoning with her finger and saying, "Come," so does Jesus. He is always ahead of you, calling you to follow even as a soldier follows his captain. He goes before you to pave the way, to clear your path, and all your life you will hear his energizing voice.

This is not only Christ's call to you, but if you are a believer, this is what you say to Christ: "Come! Come!" You look forward to his second coming. "Come, Lord Jesus" (Revelation 22:20). You will also invite him into a closer fellowship: "Come, Lord, and live in my heart."

December 17

I remember the devotion of your youth.
(Jeremiah 2:2)

Christ loves to think about his church and to look on her beauty. As the bird keeps coming back to its nest and as the traveler hurries home, so the mind returns again and again to the object of its affections. We can never look too often on the face of someone we love. It is the same way with Jesus. From the beginning of time, he was "rejoicing in his whole world and delighting in mankind" (Proverbs 8:31). His thoughts moved ahead to the time when his chosen ones would be born, seeing them through the glass of his foreknowledge. "Your eyes saw my unformed body," the psalmist writes. "All the days ordained for me were written in your book before one of them came to be" (Psalm 139:16).

When the world was set on its pillars, he was there. Many times before his Incarnation, he descended to earth in human disguise: on the plains of Mamre (Genesis 18); by the brook of Jabbok (Genesis 32:24–30); beneath the walls of Jericho (Joshua 5:13); and in the fiery furnace of Babylon (Daniel 3:19, 25). Because his soul delighted in his people, he could not stay away from them. They were never absent from his heart—he had engraved their names on his hands (Isaiah 49:16). As the names of Israel's tribes were written on the high priest's breastplate, so the names of Christ's chosen ones glitter like jewels upon his heart. We may often forget to think of our Lord, but he never ceases to remember us.

December 18

Rend your heart and not your garments.
(Joel 2:13)

Garment rending and other outward signs of religious emotion are *easily done* and *frequently hypocritical*. True repentance is much more difficult—and much less common.

People will busy themselves with the most minute ceremonial regulations, because these things *can make them proud of themselves*, but true religion is too humbling, too heart searching, too all-encompassing. Most people prefer something more showy.

Outward observances are *temporarily comfortable*. They may please our eyes and ears. They feed our sense of pride and self-righteousness. But they are *ultimately misleading*. In the day of judgment, the soul needs something more substantial than ceremonies and rituals to lean on. Apart from a living relationship with Christ, all religious observances are *totally useless*.

Heart rending, on the other hand, is *divinely caused* and *solemnly felt*. It is a private grief that is *personally experienced*, not only in form, but deep within the believer's heart. It is not something merely to be talked about, but to be keenly felt in every child of God. It is *powerfully humbling* and *completely sin purging*.

This text commands us to rend our hearts, but that is not easy. Our hearts are naturally hard as marble. We must take them to Calvary. The voice of our dying Savior has split rocks before (Matthew 27:50–51). It is just as powerful now.

O Spirit of God, help us to hear the death cry of Jesus, and let our hearts be torn in true repentance.

December 19

The lot is cast into the lap, but its every decision is from the Lord. (Proverbs 16:33)

If the Lord looks after even the casting of lots, don't you think he can arrange the events of your life? Remember that the Savior has said that even sparrows will not fall without our Father's will, and "even the very hairs of your head are all numbered" (Matthew 10:29–30). It would bring you a holy calm, my friend, if you would remember this. It would relieve your anxiety, and you could live a patient, quiet, and cheerful life—as a Christian should.

When someone is anxious, he cannot pray with faith. When he is worried about the world, he cannot serve his Master, since his mind is on himself. If you "seek first his kingdom and his righteousness" (Matthew 6:33), other blessings will come to you as well. When you fret about your circumstances, you are meddling in Christ's business and neglecting your own. It is his job to provide and yours to obey.

Take a good look at your Father's storehouse, and then ask whether he will let you starve. Think about his merciful heart; will that ever prove to be unkind toward you? Consider his unsearchable wisdom; will that ever go wrong? Finally, hear the prayers of Jesus interceding for you, and ask yourself, "While he prays for me, will the Father ever act ungraciously toward me?" If he remembers sparrows, he won't forget you. "Cast your cares on the Lord and he will sustain you; he will never let the righteous fall" (Psalm 55:22).

December 20

I have loved you with an everlasting love.
(Jeremiah 31:3)

Sometimes the Lord Jesus shares his loving thoughts with his people. He is wise enough to know when to hold back, but he often expresses his love clearly and announces it to the world. The Holy Spirit often confirms the love of Jesus, bearing witness with our spirit (Romans 8:16 KJV). He takes the things of Christ and reveals them to us. We don't hear any voice from the clouds. We don't see any vision in the night. But we have a testimony stronger than either of these, in the quiet whispers of the Spirit. If an angel should fly from heaven and tell us personally that the Savior loves us, it would be no more convincing than the Spirit in our hearts.

Ask the experienced Christians you know, and they will tell you that there have been times when they felt the love of Christ so clearly and certainly that to doubt it would be to doubt their own existence. Maybe you have had similar times of refreshing, when your faith has risen to the heights of assurance. You have enjoyed a closeness to the Lord that rules out any question of his affection for us. He wraps us in his embrace and squeezes our doubts out of us.

Listen to his sweet voice. Be assured that he loves you with an everlasting love.

December 21

Has he not made with me an everlasting covenant?
(2 Samuel 23:5)

This covenant is *divine in its origin*. God has made it with us. Yes, God, the everlasting Father, the God who spoke the world into existence, stooped from his majesty, took hold of your hand, and made a covenant with you. Isn't that a remarkable deed? Can we ever really understand the humbling that was involved in that action?

It would be incredible enough if a human king made an agreement with us. But the King of all kings, El Shaddai, the All-sufficient Lord, Yahweh of the ages—*he* has made an everlasting covenant with us.

The covenant is also *specific in its application*. David says that God has covenanted "with *me*." And this applies to every believer. It is a personal agreement. It's all well and good that he has made peace with the world, but has he made peace *with me*? Yes, says David in this verse. God has agreed with us on a personal level.

The covenant is also *eternal in its duration*. An everlasting covenant is one with no beginning and no end. This is reassuring, amid all of life's uncertainties, to know that "God's solid foundation stands firm" (2 Timothy 2:19). He has promised, "I will not violate my covenant or alter what my lips have uttered" (Psalm 89:34). I can sing this song with David, even though my house (like his) may not be as holy as I'd like. Still, "Has he not made with me an everlasting covenant?"

December 22

I will strengthen you.
(Isaiah 41:10)

God is certainly able to follow through on this promise. He has all the strength we need. My friend, until you can drain dry his ocean of omnipotence, until you can break in pieces the towering mountains of almighty strength, you have no reason to fear. Human strength will never overcome God's power. As long as the earth exists, you have reason to stand firm in your faith. The same God who keeps the earth in its orbit, who stokes the sun's furnace, who lights the stars of heaven, has promised to supply you with daily strength.

If he is able to hold up the universe, do you think that he can't fulfill this promise? Remember what he has done in the past. He spoke, and it came to pass. He created the world out of nothing; will he be unable to support his children? He holds back the thunderstorms, he rides on the wind, he holds the oceans in the palm of his hand—how can he fail you? And especially when he has put a promise like this in writing, how can you indulge the notion that he has promised too much, that he cannot come through? Do not doubt this any longer.

O God, my strength, I believe in your promise. The limitless reservoir of your strength can never be exhausted. Your overflowing storehouse will never be emptied by your friends or robbed by your enemies. I can sing forever in your strength.

December 23

Friend, move up to a better place.
(Luke 14:10)

When our Christian life first begins, we draw close to God, but only with fear and trembling. At that point the soul is very conscious of its guilt. It reacts humbly, overawed by the Lord's grandeur. With a sincere bashfulness, we take the lowest position possible in the presence of our Lord.

But in later life, as we grow in grace, we lose that sense of terror. It's not that we forget our sin or that we lose our sense of holy awe in the presence of God. But our "fear" of God becomes a reverence, rather than a dread. We are called up to a "better place," with greater access to God through Christ.

From that place the Christian walks among the splendors of deity, veiling his face, like an angel, with the twin wings of the blood and righteousness of Jesus. Humbly we approach the throne. From that perspective, we see not only his greatness, but his love, his goodness, his mercy. This is just as selfless a position as we had before, but now there is more freedom in our response to God. We are aware of his limitless mercy and infinite love, and this refreshes us. We realize that we are "accepted in the beloved" (Ephesians 1:6 KJV). So we are invited to come to an even better position of closeness to God, rejoicing in him and crying, "Abba, Father."

December 24

For your sakes he became poor.
(2 Corinthians 8:9)

The Lord Jesus Christ was eternally rich, glorified, and exalted. But, "though he was rich, yet for your sakes he became poor." Think of the rich Christian, who cannot completely commune with poor believers unless he uses his wealth to meet their needs—the same rule applies with Christ. He could never have had fellowship with us unless he had shared with us his own abundant wealth, becoming poor to make us rich. If he had remained on his glorious throne and if we had stayed in the ruins of our sin, communion would have been impossible on both sides.

In order to create this relationship, it was necessary for the rich relative to transfer his estate to the poor relatives. The righteous Savior had to give his own perfection to his sinful brothers. Giving and receiving in this way, he descended from his lofty position, and we rose from the depths. We embrace in the middle, in full fellowship.

Before a sinful soul can truly relate to the perfect God, it must lose its guilt and put on the righteousness of Christ. Jesus must clothe his people in his own garments, or he cannot let them into his palace of glory. He must wash them in his blood, or they will be too dirty to embrace.

Here is true love, my friend. *For your sake,* the Lord Jesus "became poor," so that he could lift you into communion with himself.

December 25

The virgin will be with child and will give birth to a son, and will call him Immanuel. (Isaiah 7:14)

Let's go today to Bethlehem, along with the marveling shepherds and the adoring magi, and see the one born King of the Jews. We can sing with Isaiah, "To *us* a child is born, to *us* a son is given" (Isaiah 9:6)—by faith we, too, have a claim on this newborn King. Jesus is Yahweh incarnate, our Lord and our God, yet our brother and friend. Let us adore him and admire him.

At first glance, we recognize his *miraculous conception*. The virgin birth was a thing previously unheard of and unparalleled since. The very first promise of the coming Savior referred to the seed of the woman (Genesis 3:15) and not to the offspring of man. Since the woman had led the way into sin, resulting in "Paradise Lost," it was fitting that she would bear the one to regain Paradise.

Let us bow in reverence before this holy Child, whose innocence restores glory to humanity. Also let us pray that he will be formed in us, as "the hope of glory" (Colossians 1:27).

But do not fail to note Jesus' *humble parentage*. His mother is described simply as "a virgin," not a princess or prophetess or matron of a large estate. True, the blood of kings ran in her veins. Her mind was apparently sharp, since she composed and sang a brilliant song of praise (Luke 1:46–55). But her social status was obviously humble, and the man she was engaged to was certainly quite poor. That explains the humble accommodations offered the newborn King.

Immanuel, this Jesus, is "God with us" in our nature, our sorrow, our work, our punishment, even our death. He brings us with him in his resurrection, ascension, triumph, and glory.

December 26

The last Adam.
(1 Corinthians 15:45)

Jesus stands for every person he has chosen. Under the old agreement of works, Adam stood for every member of the human race. But under the new agreement of grace, every redeemed soul has a personal interest in Christ. We are one with him, since he is the Second Adam, the Sponsor of every chosen soul in this new covenant of love. The author of Hebrews spoke of Levi being "in the body" of his ancestor Abraham when Melchizedek met him (Hebrews 7:10). In the same way, the believer is in the body of Jesus Christ, the Mediator, as he settles and confirms the new covenant. So whatever Christ has done, he has done for the whole body of his church. We were crucified with him and buried with him (Colossians 2:10–13), and even more wonderful, we are risen with him and ascended with him to heavenly positions (Ephesians 2:6).

Because of this, the church is accepted by the Father, because he sees us *in Jesus*. The body is united to the Head. Adam's righteousness was ours as long as he maintained it, and his sin was ours the moment he committed it. In the same way, everything the Second Adam does is ours, too. This is the very groundwork of the gospel. Our salvation is based on this.

December 27

Can papyrus grow tall where there is no marsh?
(Job 8:11)

Papyrus is flimsy. So is the hypocrite. He has no substance or stability. The papyrus reed is shaken by every wind, just as the hypocrite yields to every outside influence. The papyrus weathers the storm because it bends easily. And that's why the hypocrite is not troubled by persecution.

The papyrus reed thrives in the marshy ground. But if the marsh goes dry, the reed will wither. Its life is entirely dependent on circumstances. Is this your situation, too? Do you only serve God when it is profitable or respectable to do so? Do you love God only when he is providing you with material blessings? If this is true of you or me, then we are base hypocrites. We will wither like papyrus reeds.

Or can you honestly say that you have held on to your integrity when it has been inconvenient, even difficult to do so? Then there is a genuine godly vitality in you. The papyrus needs the moisture all the time, but plants that the Lord has planted can flourish even in the midst of drought. A godly person often grows best when circumstances go against him. But the one who follows Christ for profit is a Judas. Those who follow just for loaves and fishes are children of the devil. But those who follow him because they love him, these are the ones he loves in a special way.

December 28

The life I live in the body, I live by faith in the Son of God.
(Galatians 2:20)

Jesus' first command to us was "Live!" Life is absolutely essential in spiritual matters; until we have it, we have no way of participating in things of God's kingdom.

What is this life that grace confers on us? It is none other than the life of Christ. Like sap from the trunk of a tree, it surges into us—we are like branches—and it establishes a vital connection between our souls and Jesus. Faith is the firstfruits of this transaction. It is the neck that joins the body of the church to its all-glorious Head.

Faith grabs hold of Jesus with a firm and determined grip. The person of faith knows how valuable he is, and no temptation can make him put his trust elsewhere. Christ Jesus is so delighted by faith that he keeps strengthening it and nurturing it in the believer, holding it in place with his eternal arms.

So here we have pictured a living, logical, and delightful union that streams forth with love, confidence, sympathy, comfort, and joy for both bride and bridegroom. When you feel this oneness with Christ, you begin to sense your pulse beating with his—which only makes sense, since the same blood is flowing through you both. Those moments of closeness are as near to heaven as we can be on earth. They prepare us for our eternal fellowship with him.

December 29

Thus far has the Lord helped us.
(1 Samuel 7:12)

The phrase "thus far" is like a hand pointing to the past. Through poverty and wealth, in sickness and health, at home and abroad, on land and sea, in honor and dishonor, in perplexity and joy, in trial and triumph, in prayer and temptation—"thus far has the Lord helped us!"

I love to look down a long avenue of trees. It is delightful to gaze from one end to the other, perusing this long vista, a sort of verdant temple, with its branching pillars and arches of leaves. In the same way, look down the long road of your years; see the green boughs of mercy overhead and the strong pillars of God's faithfulness that bear up your joys. Do you hear birds in those branches, singing? There must be many of them, and they are all singing of the mercies of God that have come to you "thus far."

But the phrase also points forward. When someone reaches a certain point and says, "Thus far," he is obviously not finished yet. There are more trials and joys, more temptations and triumphs, more prayers and answers, more labors, more strength, more fights, more victories—leading all the way to death. Is it over then? No! There is more—being made like Jesus, thrones, harps, songs, white robes, Jesus' face, the company of believers, the glory of God, the infinite bliss. Thus far the Lord has proved himself faithful, but there is much, much more to come.

December 30

The end of a matter is better than its beginning.
(Ecclesiastes 7:8)

Look at our Lord's life. See how he began. "He was despised and rejected by men, a man of sorrows, and familiar with suffering" (Isaiah 53:3). But look how he ends up—at his Father's right hand, waiting in glory until his enemies are made his footstool (Luke 20:42–43).

"In this world," wrote John, "we are like him" (1 John 4:17). You must bear the cross, too, or you will not wear the crown. You must wade through the mud, if you want to walk that golden pavement. So cheer up, if you find yourself in difficult straits. "The end of a matter is better than its beginning."

Look at the crawling caterpillar. It is just a worm and rather ugly at that. But this is only the beginning. Now see the beautiful winged butterfly, dancing with the sunbeams, sipping at flowers, full of happiness and life. That is how it ends.

You are that caterpillar, until you are wrapped up in the chrysalis of death. "But we know that when he appears, we shall be like him, for we shall see him as he is" (1 John 3:2). So be content to be like him, in a wormlike existence, so that you may someday be like him in glory.

Consider the diamond, painfully cut by the jeweler. It seems to lose too much as the gem cutter carves it. But when the king is crowned, the diadem is placed on his head with a joyous fanfare. A glittering ray flashes from the crown—it is the very diamond that was tormented by the jeweler. Yes, you may compare yourself to that diamond. You are one of God's people, and you are going through the cutting process. Let faith and patience fill your heart, for when your King is crowned, one perfect ray of glory will stream from you. "They shall be mine," says the Lord, "in the day when I make up my jewels" (see Malachi 3:17).

December 31

On the last and greatest day of the Feast, Jesus stood and said in a loud voice, "If anyone is thirsty, let him come to me and drink." (John 7:37)

On this last day of the year, Jesus pleads in the same way with us. He longs to show us his grace. His patience has been admirable, bearing with us year after year, despite our rebellions and resistance to his Spirit. It is amazing that we are still in the land of mercy!

In his simple statement at that feast, Jesus *expresses pity*. He cried! You can almost hear the urgency in his voice. He begs his hearers to come to God. The apostle Paul knew this feeling. "As though God were making his appeal through us," he wrote, "We implore you on Christ's behalf: Be reconciled to God" (2 Corinthians 5:20). This is the deep love of a mother for her children. Surely that must touch your heart.

Jesus also *offers satisfaction*. Everything you need to quench your soul's thirst is here in Christ. For your conscience, the atonement brings peace. For your mind, the gospel brings rich instruction. For your heart, Jesus is the most worthy object of affection you could ever find. Thirst is terrible, but Jesus can remove it.

Jesus *gives an open invitation*. Everyone who thirsts is welcome. There is no other qualification. Whether it is the thirst of greed, ambition, pleasure, knowledge, or rest—the one who suffers from it is invited. The thirst itself may be bad; it may be a result of sin dominating your life. But you are not invited on the basis of your goodness. If you are thirsty, come and drink.

Jesus *presents himself*. The sinner must come to *Jesus*, not to good deeds, religious ceremonies, or biblical doctrines, but to a personal Redeemer. He is the only hope for the sinner.

There's no need to prepare. Drinking is something you just do. Any fool can drink—so can a thief or a prostitute. Your sinfulness will not bar you from these waters. You need no golden cup or jeweled chalice, just stoop to the river of life and drink. Your lips may be blistered or diseased or dirty—even that should not keep you from drinking. The stream will not be polluted by your lips; it will purify them. Jesus is your fount of hope. Hear his voice today: "If anyone is thirsty, let him come to me and drink."